Out
of
Order

ARROGANCE,

CORRUPTION,

----

and INCOMPETENCE

ON THE BENCH

Max Boot

Foreword by Robert H. Bork

BASIC
BOOKS

A Member of the Perseus Books Group

PUBLISHED BY BASIC BOOKS, *A Member of the Perseus Books Group.*

Designed by Jenny Dossin

LIBRARY OF CONGRESS CATALOGING-IN-PUBLICATION DATA

Boot, Max, 1969–
Out of order : arrogance, corruption and incompetence on the bench / by Max Boot
p.   cm.
Includes bibliographical references and index.
ISBN 0-465-05432-3 (cloth) — 0-465-05375-0 (pbk)
1. Judges—United States.   2. Judicial corruption—United States.   3. Judicial ethics—
United States.   4. Political questions and judicial power—United States.   1. Title.
KF8775.Z9B66   1998
347.73'14—dc21   97-52791

98 99 00 01 02   10 9 8 7 6 5 4 3 2 1

Contents

Foreword

BY ROBERT H. BORK

THE SUB-TITLE of this book—"Arrogance, Corruption, and Incompetence on the Bench"—sums up a judicial system that is, to put the matter mildly, not working well. All too often, it is not even performing tolerably. Yet laymen rarely have a complete understanding of what is taking place and those lawyers who do, by and large, become cynically accepting of a system they do not admire but have learned how to work, or at least to live with. This book focuses on American courts, but it may be worth noting that much of what has gone wrong occurs everywhere there is an independent judiciary, and most especially where there is a written constitution. In this context, independence is another word for power. Men and women given unaccountable power will often use it to further their own ends, not the ends of the polity which they exist to serve.

Thus, a wholly unanticipated change has occurred in the governance of all Western industrialized democracies, including the United States, perhaps preeminently the United States. Designed as governments in which legislatures would be dominant, the instruments by which policy is made, these countries have acquiesced in the increasing movement of political decisions into their courts. Judges both write and apply the constitutional law. Nor is this a mere technicality. The constitutional law judges make affects the lives of the citizenry in intimate detail by remaking the cultures in which they live.

The United States, the first government to accept courts that applied a written constitution as law, took longest for this transformation of the judiciary to occur. But the United States has become a model for other countries and the judicialization of their politics took root almost immediately.

Designed to be the least powerful of the three branches of the American government, the judiciary has steadily increased its powers so that in many areas it is both the most powerful and the final authority. In one recent term, inspired by radical egalitarianism, the Court created special rights for homosexuals; through a variant of radical egalitarianism, radical feminism, the Justices decreed the end of single sex public education at the college level; and overcome by the claims of radical individualism, the Court blocked Congress' attempt to make pornography marginally less accessible on cable television. But perhaps the worst decision in this century, a combination of egalitarianism and individualism run amok, was the creation of a constitutional right to abortion in *Roe v. Wade*, a fifty-one-page opinion containing not a line of legal argument. Two characteristics of those decisions are apparent. First, nothing in the written Constitution supports any one of them. They are entirely Court-made constitutional law, and, for that reason, illegitimate exercises of power. Second, all three decisions press our culture in a single direction, toward the fads of radical individualism and radical egalitarianism dominant in our intellectual class. The Supreme Court is an active partisan on one side of our culture wars.

Nor is this a natural and unplanned development. A majority of the justices could hardly miss the point that they have undertaken to rule where no written or customary law affords them title to do so. A large body of literature complains of their ultra vires actions, not the least vociferous of which is to be found in the opinions of their dissenting colleagues. Hardly anyone has had the temerity to employ rhetoric so unrestrained, fiery, and even violent as have the dissenters. The Court majority remains absolutely unswayed by this criticism. That they know full well what they are doing is shown by their occasional response, which never rests upon theoretical or practical justifications of their behavior, but consists entirely of the assertion that the Court has departed from the law many times in the past. That is true, but it does not support the conclusion that the Court is, for that reason, entitled to do it again. That is hardly more than a claim that past sin justifies further sin. It is as if, having worn a path of judicial activism, the Court is now claiming justification by long usage or prescriptive right, an easement across democratic authority for judicial transgressions.

The most disturbing aspect is that this behavior of judges is not an accident of United States history, politics, or the process by which we select our judges. Judicial usurpation of democratic prerogatives is just about universal wherever judicial independence is an ideal and particularly where there is a written constitution containing a bill of rights. Canada provided for judicial override of democratic decisions in its new constitution. (It also provided for a legislative response to such decisions; more about that later.) Ireland's top court has decriminalized homosexuality as have other courts that have pronounced on the subject. For example, it seems certain that within the next few years American courts will make homosexual marriage a constitutional right. Radical individualism, the privatization of morality, has been particularly powerful with respect to sexual behavior.

Whatever the context, the drive of the courts for power remains a constant. The Israeli court, for example, is said to make our Warren Court seem restrained and modest by comparison. Australia is particularly interesting because its constitution contains no bill of rights and the nation might, for that reason, be thought immune to the excesses of the judicial privatization of morality seen elsewhere. But the Australian Supreme Court has begun to work around that minor difficulty by adopting international norms, derived from treaties and United Nations' resolutions, as the law of the country. These, needless to say, are sufficiently vague to provide ample latitude for judicial innovation.

I once attended an international conference of lawyers and judges which several members of the European Court attended. Facing a union made up of widely different nations and culture, they were especially interested in how the American Supreme Court had largely obliterated the independent authority of the state governments. They were also eager to be instructed in how the American Supreme Court had found new scope for radical individualism and radical egalitarianism in our Bill of Rights. Imperialistic fervor shone from their eyes. There seems no doubt that this court will behave as all Western-style courts do. Jurists are drawn from and respond to the intellectual class. They have in common the belief that their own views are superior, more civilized and just, than those of the public or those they elect to represent them. This assumption of judicial intellectual and moral superiority is not likely to be replaced by judicial modesty, which was the virtue assumed in judges at the outset of the American republic, any time in the foreseeable future.

The same judicial arrogance is evident in the courts' dealings with criminal law. Max Boot has recounted some of the countless cases in which judges have released violent felons on probation without requiring that they serve significant, or any, time in jail. Since violent criminals continue their activities when back on the streets, this is nothing less than a judge sentencing law-abiding citizens, whom he has never seen, to serious injury and death. Such judges do not even consider that what they have done to the innocent would be the unconstitutional infliction of cruel and unusual punishment if it were done to the felon. The criminal is set free, because the judge does not believe in punishment or incarceration, so that the innocent may be murdered, raped, or assaulted.

All of this has been magnified by the Supreme Court's ruling in *Miranda v. Arizona*. *Miranda* was the culmination of a series of judicial expressions of sympathy for those accused of crime. First, the Court ruled that evidence seized by the police in violation of the Fourth Amendment (requiring a warrant in most cases and prohibiting unreasonable searches and seizures) could not be used against the accused at trial. Called the "exclusionary rule," that was a large misstep. It meant that perfectly good evidence of a crime committed by the defendant could not be submitted to the jury if the police had gained the evidence in a manner that the courts later determined not to be in accord with the Fourth Amendment. The results were often bizarre. Police who entered an apartment with a search warrant for one kind of goods, for example, were held by the Court to have conducted an unlawful search and seizure when one of them noticed a large, brand-new television set which was out of keeping with the rest of the furnishings. An officer turned the set to see the serial number and determined that the television was on his list of stolen property. The Court, in an exercise reminiscent of theological hair-splitting, held that the police had acted unlawfully and so the stolen property could not be adduced in evidence. Consider that the police, acting in accordance with a warrant, were lawfully in the room with the television set and that its appearance there was highly suspicious. There was no random search and no police brutality, only a reading of the serial number. A crime went unpunished for no intelligible reason whatever.

Confessions could be admitted only if the court determined they were not coerced. That rule made sense because of the unreliability of confessions so obtained. There was a price in criminals going free, but that price was arguably well worth paying. Matters were made much worse, in fact got out of hand, with the Supreme Court's decision in

Miranda v. Arizona. There the Court legislated a series of warnings that had to be given a suspect before he confessed. A failure to recite the formula resulted in the exclusion of even voluntarily given confessions. Police picked up a man they were sure had murdered a child. In the course of the ride back to headquarters, one of the officers, not addressing the suspect in particular, said that unless the body were found soon, the family would suffer additionally and the child would never receive a proper burial. The ride continued in silence for some time, and then the suspect, without prompting, told the officers where the body was hidden. The Supreme Court held that this was an interrogation and confession without benefit of the *Miranda* warnings so that the defendant's statement and the subsequent discovery of the body could not be used in evidence. To call the Court's decision, which resulted in overturning the conviction of a child killer, finicky or hypertechnical would be high praise.

The problem posed by the judiciary in the United States, however, goes far beyond the judges' tendency to rewrite the Constitution and apply, or fail to apply, other laws according to their personal preferences. It is one of the virtues of this book that it calls our attention as well to the problems of corruption and incompetence on the bench. On the federal bench, corruption is a rare phenomenon, but it does occur. There is the legendary case of Judge Martin Manton who sat on the Court of Appeals for the Second Circuit, and who came very close to being nominated for the Supreme Court of the United States. When it became known that Manton took bribes from parties appearing before him, he claimed innocence on the interesting ground that he took bribes from both sides, decided the case on the merits, and then returned the money to the losing party. That defense caused Judge Learned Hand, perhaps the most distinguished court of appeals judge in our history, to call Manton a moral moron. There have been several cases of venal federal judges in recent years. One of them, removed from office by conviction on a bill of impeachment, promptly ran for Congress, and, the voters' concern for judicial integrity being what it is, won.

Sometimes the solicitation is not only explicit but public. Some years ago, a partner of mine attended the annual banquet of Chicago's probate judges. The chief judge rose after dinner to deliver the annual state-of-the-bench address. He said, in ringing tones, "I understand there is a rumor that lawyers have to give the judges of the probate court Christmas presents in order to secure justice. I want to scotch that rumor right now. Justice is not for sale in the probate courts of Chicago. You need not give a judge any present to get a fair decision." He paused, and then said thoughtfully, "On the other hand, use your own judgment."

Incompetence is much more common than venality. (If it weren't, many of our judges would be multimillionaires.) Incompetence is also more apparent to the practicing bar. That sad state of affairs, the want of professional skills, is largely due, as Mr. Boot points out, to the methods by which we select judges. In most of our states, judgeships are elective offices. That is a manifestation of American egalitarianism and probably originally sprang from colonists' fears of appointed judges as agents of the Crown. Whatever its historical roots, the theory that the public is entitled to the kind of judges it wants is all right so far as it goes; the trouble is that the public is massively uninformed about both law and judges. Even when a judge perpetrates an obvious injustice, even when he or she lets violent killers walk free, the public, which may be outraged for a week, has largely forgotten the matter and even the judge's name when the next election comes around. When it comes to constitutional rulings, which affect our lives and our culture at wholesale rather than retail, the public tends to think that the Constitution means anything they like, or at least anything they do not violently disagree with.

Incumbents tend to be reelected easily, often enough aided by cash contributions from the attorneys who appear before them. One result is that the plaintiffs' trial bar has a great deal of influence on the directions the law takes and the way its doctrines are shaped. That bar is one of the few sections of the public that takes a knowledgeable and continuing interest in judges' performance. The kind of judges who are persistently plaintiff-minded in tort actions are likely also to display the soft-hearted attitudes toward criminal defendants and, reinforced by the cultural elite, tend to expand constitutional guarantees in favor radical individualism and egalitarianism, the twin excesses of that elite. The results of the tort explosion are apparent everywhere. Swings have been removed from many public parks and diving boards from pools. A large fraction of the price of a ladder reflects accident insurance costs. Many doctors have been driven from practice. A major corporation has been bankrupted by damages for the manufacture of breast implants, though there is no scientific evidence that the implants do any harm. The most effective morning sickness medicine for pregnant women has been taken off the market, not because it has ever been shown to cause any harm or birth defects, but because the cost of defending the lawsuits became prohibitive. Horrors of this sort abound, to the damage of business and consumers alike, and a major reason is the pro-plaintiffs bias, the incompetence, and the timidity of judges who often send cases to the jury when they should summarily rule the plaintiffs out of court.

We are currently regaled with news stories about outrageous monetary judgments against manufacturers of products and providers of services. Punitive damages, which do not provide recompense for injuries but punishment for the out-of-state corporation for the crime of being from out of the state, have become a national disgrace. As a member of the Department of Justice, I co-authored a report recommending, among other things, an end to diversity jurisdiction to relieve the litigation overload in the federal courts. (Diversity jurisdiction makes the federal courts available in many cases in which the parties are from different states.) Members of the bar were aghast, but I dismissed their fears as mere professional stodginess. Shortly after returning to private life I found myself representing a large corporation in a state court. Local co-counsel warned that I was about to "eat home cookin'." Sure enough, I was, and I did not like the flavor. Diversity jurisdiction now seems to me a fine invention. Running neck-and-neck with local prejudice and venality, however, is simple incompetence. Attorneys with only ambulance-chasing or lobbying experience are routinely placed on the bench. If the public does not know of these matters, lawyers do, but out of justified concern for their livelihoods, confine their protests to gallows humor among themselves. There is, for example, an ornament to the bench known locally as "Judge Necessity," because, as the aphorism has it, "necessity knows no law."

What is to be done, then, about the shambles that is our legal system? Whatever that may be, it will be a long process. As one astute and frustrated state chief justice put it, "Judicial reform is not for the short-winded." A number of cures have been proposed, most of them guaranteed to be ineffective. Switching state judiciaries from elective to appointive would have one large benefit; it would remove the influence of lawyer donations to election campaigns. That certainly would not alleviate all of the problems with state court systems, but it would remove one factor that pushes product and service tort law always in the plaintiffs' direction. It is true that the plaintiffs' bar has been highly successful in getting legislatures to draft ever stricter liability laws, but those are the forums in which policy choices should be made. There is, moreover, a better chance that the interests of potential defendants will receive a hearing in legislatures there than in courts elected with plaintiffs' bar donations. Unfortunately, defendants, who do not have make their livings from lawsuits, class actions, and contingency fees have not organized in the way that plaintiffs' lawyers have.

A shift in the route to the bench could not entirely cure the liberal mind-set that characterizes the judiciary. The tendency to go easy on criminals is apparently a long-standing characteristic of the courts. In a classic detective novel published in 1907, the protagonist complains of the laxity of English judges in punishing criminals. Nor is it easy to think of a mechanical solution of the practice of judges to ignore the limits of written constitutions in order to proclaim their own philosophies (if that is not too grand a term) as the law of the land.

Various meliorations have been offered. The United States Constitution appears to give Congress the power to restrict the appellate jurisdiction of the Supreme Court. That tactic, however, would merely shift constitutional issues to state courts, from which they could not be removed without a constitutional amendment. That would cure very little, given the very short life of public indignation about even the most egregious usurpations of democratic prerogatives by state as well as federal courts. Term limits for federal judges would similarly require a constitutional amendment and would probably make matters worse. Judges would realize that they had only a short time to write opinions that make history, and only opinions declaring rights that nobody had previously suspected of lying within the Constitution make history.

At one point, in despair over the Supreme Court's propensity for rewriting the Constitution, I suggested that the document be amended to allow majority votes in the House and Senate to override any federal court decision. The suggestion was treated with disbelief, if not indignation, as a threat to "judicial independence" and "upsetting the system of checks and balances." Well, yes, in a sense it was both of those things. The difficulty is that the ideal of judicial independence was designed to prevent political pressures from affecting the interpretation of the law. Today, the phrase serves as buzz words to prevent interference with political decisions by the courts. Judicial independence was never intended to make courts what they have become, unaccountable and uncheckable partisans in our culture wars. As for the system of checks and balances, there is no check upon the federal courts provided by the Constitution precisely because it was assumed, as Alexander Hamilton, James Madison, and others put it, that there was no need for such a check. The courts were to interpret, not create the law. Placing the federal courts under democratic restraints would in no sense violate the original understanding of their place in our government. At least, it would violate that understanding less than the present practice of the courts does.

Suggestions for the serious reformation of the judicial system ought not be treated with the combination of alarm and scorn that is their usual lot. People forget that such proposals have been consistently offered throughout our history and that they were put forward by some of our most revered public figures: Thomas Jefferson wanted to redirect the course of the courts by impeaching and convicting Federalist judges; Jefferson also proposed that the Supreme Court's constitutional rulings be binding only upon the judicial branch; both Andrew Jackson and Abraham Lincoln simply ignored court orders that they found disagreeable or threatening to the public good and Jackson agreed with Jefferson that Court decisions were not binding on the other branches of the federal government; Robert Lafollette proposed that rulings of the Supreme Court be subject to overruling by a two-thirds vote of the Senate; Learned Hand thought it probably best that the due process clause, the vehicle for the courts' political legislations, be repealed; Franklin Roosevelt proposed "packing" the Supreme Court to make it friendlier to New Deal legislation. Jefferson failed to convict a Justice of the Court on impeachment but Roosevelt's plan might have succeeded had he not presented it disingenuously as an aid to an overworked Court.

The real objection to my proposal to allow legislative override of judicial decisions is not that it is inconsistent with the proper judicial role but is, quite simply, that it would not work. The belief that the courts and their decisions are sacred is too strong. Canada's new constitution provides not only for judicial review of statutes and official acts but for a reciprocal legislative power, both in the Parliament and in the provincial legislatures, to override the acts of the courts. Canada had no long history of judicial supremacy, as we do, and deliberately provided for a democratic check on the courts. If a legislative override would succeed anywhere, it should be in Canada. Legislative efforts to exercise the power given the legislatures by the constitution nonetheless provoked cries of outrage. They are, it is said, impermissible attempts to interfere with judicial independence, and that notwithstanding that the constitutional provision for just such interference. The courts are, apparently, more sacred than the Constitution. The same thing is true in the United States, and it is predictable that a legislative override, were one provided by amendment to the Constitution, would rarely be attempted and even more rarely succeed. The power and independence of the courts lies not in the historical or textual meaning of the Constitution but in moral intimidation.

Nor is this situation likely to change of itself. Our history demonstrates that the courts respond to the dominant social and cultural forces in American life. In the last century that elite consisted of the business class. In this century, the cultural elite is the intellectual class, broadly defined (very broadly defined as the class that makes its living from words and symbols, from the wholesaling or retailing, though rarely the creation, of ideas). In any information age, a time of the supremacy of words and symbols, that situation is likely to continue far into the future. It may even be permanent. For reasons I have gone into elsewhere, the intellectual class is by nature liberal to left-wing. That class combines radical individualism and radical egalitarianism, and those tendencies are clearly observable in the work of the courts.

The courts are both weapons and prizes in our culture wars. If that is true, it means that the courts will alter their behavior only as the culture around them changes. That is a large order, but the change, if there is to be any, must proceed by informed criticism of each of the cultural institutions that creates the present climate. That is the virtue of this book by Max Boot. Our courts are behaving badly and the public, to the degree it can be brought to understand that, will exert force for reform, a reform that must be structural as well as intellectual and moral. Mr. Boot contributes to the necessary understanding of what has gone wrong and why.

Introduction

"JUSTICE," observed Daniel Webster, "is the ligament which holds civilized beings and civilized nations together." And judges are the ligament that holds justice together. Wearing their black robes, banging their gavels, these men and women are the priests of our civic religion—the Law. They embody the fondest hope of our society that wrongdoers will be punished, victims succored, and justice done. That all disputes, public and private, will be resolved fairly and impartially. Ultimately, judges are the final guarantors that we live, as the ideal has it, in a society ruled by laws, not by men.

How well are judges doing their job today? To answer that question, ask yourself another one: How well is the legal system doing today?

Start with criminal justice. Many Americans view the courts as a revolving door for violent offenders. And with justification. Just look at the headlines: Little Polly Klaas slain. Her killer had served just half his sentence on a previous kidnapping charge. . . . Michael Jordan's father murdered. Two thugs who compiled long rap sheets but little time behind bars are convicted. . . . O. J. Simpson (need I say more?). Crime statistics may be falling, but few Americans will feel safe as long as so many hardened criminals are roaming free.

Then there's the civil justice system. Its reputation has been badly tarnished by a long series of absurd awards: A doctor wins $2 million because of an invisible paint scratch on his BMW. . . . A grandmother gets $2.9 million because she spilled some hot coffee on herself. . . . A railroad gets socked for $3.4 billion in damages after an accident that caused neither serious bodily injury nor significant property damage. It doesn't much matter that most of these stratospheric sums are reduced on appeal. The underlying problem is that the courts seem to be operating under the same principle as a lottery: getting a lot for almost nothing.

When the dominant metaphors in most people's minds for the justice system are a "lottery" and a "revolving door," you know something has gone profoundly wrong. Ambrose Bierce defined justice as "a commodity which is a more or less adultered condition the State sells to the citizen as a reward for his allegiance, taxes and personal services." Well, we still pay taxes, but we're not getting much justice in return.

Much of the blame for what ails our justice system seems to fall on lawyers. The World Wide Web is packed with sites posing such vital questions as "What's the difference between a lawyer and a vampire?" (The answer, in case you're wondering, is "A vampire only sucks blood at night.") But nobody's making fun of judges. In the 1997 movie *Liar Liar*, for instance, the lawyer played by Jim Carrey is congenitally unable to tell the truth, while the judge comes across as a stern, but fair, authority figure. And have you heard any good judge jokes lately?

At first blush, this popular image is puzzling. After all, a judge is a combination of two of the most reviled figures in American life—a lawyer *and* a politician. But somehow donning the black robes confers instant credibility and esteem on even the most notorious political operator or corner-cutting attorney. Most people seem to assume, without giving the matter much thought, that anyone accorded so much respect ("Your Honor") and power must be worthy of the position.

In fact, I fell into this trap in my own work. For several years, until becoming features (or op-ed) editor in mid-1997, I wrote about the legal system for the editorial page of the *Wall Street Journal*. I authored numerous editorials, feature articles, and Rule of Law columns calling for legal reform, primarily in the civil justice arena. While I occasionally wrote about judges, most of my focus was on the kings (and queens) of torts who make millions by pursuing personal injury claims—often claims with little factual foundation. These bombastic plaintiffs' lawyers frequently responded with personal invective and even threats (never carried out) of lawsuits against the newspaper and me. This only redoubled my determination to hold these multimillionaire attorneys responsible for their excesses. In my zeal, however, I now realize I was overlooking the real problem with the legal system—judges, not lawyers.

Sure, lawyers engage in unethical, slimy, underhanded behavior. (Are you surprised?) But lawyers profit from their behavior only when judges let them. Attorneys are rational actors; they react to economic incentives. And who creates those incentives? Judges. The folks wielding gavels aren't doing their job if they create technicalities that allow wily defense lawyers to get guilty clients off the hook or if they allow roguish plaintiff's lawyers to become richer than Donald Trump by bringing dubious injury claims.

So what are judges doing? Instead of devoting time to their traditional duty—adjudicating cases fairly and efficiently—all too many jurists are becoming consumed with tasks once reserved for legislators. In the process, they're wielding unprecedented power over our lives.

Whether you think that's good or bad usually depends on your political perspective. Favor abortion? Then you like the Supreme Court guaranteeing abortion on demand. Oppose the use of racial preferences by government? Then you like the courts' overturning many of these programs. Want to limit the terms of your congressman? Then you don't like the courts telling you that's verboten.

The striking thing about all these rulings is how both the left and right now take it virtually for granted that such important issues should be decided by unelected judges rather than elected legislators. Yet voters never made this choice consciously; the gaveling set simply grabbed power for itself. The expansion of judicial fiat is especially striking when you see men and women in black robes personally running institutions ranging from prisons to schools. Judges are even levying taxes. Whatever happened to "no taxation without representation"?

Since these developments have occurred at the same time that the civil and criminal justice systems appear to be breaking down, it's no surprise that this has led to a backlash against the black-robed set.

Attacking liberal judges has long been a staple of Republican political campaigns, from Richard Nixon to Bob Dole, though with the exception of Ronald Reagan, few Republicans have done much to rein in the judiciary once in office. In recent years, however, the rhetoric against activist judges has been turned up a few notches in some of the more feverish swamps of the right.

Tom DeLay, the bug exterminator turned congressman, has talked of squishing judges through the impeachment process simply for issuing bad opinions. In 1996, *First Things*, a conservative quarterly, staged a symposium in which the editors suggested that "judicial usurpation of power" may have led us to a point "where conscientious citizens can no longer give moral assent to the existing regime." When prominent intellectuals of the right, not the left, start muttering about the American government as a "regime," that's a pretty good sign that judicial activism is triggering powerful opposition.

Unfortunately, extremist talk like that found in *First Things* only discredits legitimate criticism of judges, much as the John Birchers gave anticommunism a bad name for so many years. It's important to stress that there's no inherent reason for concern about junk judges to be a right-wing or Republican issue. Anyone who wants decent, democratic government ought to be concerned about judges who misbehave, or exceed their authority, or issue unjust decisions. Conservatives may be decrying activist judges today, but in the 1930s, it was liberals who were upset about conservative activism from the bench. The pendulum could swing back again.

The case against judicial abuse of power, the case this book will lay out, isn't about politics or ideology. It's simply about making the third branch of government more accountable to the folks who pay its bills.

A Few Words About This Book

This book is the natural outgrowth of my work writing about legal issues for the *Wall Street Journal*'s editorial page, and before that for the news pages of the *Christian Science Monitor.* During the course of my research, I drew not only on my firsthand reporting on the justice system but also on the reporting of others, law review articles, various statistics, conversations with judges and lawyers, and of course the decisions issued by countless courts. What I have produced is not intended to be a dry, academic text on the role of judges. Nor is it intended to be a comprehensive survey of every area of the law. It is, rather, a polemic, passionate at times, about what I view as some major failings of the justice system that have gotten far too little attention so far.

In recent years, there has been no shortage of excellent books—by such distinguished authors as Peter Huber, Walter Olson, Robert Bork, Harold Rothwax, and Philip Howard—decrying various shortcomings of the American legal system. But no book, to the best of my knowledge, has covered more than one or two areas of the law (for example, criminal or civil) and few, with the exception of those dealing exclusively with constitutional matters, have focused on the judge as the locus of our problems. This book, by contrast, aims to show precisely how judges have contributed to the revolving door in criminal justice; to the lotto mentality in civil justice; and to the loss of democracy in constitutional law.

Chapter 1 offers a general overview of the problem with incompetent and arrogant judges, from Lance Ito (who blew the O. J. Simpson trial) to Sol Wachtler (who was convicted of harassing a former mistress). My argument is simple: We have too many "benchwarmers" in the legal system, and they can cause an awful lot of damage because there aren't enough mechanisms in place to hold judges accountable for their conduct. The succeeding chapters expose the costs of this shortcoming.

Chapter 2 looks at criminal sentencing, from bail to the death penalty, and argues that too many judges are bringing a pro-defendant attitude to the bench, with disastrous results for society. Chapter 3 is also concerned with criminal matters—specifically, the exclusionary rule and *Miranda*, both court-invented devices that can only serve to set the guilty free. Note that in neither chapter do I join in the criticism of judges who, on rare occasions, reverse a jury decision and set a defendant free because they're genuinely convinced of that person's innocence. That is what judges are supposed to do when confronted with evidence that a miscarriage of justice has occurred. My focus is strictly on judges who don't deal harshly enough with those who are manifestly guilty.

Chapter 4 begins an examination of constitutional law. I review a number of cases—from panhandling to abortion—to show how the will of the voters is often unfairly thwarted by activist judges bent on reading their own social nostrums into the law. Chapter 5 explores a corollary problem: judges who use court decrees to intervene directly in the business of government and take over jails, schools, and other institutions.

Chapter 6 addresses the civil justice system. Here I argue that judges are failing in their duty to stop juries from issuing out-of-control damage awards based on flimsy evidence. Chapter 7 examines how the runaway litigation system has resulted in more and more ethics problems for the bench—such as judges taking campaign donations from lawyers who appear before them and sometimes even actual bribes.

Chapter 8 is my attempt to offer some prescriptions, however tentative, for what ails the legal system. My answer (at the risk of giving away the denouement at the start of the plot), in essence, is this: We need more public criticism and exposure to hold judges accountable for their actions. And that is precisely the aim of the book you now hold in your hands.

The Freedom of Information Act is designed to uncover evidence of doings the government would rather keep quiet, in the expectation that this will lead officials to avoid improper behavior. Think of this book as a Freedom of Information Act for the third branch of government: We're going to peel back the black robes of the judiciary and see what we find underneath. It may not be a pretty sight, but it's a first step toward better government.

Out
of
Order

CHAPTER I

The Injudicious Judiciary

JUDGES WHO ARE

INCOMPETENT AND

OUT OF CONTROL

Judge — a law student who marks his own examination papers.
H. L. MENCKEN, *A Mencken Chrestomathy*

YOU GET TO Hayneville, Alabama, by turning off the interstate and heading down a two-lane country road. You drive past countless acres of cattle, catfish farms, and cotton. Finally you zip into a small, tired town where the only industry seems to be government—as in welfare, agricultural assistance, rural health services, Head Start—and the only imposing structure is the county building. This is the seat of Lowndes County, population 12,658.

On the second floor of the dilapidated if still grand structure, you find a cavernous chamber with rows of pewlike benches and, incongruously, a cage in the corner (for incarcerating miscreants on the spot?). Welcome to the courtroom of Judge A. Ted Bozeman.

At Hayneville's lone diner, where the blue plate special is often chicken-fried steak, a sign proclaims: "This ain't Wendy's—you'll eat any damn way we fix it." The motto of Judge Bozeman's courtroom seems to be: "You'll be tried any damn way we fix it."

I visited this Backwoods Blackstone in the fall of 1996 to see post-trial motions in the biggest judgment ever against America's largest corporation—an award of $150 million in compensatory and punitive damages against General Motors. I went there to find out how lawyers can make such a big killing. But in the process I discovered something else: the vital, indeed central role, that judges play in creating disorder in our courts. The case *Hardy v. GM* opened my eyes to a problem that doesn't get half the ink lavished on unprincipled pettifoggers but is arguably twice as important.

Alex Hardy, the plaintiff in the case before Judge Bozeman, flipped his Chevrolet Blazer over at 2:30 A.M. one night in 1991 and became paralyzed. A test administered hours after the wreck found he wasn't drunk. But immediately after the accident he told an eyewitness that he'd fallen asleep at the wheel; at the hospital he told a doctor he'd had "a few beers at a party prior to his accident." The severity of his injuries is no doubt explained by the fact that he wasn't wearing a seat belt.

Out of this quotidian tragedy, James Butler and Jere Beasley—the plaintiffs' lawyers—crafted a masterpiece of innuendo and insinuation. They claimed that the accident occurred because the Blazer's axle spontaneously snapped, an implausible suggestion fully rebutted by GM's engineering evidence. Then they claimed Hardy was injured not because he wasn't wearing a seat belt but because the door latch snapped open and he was ejected while the vehicle was turning over. Although GM argued that the door had never even opened, Hardy's lawyers labeled this a defect. No doubt, if the latch had failed to with-stand a nuclear explosion, they would call that a defect, too.

Butler and Beasley propounded an elaborate theory, complete with dis-torted company documents, about how the "big bosses at GM" conspired to foist killer door latches on the public. As evidence, they pointed to 211 side-door ejections in GM cars, many of which have led to lawsuits and settlements. But since there are some 30 million GM cars with these latches on the road, that represents an underwhelming failure rate of .001 percent. GM statistics show that its latches actually perform better than those of most competitors, and the National Highway Traffic Safety Administration has refused to take any action against the automaker.

Before the Hayneville trial, another set of plaintiffs' lawyers had presented a virtually identical case of GM door-latch failure in Brazoria County, Texas, another blue-collar, pro-plaintiff jurisdiction.

They sought some $110 million in punitive and compensatory damages. The jury ruled for the defense, finding no defect and no liability.

Even some members of the Hayneville jury didn't seem to buy the Butler-Beasley line. "I don't feel like all the GM door latches are bad," juror Sidney Logan Jr. told me. "I ain't got nothin' against GM 'cause I use GM motor products myself." Yet the all-black jury decided unanimously to award $150 million—*$150 million*—to Alex Hardy, who, as it happens, is also African American. Logan explains the jury's reasoning: "He got paralyzed. I figured we should give him something."

This is, in short, jury nullification—issuing a verdict that flies in the face of the law—and Judge Bozeman allowed it to occur. (To find out what's wrong with nullification, read on.) He even let the plaintiffs rig the jury selection. The jury pool—twenty-four blacks and eleven whites—was representative of Lowndes County's population distribution. But the plaintiff's lawyers used peremptory challenges to strike ten whites, leaving an all-black jury. (The eleventh white had been involved in a similar accident and was knocked off the jury by GM.) The Supreme Court has held that using peremptory challenge in a racially biased manner is unconstitutional, and the defendants objected to the plaintiffs' tactics, but Judge Bozeman decided the plaintiffs' conduct was perfectly acceptable.

It's hard to overestimate the significance of this apparent dereliction of duty. The previous year, according to the *Detroit News*, "a Lowndes County jury found for GM in another wrongful death case—after a different trial judge insisted on a jury that included both races."

Nor did Judge Bozeman seem particularly perturbed by possible juror misconduct during the trial. On the penultimate day of the trial, one of the defendant's paralegals overheard a juror lean over to a plaintiff's attorney and declare, "How long are we going to have sit here and listen to these lies?" GM, citing state court precedents, argued that the judge had a duty to determine whether "this juror had decided the case prior to the close of the evidence and whether she had—due to her strong feelings—influenced other jurors."

But Bozeman refused to take any action, explaining that the juror "could express her feelings out loud as long as others aren't influenced by that because that's her thought pattern." It's unclear how he knew the juror hadn't committed misconduct since he never bothered to question either her or other members of the panel.

General Motors' lawyers suggest that the judge was more than inattentive; they argue that because of his links to the Beasley law firm, the plaintiff's lawyers, he had a conflict of interest in handling the trial. At the time that Bozeman volunteered to take over the Hardy case from another jurist—early April 1996—Bozeman's wife, Mildred, was suing a national insurance company. She was being represented by the Beasley firm, to which she had been referred by the judge's son, also a lawyer. This was not a giant class action suit with numerous plaintiffs; Mildred Bozeman was the sole plaintiff in this potentially lucrative case. In addition, the judge's other son apparently worked as an investigator for the Beasley firm.

GM says it knew nothing of this when its lawyers first appeared before Bozeman at a pre-trial hearing on May 2, 1996. Negotiations for a settlement between the two parties were then in full swing. GM later stated in court filings: "Several rulings made at the May 2 hearing—most notably Judge Bozeman's indication that he intended to exclude evidence that Mr. Hardy was not wearing his seat belt—significantly affected the settlement value of the case." It was not until another hearing on May 8 that Bozeman revealed, "to the astonishment of General Motors' counsel," his apparent conflict of interest.

Bozeman declared in court that he had not been aware that his wife was being represented by Beasley's firm until April 29, when one of Beasley's colleagues called and broke the news to him. (Perhaps Mildred Bozeman had so many lawyers on retainer that the judge couldn't keep track of them all?) Instead of immediately disclosing the conflict to GM, Judge Bozeman acceded to the plaintiffs' request that he give them "a few days to research" and "see what happens." Consequently, the May 2 hearing and settlement talks proceeded apace with GM still in the dark. In fact, says the company in legal filings, "If this case had settled on May 8, General Motors possibly would never have known about Judge Bozeman's relationship with plaintiffs' counsel."

As it was, settlement talks fell apart, necessitating the May 8 hearing. The day before, the Beasley firm withdrew as counsel for Mrs. Bozeman. The judge announced that this solved all the problems and refused to recuse himself from the case. GM asked the state supreme court to kick him off the proceedings, but the justices never ruled on the motion, so Bozeman stayed on the case. Meanwhile, the state Judicial Inquiry Commission absolved Bozeman of wrongdoing, concluding that Beasley's withdrawal as counsel for Mrs. Bozeman had remedied the conflict, if any had existed in the first place. But GM continues to argue that the nine-day delay in notifying the company of the conflict gave an unfair advantage to the other side.

Judge Bozeman's attitude toward the proceedings became evident at the posttrial hearing, where GM petitioned for him to overturn or reduce the damage award. Jere Beasley kicked off the hearing with a rant against outsiders who might find something fishy about this outsize verdict. Having once served as George Wallace's lieutenant governor, he is well versed in stoking populist passions for his own gain (in this case, a share of potentially $50 million in fees, though he wouldn't divulge the actual amount). So Beasley thundered that GM was guilty of "close to criminal" conduct for spreading "false information" to its "surrogates and lackeys," including this author, sitting in the front row of the spectators' section. "They went out and put out false information about this trial, false information about the court, they even attacked the jury!" he exclaimed in mock horror.

A jurist of any standing and independence would undoubtedly have put a quick stop to Beasley's rant, apropos of nothing. But the lawyer's sallies against the out-of-town defendants found a receptive audience in Judge Bozeman. The judge waxed indignantly about "all kinds of publicity about me" and about "this trial" that "was false." In short, he joined Beasley's populist pose, designed to poison the atmosphere against the out-of-state defendants—from "Dee-troit," as the local lawyers pronounced with relish.

The judge's attitude should not be surprising, given his background. He grew up in the area; received a bachelor's degree from something called Huntingdon College and a law degree from Jones Law School, a night school not accredited by the American Bar Association; practiced some law; and then in 1976 won election as a district judge, the lowest level of the state judiciary. He was to remain on the bench, never advancing, until the end of 1997, when he retired to make way for the next Judge Bozeman, his daughter. A. Ted—as he preferred to be known—won successive elections, reports a local newspaper, on the strength of the "mom vote" because the judge had a reputation for being tough on "deadbeat dads."

None of this is necessarily good preparation for trying a mega-case involving one of the world's largest corporations. Indeed Judge

Bozeman's command of the courtroom during the post-trial motions never appeared especially strong. When the lawyers would make motions, for instance, objecting to a witness's testimony, all eyes would turn to the judge for a ruling. He would get a deer-in-the-headlights look, a goofy grin would flit across his face, he would mumble something under his breath, and then the proceedings would continue—without anyone having any idea what he had just ruled. At other times, he appeared to be dozing on the bench. Afterward, observers broke into two camps: One camp held that the judge was in dreamland, the other that he was simply resting his tired eyelids.

What no one could dispute was that at one point during the proceedings, while a learned Yale professor was holding forth solely for the judge's benefit (no jury was present), Bozeman wandered into the audience, put his arm around one of the lawyers, and started whispering to him. "Go ahead, I'm paying attention," he insisted to the startled attorneys.

With such an alert jurist presiding, it should be no surprise that GM decided not to wait for the court's ruling on setting aside the $150 million verdict. It simply settled the case quietly. Never mind the merits: An out-of-state defendant can't get justice in a place like Lowndes County.

Why Judges Matter

GM'S ADVENTURES IN Alabama's legal wonderland illustrate the problems that judges of dubious competence can cause. Yet this is a concern that all too rarely captures public attention. Apart from a few high-profile trials—the O. J. Simpson and Timothy McVeigh cases come to mind—virtually the only sustained discussion of judging occurs during Supreme Court nomination hearings.

When they're not degenerating into name-calling about "back-alley abortions" and "high-tech lynchings," these debates are usually conducted at a rarefied level, with terms like "natural law" and "substantive due process" freely tossed around. Whatever your opinion about the political desirability of a particular nominee, there's usually no question that the candidate, whether Robert Bork or Stephen Breyer, is highly intelligent, experienced, learned, honest, and so forth. But drawing conclusions about most judges by observing Supreme Court nominees is like drawing conclusions about sandlot baseball players by observing the New York Yankees.

The vast middle ground of American judges, it is fair to say, is far removed from the world of a Bork or a Breyer. Indeed, no one would confuse A. Ted Bozeman with a Supreme Court candidate. Yet judges like Bozeman are, arguably, more important to the future of the legal system than the nine members of the Supreme Court. These ordinary judges—who are likely to work for a state, not a federal, court; who are likely to preside over trials, not appeals; and who, in all likelihood, will never to be written about in the *New York Times*—are the ones responsible, on a daily basis, for making the wheels of justice turn.

It is a heavy burden. True, American judges enjoy less power than their European counterparts, who usually make the fact-finding decisions that in this country are generally reserved for juries. But U.S. judges can't escape responsibility for what goes on in their courtrooms, even if many of the ultimate decisions are made by juries.

In the first place, the vast majority of criminal and civil cases—more than 90 percent—are settled, not tried before a jury; judges guide these settlements and can shape the final outcome through their rulings on various motions. Even when cases do go to a jury, judges can influence the jurors through their comments and instructions. They can tilt their rulings on motions in favor of one side or the other. When all else fails, they can intervene directly and issue a verdict from the bench, notwithstanding what the jury says (the only limitation being that a judge can't find a defendant in a criminal case guilty). And judges play an outsize role in the penalty phase of the trial, ultimately deciding how much, if anything, in damages a plaintiff collects in a civil action and how much, if any, jail time the defendant receives in a criminal case.

Judges are supposed to use all this power to make sure that justice is done, that at some basic level the verdicts issued in their courts display a certain degree of reasonableness. "The judge," according to the great jurist Benjamin Cardozo, "is under a duty, within the limits of his powers of innovation, to maintain a relation between law and morals, between the precepts of jurisprudence and those of reason and good conscience."

Alas, today too many judges aren't doing their duty; law is diverging, as in the *Hardy v. GM* case, from the dictates of reason and morality. The cause for this failure, I believe, is that we have too many judges presiding in our courts whose arrogance far surpasses their competence.

So what else is new? you may say. And with reason. It's probably true that the bench has always had its share of petty tyrants and nincompoops. But today it matters more—simply because the law matters more. Since 1960, the number of lawyers has grown far faster than the population. The number of pages in the *Federal Register*, the annual listing of all the government's new regulations, has skyrocketed in the same period. So has the number of civil and criminal cases.

All this has vastly increased the power of the judiciary and has expanded its control over our lives. Thus, what could have been shrugged off as a petty annoyance a hundred years ago—bad judges issuing bad decisions—today assumes the proportions of a much more substantial problem. In this chapter, we'll examine the dysfunctional process for selecting and monitoring judges and focus on one of its consequences: judges who display a dismaying degree of high-handedness in both their personal and professional conduct.

A Good Judge Is Hard to Find

There's a Dilbert cartoon I'm fond of: Dilbert and a coworker are told they're being passed over for a promotion to district manager. The boss explains that their "technical knowledge is too valuable to lose." Therefore, he announces, "The only logical choice is to promote Al"—a dweeb staring vacantly into space—"because he has no valuable knowledge."

That's actually a good summary of the judicial selection process and helps to explain why we have so many "benchwarmers" in our courts. The American way of picking judges is practically designed to exclude the best and the brightest; thus, we wind up with the likes of A. Ted Bozeman. "Most judges, even Supreme Court Justices, have been plucked from well-deserved intellectual obscurity," writes one observer.

To be sure, there are some notable exceptions. The federal appeals courts, the U.S. Supreme Court, and a few state supreme courts draw some of the smartest people in government service—the likes of federal appeals judges José Cabranes, Amalya Kearse, Richard Arnold (all

Democratic appointees); and Frank Easterbrook, Alex Kozinski, and Laurence Silberman (all Republican appointees).

But for the most part, lawyers of towering intellect and ambition don't wind up on the bench. Attorneys of great drive, who aren't afraid of unrelenting toil and pressure, who flourish in an environment of high risks and high rewards, will naturally gravitate to the major law firms, where starting associates earn more than most judges. Lawyers with a burning desire to change the world will usually go off to law school faculties or public interest law firms.

The best of this lot will often resist the siren song of the bench. I know of one law professor, one of the most brilliant in the country, who was offered a federal judgeship in the 1980s—not a mere state appointment—and flatly turned it down. The person telling me this story, who worked in the Justice Department at the time, explained, "He felt that he could have more influence if he stayed at the university. And he was probably right."

Who winds up wearing black robes, then? All too many backslappers and palm greasers, toadies and lickspittles. Would-be judges have to spend years ingratiating themselves in political circles, running errands and doing favors, before they're finally picked for the bench. Most judges aren't selected on merit, any more than politicians are. They're usually selected because of political pull and, increasingly these days, because of skin color or gender. As Curtis Bok once noted: "It has been said that a judge is a member of the Bar who once knew a governor." That's not quite true; sometimes you have to know a legislator, too.

It's hard to generalize about judicial selection, since each state does things a bit differently, often choosing different levels of judges in different ways. But here's how judicial selection works, broadly speaking, across the country:

- Eight states give the governor almost complete power over judicial selection, with no input from voters. In Rhode Island, the governor can appoint judges for life; in Massachusetts and New Hampshire, until age seventy.

- Nine states allow the governor to pick judges who are then subject, after a year on the bench, to a straight up-or-down retention vote. This system of "merit selection" is known as the Missouri model, named for the state where it was first implemented in

1940. In these states, judges are nominated for the governor's consideration by political and legal worthies who meet in secretive selection committees.

- Seventeen states select judges through nonpartisan elections, which in practice doesn't differ much from the Missouri system, since many, perhaps most, of the judicial candidates are first appointed by the governor to fill unexpired terms after a previous judge has died or quit. They then run for election as incumbents—and invariably win.

- In three states—Connecticut, Virginia, and South Carolina—judges are picked by the legislature, so former legislators tend to be heavily represented on the bench.

- The remaining thirteen states use partisan election, where there's not even the pretense of sorting candidates based on qualifications and politicos simply campaign for judicial office as they would for student council president, congressman, and other disreputable posts. *A favorable ruling in every pot!*

No matter which variant a state employs, the winners are inevitably chosen based more on their skill at glad-handing than opinion writing; in other words, based on political rather than judicial skills. The method of picking federal judges is little better. Again, the overriding consideration—sometimes the *sole* consideration—seems to be the candidate's service to the party in power. Indeed, an academic study found that between 60 and 70 percent of appointees to the federal courts, from Franklin Roosevelt to Ronald Reagan, were politically active prior to their selection, and more than 90 percent belonged to the same political party as the president who appointed them.

This glad-handing approach can sometimes produce comic consequences. In 1996, for instance, President Bill Clinton nominated to the U.S. Court of Appeals for the Eleventh Circuit—one of the most important judicial posts in the country—a Miami plaintiff lawyer named Charles "Bud" Stack. His chief qualification seemed to be that he had raised more than $7 million for the 1992 Clinton-Gore campaign. His nomination was scuttled only after he revealed during a Senate Judiciary Committee hearing that he had never heard of

Adarand Constructors, Inc. v. Peña—the most famous Supreme Court case of the previous term, which had struck down most federal racial preferences.

This know-nothing system of picking judges stands in stark contrast to the way judges are chosen elsewhere. In many civilized countries, including most of those in continental Europe, being a judge is a lifelong occupation, a part of the civil service. Applicants undergo a rigorous testing process after law school, then they're trained and given low-level judgeships, where they have to prove themselves before being promoted to more senior positions. In Germany, for instance, a judge must spend three probationary years on the bench before applying for life tenure. In France, candidates must generally have twenty-five years of lawyering experience or pass a competitive examination after twenty-eight months of training at the Ecole Nationale de la Magistrature. In democratic and egalitarian America, however, more testing is required to get a driver's license—to say nothing of a liquor license or a taxi medallion, which are *really* hard to get—than a judge's gavel.

A Process That Produced a Crackhead

Michael Gallagher could testify about how easy it is to become a judge. He should have had some time to reflect on that subject while in prison.

In 1995, he pled guilty in federal court to possession of cocaine with intent to distribute. At first he was sentenced only to a residential drug treatment program, but after testing positive for cocaine, he was ordered to spend a year in prison and pay a $20,000 fine. At the time of his arrest, this crackhead was a judge on the Common Pleas Court of Cuyahoga County (Cleveland), Ohio. Prosecutors said that Gallagher was arrested right after he offered an undercover Drug Enforcement Administration (DEA) agent a couple of lines of cocaine in the judge's own bedroom.

The judge reportedly called himself "Chef Boyardee" in allusion to his ability to cook powder cocaine into crack. He also drank heavily and smoked marijuana in front of his children; he was polite enough, however, to adjourn to another room of his house when he used crack. He caroused with a hooker named (no kidding) Sunday Lamb and even asked her to marry him; she refused.

The judge made no secret of his unconventional views. In court, after sentencing a drug user to probation, he proclaimed that he favored the legalization of drugs and that drug abuse was a victimless crime. He frequently appeared disheveled at work and sometimes referred to lawyers as "dude" and "man." "He was terribly addicted to cocaine," Gallagher's lawyer told me. "It was a pathetic situation."

How on earth did Gallagher ever become a judge in the first place? Simple: He ran. In 1990, the thirty-three-year-old attorney decided to seek office after he got mad at a judge who refused to reduce the drug sentence of one of his clients. "Your honor!" he hollered. "I'm going to run against you next time!" He carried out his threat, though he didn't seem to do much campaigning after paying his $50 filing fee.

Gallagher had more negatives than Newt Gingrich: A graduate of Cleveland-Marshall College of Law, he received one of the lowest ratings ever given out by the Cleveland Bar Association in its surveys of judicial candidates. In addition, in 1986 he had been convicted of assaulting his ex-wife and trying to suffocate her with a bath towel.

Despite these shortcomings, he easily beat three better-qualified candidates—largely, it appears, on the strength of his name. "Candidates with the name Gallagher, like other Irish names such as Sweeney and Corrigan, have traditionally done well in Cuyahoga County," reported a Cleveland newspaper, in all seriousness.

Oh well, *that* explains it.

It should give us pause that someone like Michael Gallagher so easily won a judicial election. It's much harder to imagine a crackhead getting elected to Congress or even to a state legislature. We pay a lot less attention to judicial candidates, so we get a much lower quality candidate.

And although there may be few crackhead judges, there are plenty of successful judicial candidates just as unqualified as Michael Gallagher. Occasionally, a few first-rate minds also make it onto the bench, but only, it seems, by accident. The system is designed to produce political mediocrities, not independent thinkers. Ted Bozemans, not Learned Hands. Hence the old joke: What do you call a lawyer with an IQ of 80? Your honor.

Incompetence in the Courtroom

THE PROBLEM of low-quality candidates getting picked for the bench is compounded by the fact that larval Cardozos receive little or no training. This is no small concern, since being a judge requires considerable technical skills.

Trial judges must rule on evidentiary matters, decide summary judgment motions, keep control of a courtroom, and instruct a jury. Appeals judges must "distinguish" cases (the process of deciding which precedents apply to the case before you), interpret statutes, and write opinions (or at least supervise clerks who write opinions). These are not skills the average lawyer picks up during the ordinary course of a career. Many of those appointed to the bench don't even have trial experience (which isn't at all unusual, since, TV depictions notwithstanding, many lawyers never see the inside of a courtroom). Yet once on the bench, they're simply expected to be competent from day one, the only real check on them being appellate courts, which are unlikely to catch and correct every mistake inept trial judges commit.

The system essentially operates on an optimistic, if perhaps unrealistic, premise: that lower court judges, through a process of trial and error, will eventually learn to do their jobs properly. But no number of appellate reversals is likely to teach a judge the most essential qualification for his job. This is that elusive quality know as judiciousness, which my dictionary defines as "having or exhibiting sound judgment; prudent."

Not many of us could claim to be "judicious." I couldn't. But then I'm not a judge. Unfortunately, too many of those wielding gavels aren't judicious either. It's not just judges in rural Alabama that don't measure up. In fact, the most famous judge in America makes A. Ted Bozeman look like Oliver Wendell Holmes by comparison.

How Not to Run a Trial

The O. J. Simpson trial has been called a circus, but that's doing a grave injustice to Ringling Brothers and Barnum and Bailey, which run a tightly choreographed show. The Simpson trial was simply a mess—chaos in the courtroom, the judicial equivalent of the 1992 Los Angeles riots. Part of the culpability can be apportioned to the prosecutors, who bungled their courtroom presentation, and to the defense attorneys, who threw more sand than usual into the gears of justice. But no man shoulders more responsibility than Judge Lance Ito of the Los Angeles County Superior Court. "I blame Ito 100 percent for allowing it all to happen," writes veteran prosecutor Vincent Bugliosi.

The judge's faults would take a book to sum up, but since far too many tomes already have been devoted to the Trial of the Century, we need only sketch the broad outlines of the indictment against Lance Ito.

Count One: "Judge Ego" was fatally lacking in the gravitas needed to preside over a major trial. During one break scheduled for fifteen minutes, the judge became so engrossed in conversation with Larry King that finally, after about forty minutes, the Suspendered One asked him, "Don't you have to get back to court?"

Count Two: Ito allowed TV coverage to warp the trial proceedings. "Cameras caused all the lawyers to change our approach and our style," prosecutor Christopher Darden later recalled. "Everyone became long-winded and abrasive. Often without meaning to, we tailored our arguments to the millions of people watching and the experts second-guessing our every move." (At least Judge Bozeman was smart enough not to let cameras into his court to watch the fiasco unfolding therein.)

Count Three: The judge lost control of his own courtroom. Nothing came to symbolize Ito's lack of control better than an exchange between F. Lee Bailey and Marcia Clark. The defense lawyer took out a glove he wanted to use during the questioning of Mark Fuhrman. Clark examined the glove for a minute and said, "Size small—I guess it is Mr. Bailey's," an obvious reference to the folklore linking a man's hands with another part of his anatomy. Such were the weighty legal issues being batted around in Ito's court.

Count Four: Ito allowed the trial to drag on for far too long. By the time it was all over, the jurors had endured more than eight months of proceedings, including 45,000 pages of trial transcripts, 1,105 pieces of evidence, and 133 witnesses.

Count Five: The most serious error Ito made was allowing the defense to play the "race card," to make the trial about Mark Fuhrman, not O. J. Simpson. This error seems especially glaring in hindsight, since a seventeen-month-long Los Angeles Police Department (LAPD) investigation determined that none of the brutality and abuse charges against Fuhrman were true.

Yet Ito allowed F. Lee Bailey to cross-examine Fuhrman about his use of the word "nigger" (what's the relevance of this in a murder trial?); he allowed into evidence snippets of the Fuhrman tapes in which he used the "n" word; and, until overridden by an appeals court, he even planned to inform jurors, in contravention of the California Evidence Code, that they could take into account Fuhrman's invocation of his Fifth Amendment right not to testify further. To cap off the proceedings, Ito allowed Johnnie Cochran to compare Fuhrman with Hitler in his closing statement, in which he called the LAPD detective a "lying, perjuring, genocidal racist."

What Johnnie Cochran managed to do, his denials notwithstanding, comes down to two words: jury nullification. A prominent judge has explained that nullification occurs whenever a juror "based on his own sense of justice or fairness refuses to follow the law and convict in a particular case even though the facts seem to allow no other conclusion but guilt." There is some debate in fashionable academic circles about whether nullification is proper, but legally speaking, it is not a close call. Nullification is illegal. Period. As one appeals court has ruled: "A jury has no more 'right' to find a 'guilty' defendant 'not guilty' than it has to find a 'not guilty' defendant 'guilty', and the fact that the former cannot be corrected by a court, while the latter can be, does not create a right out of the power to misapply the law. Such verdicts are lawless and a denial of due process and constitute an exercise of erroneously seized power." It's hard to imagine a greater dereliction of duty by a trial judge than allowing such a "lawless" verdict to take place in his courtroom—yet that's precisely what Ito did.

Of course, it's possible to object that *The People of the State of California v. Orenthal James Simpson* was so sprawling, so complicated, so media-saturated that no judge could have managed the case. It's possible, except for one thing.

Another judge *did* manage to try O. J. Simpson fairly—the judge who presided over the civil trial where O.J. was held liable for $33.5 million in compensatory and punitive damages. Judge . . . Well, what was his name? If you don't remember, that's a good sign. It means that this judge did his job—running a trial instead of becoming a pop icon. His name, for the record, is Hiroshi Fujisaki and it's a fair bet you'll never see Jay Leno hosting a group of Dancing Fujisakis. He made the trial move briskly, he didn't allow the attorneys to act up, and, perhaps most important, he made sure that all cameras were checked at the courthouse door.

Many people connected with the Los Angeles criminal justice system still insist that Lance Ito is a fine jurist who got a bum rap for making mistakes in one case. It's undoubtedly true that he is energetic, intelligent, and well-intentioned. But he also seems to be remarkably unburdened by sound judgment. It's notable that Ito muffed the only other high profile case he's presided over—the conviction of savings-and-loan kingpin Charles Keating on state charges of securities fraud.

A federal judge overturned the jury's conviction on the grounds that Ito had botched the jury instructions. In the first place, U.S. district judge John Davies held that Ito had misread the statute and had erroneously told jurors they could convict Keating without a finding of mens rea (criminal intent). Second, Judge Davies ruled that Ito's specially crafted instruction—which allowed the jury to convict Keating of "aiding and abetting" the sale of bonds—created a "novel" offense and "violated his [Keating's] rights under the United States Constitution." In sum, Judge Davies wrote, Keating's conviction was based on a "nonexistent and erroneous legal theory," a theory created by—who else?—Lance Ito.

Judge Ito's handling of the Simpson and Keating cases illustrates the disastrous consequences of a judge being out of his depth. And as we've seen, judicial selection, American-style, is practically designed to produce more than our fair share of such less-than-competent jurists.

The Least Accountable Branch

But surely there must at least be mechanisms to monitor judges once on the bench and remove those who don't do a good job. Aren't judges accountable to the voters, or legislators, or *someone*? In theory, yes, but ask yourself a question: Can you name a single judge who appeared on your last ballot? *A single one?*

Few voters pay attention to judicial elections, except under the most extraordinary circumstances, such as the elections that led to the banishment of ultra-egregious California Supreme Court chief justice Rose Bird in 1986 and Tennessee Supreme Court justice Penny White in 1996. In most cases, voters dutifully troop to the polls, only to be confronted with long lists of unknown aspirants, all vying for judge-ships. They might as well be lists of subatomic particles or angel food cake ingredients, for all the good they'll do the average citizen.

The default position that most people adopt is simply to vote for the incumbents. Term limits proponents often bemoan the high reelection rate of congressmen; well, judges are voted out of office only slightly more often than Prince Rainier of Monaco, and their terms (often ten to fifteen years) rival that of the late, unlamented Romanian president Nicolae Ceausescu. To be exact, only 1 percent of judges who have faced retention elections have been removed by the electorate.

Obviously, voters don't do a great job of watching judges and judi-cial candidates. And who can blame them, when they have so many more important things to do, like eating, sleeping, and paying bills. So who oversees the third branch of government? Journalists occasionally take jurists to task, but the judges and their sympathizers in the legal community always scream that any outside criticism of a judge's ruling is tantamount to constitutional treason. Legislators also occasionally oversee the third branch of government, but, as you might imagine, a subject that doesn't grip their constituents doesn't hold much interest for most politicians.

Judges, then, are for the most part watched by . . . judges. Most states have some kind of judicial review commission, usually made up of judges, sometimes with lawyers and laymen also serving. Their pro-ceedings are usually conducted in private, and the punishments they mete out are as rare as they are lenient. How could it be otherwise? Just imagine if the only check on butchers were other butchers, the only check on investment bankers other investment bankers. How much oversight would there be?

In Chapter 7, we'll see how this lack of oversight can breed conflicts of interest and even outright corruption by judges. The relevant point here is that judges can get away with a lot of behavior that's (merely) unethical, behavior that they simply wouldn't tolerate of the litigants or lawyers who appear before them in court.

What a State Judge Can Get Away With

James Dee Heiple may be virtually unknown outside Illinois, but within the state his name has become a byword for judicial unaccountability. He was elected as a Republican to the Illinois Supreme Court in 1990. Four years later, he wrote an opinion wrenching three-year-old Baby Richard away from the only family he'd ever known—his adopted parents—and returning custody to his biological father.

In reaching its decision, the state Supreme Court overrode all precedent, several statutes, and the rulings of two lower courts, which had determined that the biological father was unfit because he hadn't expressed an interest in the child soon after he was born. In Justice Heiple's opinion, all that didn't matter because the biological father claimed he had thought his child was dead—the mother, his ex-girlfriend, had deceived him after being dumped—and therefore he had been unable to exercise his paternal rights in a timely manner. There was, in fact, some dispute over whether the father had known or not, but the point is, it shouldn't have mattered—a law's a law. And in this case, the law clearly favored the adoptive parents. The Supreme Court ruled otherwise without even bothering to find out what was in the best interest of the baby, who was taken out of a loving and comfortable home, sobbing and protesting, crying, "Please don't send me away."

This decision was lambasted by critics ranging from *Chicago Tribune* columnist Bob Greene to Governor Jim Edgar. The judge didn't take kindly to being brought to task for his high-handed ruling. In his final opinion in the case, Justice Heiple lashed out at his critics in a shockingly injudicious manner. He accused Greene of "journalistic terrorism" and suggested that the governor "return to the classroom and take up Civics 101." All this, mind you, in an official court document. A law professor accurately characterized Heiple as "petulant" and "thin-skinned."

Heiple's out-of-court conduct did nothing to dispel these impressions. He's been stopped repeatedly for violating the traffic laws. And just as repeatedly, police have testified, he flashed his court ID, not his driver's license, to escape punishment. Matters went still further in the early morning hours of January 27, 1996.

After the judge was pulled over by a cop in his hometown of Pekin, Illinois, he allegedly drove off without permission. The police pursued him, sirens wailing, but the judge didn't pull over until he reached his home. According to the police report, he demanded of them, "Do you know who I am?" and "Do you know what you're doing?" He was arrested for disobeying a police officer and speeding, among other charges.

He pleaded no contest to those charges and paid a $200 fine, though he later insisted that the police account was misleading and that the cops had "baited" him to fight. He further asserted that one of the small towns where he'd been pulled over had a policy of not ticketing judges, an assertion adamantly denied by the local police chief, who declared, "He's just trying to get himself out of the trouble he's in."

Oh, the lengths Heiple went to to avoid any more trouble. He appointed as chairman of the Illinois Courts Commission, which is in charge of disciplining judges, his closest friend on the Supreme Court, Moses Harrison II. In so doing, he violated a tradition that the post goes to the court's second-ranking member. Just ten days after he appointed Harrison, Heiple himself was charged with misconduct before the commission. He insists that he had no idea at the time of the appointment that he would be charged. But the Judicial Inquiry Board, the tiny, understaffed agency that prosecutes these cases, determined that Heiple knew at the time he appointed his friend Harrison that he was under investigation. The prosecutors charged that this appointment "created an unacceptable appearance of impropriety."

The Illinois Courts Commission has never exactly been an agency staffed by Elliott Nesses. In its thirty-three years of existence, it has disciplined . . . thirty-three judges. And only five of those were removed from the bench. In this case, the commission, led by Heiple's close friend, proved more than accommodating. After giving Heiple every break imaginable, the commission "censured" him—a slap on the wrist. Although Heiple finally stepped down as chief justice under threat of impeachment, he remained on the high court.

"The judicial disciplinary process is in deep trouble," commented Illinois lieutenant governor Bob Kustra. "This one man, Heiple, is about to destroy whatever credibility the courts have left in Illinois."

Federal Judges: Unaccountable for Life

Federal judges are, by and large, of higher quality than their state counterparts. But the problem of accountability is, if anything, worse on the federal bench. Few people, indeed, even few senators, pay attention to the selection of most federal judges. Many of them are confirmed by the Senate without even a recorded vote. Once on the bench, these judges can do pretty much what they like.

As one commentator writes:

> A federal judge can be lazy, lack judicial temperament, mistreat his staff, berate without reason the lawyers who appear before him, be reprimanded for ethical lapses, verge on or even slide into senility, be continually reversed for elementary legal mistakes . . . and misbehave in other ways that might get even a tenured civil servant or university professor fired; he will retain his office. His pay cannot be lowered, either—and neither can the pay of a good judge be raised.

That's not the assessment of some critic of the judiciary (like me); those words were written by Richard Posner, himself a sitting federal appeals judge.

The basic problem is that federal judges have lifetime tenure, and they have the power to overrule almost any decision made by another branch of government, state or federal. Their decisions, not to mention their ethics, are lightly overseen by their colleagues. There is, naturally, some pressure on federal judges to do a good job because otherwise their reputation among their friends and colleagues would suffer. But even when overruling district judges, appeals courts are usually loath to criticize the judge below, since after all, they're all in the same business, often in the same building, *for life*, and have to get along together.

Under a 1980 law, many of the appeals and district court judges in a judicial circuit (there are thirteen in the United States) sit together on a judicial council overseeing each other's conduct. These councils operate largely in secret and, at any rate, don't have the power to do anything beyond scolding recalcitrant judges. Even that power is exercised infrequently—which is no surprise, since this is the fox guarding the henhouse.

The Senate, of course, has the power to impeach, but impeachment occurs about as often as judges appear publicly in the nude. As Thomas Jefferson commented, the impeachment provision of the Constitution "is not even a scarecrow." In all of American history only thirteen federal judges have been impeached, and just seven of those convicted, though the pace is picking up: Three of those convictions, all of Carter appointees, have come since 1986.

We all know, thanks to Lord Acton, what comes from absolute power, and nobody in our society, with the possible exception of college football coaches, has as much unchecked authority as federal judges. Brian Duff, or rather Brian Barnett Duff—the middle name is of no small consequence, as we shall see—is a perfect exemplar of how much a federal judge can get away with.

Duff was a middling Republican politico—he served in the Illinois General Assembly and lost a race for state secretary of state—before becoming a Cook County Circuit Court judge. In return for his political work, then senator Charles Percy secured a federal judgeship for him from President Reagan.

Duff's temper on the bench was legendary. In 1979, when he was still a state judge, he became irate at his clerk—she says it was because she handed him a file in a way he didn't like; he says it was because she refused to work on election day. Whatever the cause, tempers flared. He threatened to hold her in contempt of court. She claims that he then ordered her arrest and held her for an hour. The judge says that all he did was ask her to leave the courtroom and go to the basement for the rest of the day. Either way, what an unprofessional way to treat a coworker!

The Chicago Council of Lawyers reported in a 1991 survey of federal judges that Duff's "outbursts go far beyond the range of irascibility that judges sometimes show toward lawyers." The evaluation added, "Some lawyers report that the only way to avoid Judge Duff's ire is to grovel and constantly flatter him."

That groveling could sometimes take bizarre form. During one period, Duff became fixated on his middle name. He insisted that it be included in all petitions and briefs submitted to him; his clerk even turned away documents that lacked the requisite "Barnett." "I did want my middle name used," the judge acknowledged to me, "and for legitimate reasons"—namely, that he's very proud of his middle name, which has genealogical significance to his Boston Irish family.

His behavior grew odder the longer he stayed on the job. "Observers in his courtroom," a newspaper reported in 1996, "say Duff has been seen sleeping on the bench, has read opinions that had been issued months previously and made unintelligible comments in court."

That year, Duff delayed for twelve months the narcotics trial of Larry Hoover, notorious leader of the Gangster Disciples in Chicago, despite government pleas that one witness in the case had already been killed and more might be harmed if the trial didn't start right away. The judge told me he was too busy with other cases—not to mention trips to England and Ireland that he was really looking forward to—to hear the case right away. After postponing the proceedings, Duff slapped a gag order on all concerned, forbidding them to discuss the case with the media. "If I find someone talking to the press, I'm going to bore them a new orifice," the judge memorably declared. (Duff now explains: "I thought it was better than something really dirty like anal aperture.") Larry Hoover wound up being convicted in a timely manner, but only after the case was reassigned to another judge.

In another case, a sprawling class-action suit brought by the American Civil Liberties Union (ACLU) alleging that Illinois had mismanaged its mental health system, the judge's conduct was even more dubious. In 1994, he met in his chambers privately for three and a half hours with "experts" he had appointed to investigate conditions in the mental health system. Duff refused to reveal what went on behind closed doors, but it emerged that the experts were attempting to persuade the judge to accept their pro-plaintiff conclusions, a breathtaking violation of the rule against judges holding ex parte communications on the merits of a case—that is, holding discussions where both sides are not represented.

The judge appeared to be so firmly on the plaintiffs' side that he pushed for significant concessions from the defendants—the state—in settlement talks. And he became quite agitated when he found out that the governor of Illinois, Jim Edgar, wasn't personally going to get involved in the negotiations. Of course, this was only one of many suits naming the governor as a defendant in his official capacity; it would be unwise, as well as impossible, for him to become personally involved in all of them. Nevertheless, Duff threatened the state with retaliation if it didn't produce Edgar.

"Do you know how many cases that I have in this courtroom right now that the Governor is very, very concerned with?" the judge demanded of the state's attorneys. "Do you?" To leave no doubt about his meaning, Duff then mentioned that opponents of a recent revenue bill worth "hundreds of millions of dollars" were seeking an injunction from him to block its implementation. "Does that mean that I'm not important to the Governor or that somehow or other I'm being pretentious?" Duff huffed.

Duff refused to recuse himself from the case, so the state eventually moved to disqualify him, despite the judge's eloquent warning that the lawyers would be in "deep doo" if their motion failed. In the event, it did not. A panel of the U.S. Court of Appeals for the Seventh Circuit removed Duff from the case. The judge, the panel wrote, had become "excessively cozy" with the experts, leading a "reasonable observer to be seriously concerned about the court's ability to conduct the trial impartially."

The Seventh Circuit ruling should not have been unexpected; Judge Duff's reversal rate, at 32 percent, was the highest of any U.S. district judge in Chicago. To add to the pressure on him, the *Chicago Tribune* reported that the Justice Department filed a sealed disciplinary complaint with the Judicial Council, claiming that the judge was biased against prosecutors, a not unreasonable conclusion in light of his decision in the Gangster Disciples case. (Duff's only comment to me: "If there was a sealed complaint, I never saw it.")

Amid this controversy in October 1996, the sixty-six-year-old judge announced that he would take "disability retirement," citing his history of heart trouble and denying that he was "being forced out." But don't forget, Duff is a federal judge, so there's really no getting rid of him. He immediately went on "senior status," which means that he continues to draw his $133,000 annual salary and to preside over a reduced caseload.

Not long after his "retirement," Duff ruled on a hotly contested challenge to the ward map used to elect city alderman. Injudicious judges, it seems, neither retire nor fade away; they just go on undermining justice.

Gavelitis: The Disease of the Bench

A JUDICIAL selection process that often results in bumbling candidates being chosen. A judicial oversight process that rarely punishes judges for even flagrant misconduct on the bench. Put those together, and what do you get? A breeding ground for a disease I call "gavelitis."

This dread disease can be caused by wielding a gavel in the line of duty, and its symptoms include advanced pomposity, pathological sanctimoniousness, congenital self-importance, and aggravated eccentricity. Judges suffering from this disease grow so arrogant, so out of touch, so remote from everyday life that they think the normal rules of good behavior and human decency don't apply to them.

It's not hard to understand how judges can fall prey to this malady. After all, when you wear a black robe, everyone—staff, litigants, even haughty maître d's—bows and scrapes and genuflects before you. All your witticisms are suddenly hilarious, all your observations astute, all your suggestions readily adopted. Your fellow man invariably addresses you as "Your Honor" or "Judge." Nobody's ever mean to you and if they are, why, you can lock them up.

You think: How unusual . . . How wonderful . . . How fitting. That kind of obsequiousness is heady stuff in our rude, egalitarian society.

Is it any wonder then that so many judges issue high-handed orders from the bench—for example, ordering a New Jersey library to admit a smelly vagrant or telling an Arizona prison to make "hot pots" for cooking available to inmates—rulings that fly in the face of common sense and public opinion. In later chapters we'll examine many such decisions on their legal merits (or lack thereof). But first, it's important to point out that though these opinions are always cloaked in thick swathes of impressive-sounding legal jargon, they are often naked reflections of the judges' own lust for power. As a veteran judge once told me (not for attribution, of course): "Judicial activism is a psychological, not a jurisprudential, problem." What he meant, I think, is that activist judges—judges who expand their authority at every turn—are unable to exercise the self-control needed to rein in their self-aggrandizing impulses.

If that theory is correct, it stands to reason that some of the gavel wielders who are unable to control themselves in their public lives would be similarly troubled in their private lives. It's instructive, then, to see how gavelitis infected the conduct, official *and* unofficial, of one of America's leading judges.

Madness—or Gavelitis?

Sol Wachtler, the former chief judge of New York State, has gained a certain measure of notoriety and fame for his shocking downfall—he was sent to prison after harassing a former girlfriend—and his instant redemption on the talk-show circuit. His memoir, *After the Madness*, is a case study in judicial arrogance.

During his twenty years on the New York State Court of Appeals—the last eight as chief judge—Wachtler helped secure the court's reputation as among the most activist in the country. He proudly recalls, for instance, that he wrote an opinion striking down New York's blue laws governing Sunday closings. He doesn't explain why, after hundreds of years, the laws had suddenly become unconstitutional. Nor does he seem greatly troubled by the fact that the court had made an essentially legislative decision that had little basis in the law. "I had been given the responsibility of applying . . . contemporary standards in the explication of statues and the definition of constitutional rights," he proudly avers—and never mind what the drafters of those laws may have thought.

Throughout the book, Wachtler thumbs his nose at society's desire to punish criminals. He opposes the death penalty and suggests that "we should continue to explore alternatives to imprisonment"—the same old nostrums he implemented on the bench, even as crime rates soared. His soft-on-crime outlook was, understandably, reinforced by his stay in jail, where he seemed to fall for every inmate's sob story, leading him to conclude: "There are many people here in Butner [prison] who don't belong here."

Gavelitis became more pronounced near the end of Wachtler's stay on the bench. In 1991, while New York faced a crippling budget shortfall, Wachtler proposed a budget that increased funding for the state courts. Governor Mario Cuomo resisted his request, complaining that the chief judge was "refusing to share the burden of the state's fiscal crisis." So the chief judge sued the governor. Wachtler writes haughtily that "the governor sought to treat the budget submitted by the judiciary as if it were a budget submitted by one of his departments, as if it were an agency of the executive branch." The governor apparently didn't realize that judges enjoy a privileged position that allows them to gorge on taxpayers' money while the rest of government is tightening its belt.

Wachtler's fall finally came in 1992. He was arrested by the FBI, and convicted, for terrorizing his former girlfriend, Joy Silverman, and her fourteen-year-old daughter by writing what he now describes as "outrageous and harassing letters."

"How could my judgment have been so skewed as to blind me to the ruin I was bringing to a career, a profession, and a marriage, all of which I had nurtured for over forty years?" Wachtler asks. The answer he gives is that he was "sick," suffering from manic depression and self-medication. But most manic depressives don't violate the law; and in Wachtler's case, it was a strangely sudden outbreak of the disease from a man quite advanced in years and with no previous history of erratic behavior.

His book, perhaps inadvertently, offers another possible explanation for his bizarre behavior: Years of judging had convinced him that the standards he enforced for others didn't apply to him. "When I went into a place where the public gathered," he recalls, "the smiles and nods of approbation; the greetings and salutations—'Your Honor,' 'If it pleases the Court,' 'The Honorable,' 'Mr. Justice,' 'Chief Judge,' and, best of all, 'Judge'—the donning of the black robes; everyone rising on command when you enter a courtroom; it all meant so much to me. I wallowed in my vanity."

Most judges who wallow in their vanity do not, of course, send condoms in the mail to fourteen-year-old girls. As we shall see in the rest of this book, their hubris manifests itself in a manner far more destructive to society as a whole—through their decisions.

I hasten to add that we should not draw any overgeneralizations from Sol Wachtler's example. I do not mean to suggest that *all* proponents of judicial activism suffer from gavelitis in their personal lives as well. Far from it. William J. Brennan Jr., for instance, was not only one of the most activist Supreme Court justices of the twentieth century but also, by all accounts, one of the nicest and most pleasant. By contrast, Antonin Scalia, one of the least activist supremes, reportedly displays strong traces of gavelitis in his abrasive dealings with fellow justices, litigants, and even, on one occasion I'm familiar with, moot court participants at Harvard Law School.

This shows how arrogance can infect the conduct even of judges who take a humble view of the judiciary's powers. All the more reason to think that other judges—unrestrained by Scalia's jurisprudential philosophy—are apt to succumb to hubris in both their private and public conduct. The symptoms of gavelitis are seldom as striking as in the Wachtler example, but that doesn't mean that the disease isn't lurking, in a less virulent form, behind many another black robe.

What's Missing on the Bench

IT IS SAID that a fish has no conception of water; after all, it has nothing to compare it to. Likewise, it's hard to understand how truly awful some occupants of the bench are until we have a point of reference, a "benchmark."

There *are* judges who manage the rare feat of being dignified without becoming pompous; acting decisively, but never impetuously; and projecting an air of command, while avoiding overweening arrogance; in short, judges who manage not to catch gavelitis. One such jurist comes to mind: Richard Matsch, chief U.S. district judge in Colorado, who presided over the trial of Oklahoma City bomber Timothy McVeigh.

Though appointed to the bench in 1974 by President Nixon, Matsch is no Republican role model; he presided over a two-decade-long court decree mandating busing in Denver schools. But despite that bit of judicial activism, Matsch showed himself to be a model judge in his handling of the McVeigh matter.

It was a notable feat that the trial lasted a mere six weeks, not the eight months of the Simpson case. Much of the credit goes to Judge Matsch. He strictly limited sidebar conferences and kept the lawyers from stalling with curt commands to "move on!" Unlike Lance Ito, he demanded punctuality in court—and got it.

At one point during the pretrial motions in January 1997, defense lawyer Stephen Jones stopped his argument and asked, "Judge, it's twelve o'clock. Do you want us to break?" Matsch laconically replied: "Well, I have it as two and a half minutes before twelve. But I suppose we can break early if we can make up the time at the end of the day."

Also unlike Ito, Matsch kept the trial focused on the main issues. He refused to allow the defense team to introduce wild theories about some foreign conspiracy that could have been responsible for the Oklahoma City blast. He even limited testimony about the problems of the FBI lab strictly to the lab's handling of evidence in this case.

But Matsch couldn't be accused of unfairness to the defense. He moved the trial out of Oklahoma City to make the proceedings as impartial as possible. He allowed the defense lawyers to spend copious amounts of public money preparing their case. He delivered jury instructions favorable to the defense. And after McVeigh was finally convicted, the judge barred emotional evidence from the death penalty phase, lest the trial turn into a "lynching." All this made the guilty verdict virtually appeal-proof.

Perhaps the best thing that Matsch did was to prevent the proceedings from becoming a media jamboree. Cameras are of course barred from all federal trial courts. But Matsch went much further. He slapped a gag order on the attorneys to prevent them from trying the case in the press. He shielded the privacy of the jurors from the news media. And he closed key parts of the evidence to reporters' scrutiny.

It's possible to quibble with this or that decision, but the result is indisputable: Judge Matsch delivered justice for the 168 victims of the Oklahoma City bombing. And he helped restore some luster to a criminal justice system badly tarnished by the Simpson trial.

Conclusion: A Matsch-less Judiciary

THE PROBLEM is that the bench seems to boast many more judges like Ted Bozeman (the judge in the $150 million GM case), Michael Gallagher (the crackhead judge), Brian Duff (the tyrannical federal judge), and Lance Ito (no explanation needed) than Richard Matsch. This is perhaps inevitable; bad judges will always outnumber good ones, for as Alexander Hamilton noted in *Federalist No. 78*: "[T]here can be but few men in the society who will have sufficient skill in the laws to qualify them for the stations of judges. And making proper deductions for the ordinary depravity of human nature, the number must be still smaller of those who unite the requisite integrity with the requisite knowledge." But at least we can try to curb the consequences of this shortfall by increasing public oversight of judges and paying greater attention to the judicial selection process.

That we haven't, so far, has created many of the problems that will be discussed in the rest of this book: criminals getting loose; civil defendants being socked for unfair damage awards; voters losing the power to decide a host of controversial issues. We can and should discuss legislative fixes for each of these specific problems. But until we focus on the problem of bad judges, we're never going to improve our legal system as a whole.

CHAPTER 2

"Perverse Failures"

[J]ustice, though due to the accused, is due to the accuser also. The concept of fairness must not be strained till it is narrowed to a filament. We are to keep the balance true.

JUSTICE BENJAMIN CARDOZO, *Snyder v. Massachusetts*

KEVIN ROBERSON was furious with a former girlfriend. She had called from a friend's house and they had gotten into an argument over the telephone. So he glanced down at his Caller ID feature and figured out where she was calling from. He drove over there. Once he arrived, witnesses later testified, she ran into the shower and tried to hide from him. But he found her, pistol-whipped her, and then shot her in the chest with a 9 millimeter semiautomatic. He left her three little children—two girls, ages four and five, and a one-year-old boy—as orphans.

What makes this tragedy even more disturbing is that it could easily have been prevented. At the time of the shooting, Roberson was awaiting trial in five cases, and he was still on probation for five other crimes. It didn't take a genius to see that Roberson was not somebody who should be on the street; though only twenty-three years old, he'd already piled up fourteen convictions. In one case, still pending at the time of the Caller ID murder, Roberson had been charged with shooting up a house; two bullets had landed on a mattress where two boys—ages three and six—were sleeping.

But Judge Terry McDonald, of the 186th District Court in San Antonio, Texas, simply refused to crack down on Roberson. Prosecutors had tried to revoke Roberson's probation, but McDonald refused. On February 23, 1995, Roberson walked out of jail on a $5,000 bond set by Judge McDonald. A month later, Roberson's former girlfriend was dead.

"I look for the good in people," Judge McDonald explained to me. "[T]he easy thing for a judge to do is to send everyone to prison and disregard the fact that some crimes are committed by basically good people who deserve a second chance." Critics have a simpler explanation for the judge's conduct. "He is pro-defendant," said one lawyer.

Among the reasons given in the Preamble to the Constitution for the creation of our government is to "establish Justice" and "insure domestic Tranquillity." A big part of this mandate falls on judges. Society is endangered when kind-hearted judges like Terry McDonald don't crack down on thugs. And there are certainly plenty of occasions when McDonald didn't seem to do enough—even when he had murderers in his courtroom.

Consider the case of Danny Gonzales, age nineteen. He pled no contest to murder after taking part in a gang shooting that left two teenagers dead and two others injured. Judge McDonald wasn't convinced that Gonzales had pulled the trigger, only that he had driven the car from which the shots were fired, even though two witnesses under grants of immunity both fingered Gonzales as a shooter. McDonald told me that in his opinion, the prosecution had made a "bad choice" to offer those witnesses immunity. So over the protests of prosecutors, the judge sentenced Danny Gonzales to ten years' "deferred adjudication"—meaning that he didn't have to go to jail, and after ten years he could have the crime expunged from his record.

In another murder case, involving a defendant charged with going on a rampage in a grocery store warehouse that left one man dead and another wounded, Judge McDonald allowed the suspect to walk out of court before trial by lowering his bail from $150,000 to $50,000. In his own defense, McDonald claimed to me that Texas law at that time "did not permit the trial court to take into consideration the safety of the community in setting bonds" or to set bond "in excess of fifty thousand dollars."

In support of these propositions, McDonald mailed me some Texas criminal court precedents. Upon close examination, however, those cases don't back up his contentions. It's true that the judge was well within his rights to reduce bail to $50,000, but he wasn't *compelled* to set such a low bail. In other cases, Texas appeals courts had approved bail of $75,000–$100,000 for defendants charged with murder or even lesser offenses. Furthermore, while the law declares that "the primary purpose of an appearance bond is to secure the defendant's presence in court for trial," the law also states that a judge could "take the safety of the victim or his family into consideration."

"There are judges who will go out on a limb and set higher bail and they are reversed only infrequently," one assistant district attorney in San Antonio told me. "You can walk the line and do the right thing." But that's not what McDonald chose to do in this instance. His decision is one that the victim's relatives find hard to fathom. "This guy cold-bloodedly murdered my brother and he sought out others," said the victim's sister. "This guy is out walking the streets, happy, going about his life. He's not feeling any of what we're feeling."

Similar anguish was expressed by the family of Charles Perez Resendez, a homosexual high-school substitute teacher. He was out on the town on New Year's Eve 1989 when he picked up a twenty-one-year-old marine cadet. The marine later testified that he was "the most drunk I have been in my life" and that he woke up in a hotel room, partially naked, with Resendez lying next to him and a used condom on the floor. The marine was so upset that he beat Resendez to death. He later changed his story about what had occurred and eventually claimed that Resendez had drugged and raped him. Although this claim was far from proven (it appears the district attorney simply accepted the marine's account), Judge McDonald gave him a ten-year suspended sentence as part of a plea bargain. "The circumstances of the offense and the defendant's lack of criminal history were the basis for my decision," the judge told me.

"Where is the justice?" cried Resendez's brother. "We believed in the system and nothing happened. They [the district attorney's] office kept telling us, 'Don't worry about it, the guy will be punished for what he did.' Only he wasn't."

The judge's indulgent attitude toward defendants should perhaps not be surprising, given his background. A former law school professor and a veteran criminal defense lawyer, he briefly worked for the Bexar County district attorney's office but was fired after being accused of giving a too-lenient plea bargain to a defendant represented by his former law firm. "I offered five years," McDonald recalled nonchalantly. "The D.A. felt forty was appropriate." He was elected to the bench as a Democrat in 1990 and was narrowly reelected over a Republican challenger in 1994. Terry McDonald seems to personify the give-criminals-another-chance views so prevalent among the more enlightened occupants of the bench.

While this judge is coddling criminals in his court, a criminal in his own family is being coddled by other judges. His son, Sean McDonald, age nineteen, pleaded guilty in 1994 to robbing a Stop-N-Go convenience store; the younger McDonald allegedly held the clerk in a headlock while an accomplice beat him with the Club, an automobile antitheft device. Sean was sentenced to ten years' probation. He violated the probation by testing positive for cocaine. Yet he was given another shot at probation, even though the presiding judge acknowledged, "He's been a consistently bad boy." (Judge McDonald's only comment: "My son was not convicted and has nothing to with [*sic*] what I do professionally or personally." It's true that Sean wasn't officially "convicted"—but only because he received a sentence of "deferred adjudication" from a lenient judge. He would receive a conviction and jail time if he violates the terms of his ten-year probation.)

Oh, one bit of good news. Judge McDonald may finally be learning. After Kevin Roberson pled guilty in the Caller ID murder case, McDonald sentenced him to life in prison over the objections of defense lawyers. That doesn't mean Roberson will actually serve life— according to prosecutors, he'll be eligible for parole in forty to fifty years—but it certainly represents a welcome break with precedent in McDonald's court.

Why We Need Tough Judges

SOME READERS might think: Why worry about lenient judges like Terry McDonald? Aren't crime rates coming down anyway? Isn't the war on crime already won? How much damage could judges be doing?

It's true that crime rates have fallen in the 1990s. But before popping open the bubbly, consider a couple of sobering caveats.

First, crime is still high by historical levels. In 1960, to select a year at random from the "good ol' days," 160 violent crimes per 100,000 people were reported. In 1995, after a falloff of several years, the figure was 685 violent crimes per 100,000—more than four times as high. "Crime is down but that's only because things were so bad before," notes James Fox, a criminologist at Northeastern University.

The second point of caution concerns the future. It doesn't look good. The number of fourteen- to seventeen-year-old boys is projected to increase by about 500,000 in the next few years. Since about 6 percent of young males commit half the serious crimes in that age group, we can expect 30,000 additional violent criminals on the streets. Worse still, reports criminologist John DiIulio, "since the 1950s each cohort of young male criminals has done roughly three times as much serious crime as the cohorts before it."

This ticking "crime bomb" suggests we have no room for complacency about crime. We need a judicial bomb-disposal squad to protect us against this looming danger.

How to Combat Crime

In addressing the crime problem, there are still those who insist on bleating about "root causes." After I'd written an article for the *Wall Street Journal* criticizing the excesses of some judges in setting criminals free, Catherine Richardson, president of the New York State Bar Association, wrote a letter to the editor in which she argued, "If we are ever to rid our society of crime, the war must be fought by addressing the root causes of crime—poverty, prejudice, injustice, alienation and fear. This is a battle that cannot be won by beefing up police, building more prisons or asking the judiciary to cave in to populist sentiments and abandon the rule of law."

Similar sentiments—call it the "root causes" view—are often expressed by many gavel-wielding philosophes. "I now know," writes former New York chief judge Sol Wachtler, "that long prison sentences are not the answer, either in New York State or nationally."

This helps to explain why so many judges like Terry McDonald are as lenient as they are: They think that they're fighting a losing battle. They believe that society's resources should be devoted to crime prevention, not to punishing criminals once caught.

This is a view that can't be dismissed out of hand, as many on the right are wont to do. Obviously crime *is* associated with poverty. It's undeniable that—with a few notable exceptions, like the Menendez brothers—denizens of Beverly Hills are less likely to commit crimes than those living in South Central Los Angeles. But the cause and effect here isn't clear. It's hard to believe that poverty alone causes lawlessness when the murder rate dropped nearly 40 percent between 1933 and 1940 in the midst of the Great Depression. Poverty doesn't just cause crime; crime also causes poverty. After all, if it weren't for problems with gangs and drugs, neighborhoods like South Central L.A. and the South Bronx would be a lot more congenial to employers. One can convincingly argue, then, that to address the poverty problem we first need to address the crime problem—*not* the other way around.

The larger point is that the whole debate over the causes of crime is a giant irrelevancy, at least from the standpoint of public policy. Even if we assume that poverty, prejudice, and so on *are* the "root causes" of crime, what can we do about it? We've tried social welfare spending— more than $1 trillion since the Great Society—and by any objective measure, the problems of inner cities today are worse than ever. A comprehensive, congressionally funded study has determined that even programs expressly designed to prevent crime, such as boot camps, midnight basketball, neighborhood watches, and drug education, have little impact. These are all favorite solutions of judges who believe that we need "alternatives" to incarceration—and none of them work.

Proponents of lenient sentencing—including many judges—would undoubtedly argue that a drop-off in sentences would have no impact on crime. After all, isn't crime the product of "root causes," not of society's failure to incarcerate? This view isn't supported by the evidence. From 1980 to 1992, states that increased incarceration the most saw violent crime decrease by 8 percent. By contrast, the ten states with the lowest increases in incarceration saw violent crime increase by 51 percent.

One of those states is Texas. In the early 1980s, the Lone Star state reduced the time that prisoners served in order to open up prison space for new offenders. Between 1980 and 1989, the average prison term served fell from 55 percent of the sentence to about 15 percent. The "expected sentence" for serious crimes—average time served, reduced by the probabilities of arrest, prosecution, conviction, and sentence to prison—fell 43 percent in Texas during the 1980s, while it increased 35 percent in the nation as a whole. At the same time that jail sentences in Texas were dropping, the rate of serious crime in the state rose by around 29 percent. By comparison, the national rate was falling at this time by almost 4 percent. As a Justice Department report pointed out, "it strains credulity" to believe that this was just a coincidence.

The experience of the Lone Star State demonstrates that even if we can't address the "root causes" of crime, we can addresses its consequences by putting felons behind bars. Often, the debate over incarceration gets twisted up in philosophical pretzels about deterrence, morality, retribution, and vengeance. These are all complicated concepts that are certainly worth discussing. But the best justification for imprisoning criminals is actually pretty simple: As columnist Ben Wattenberg puts it, "A thug in prison can't shoot your sister." If judges keep that perspective in mind, perhaps they'll be less indulgent with criminals.

Are We Imprisoning Too Many People Already?

The conventional wisdom, heard from judges and journalists alike, is that our criminal justice system is already too punitive. The Sentencing Project and other liberal critics of the system assert that the United States imprisons more people—especially young black men—than anyplace else on earth. This criticism ignores the fact that the United States also has the highest crime rates in the Western world. In fact, if you control for crime rates, you find that the United States doesn't imprison any more people than Canada or Britain.

If the goal is to deter criminals, we're actually not imprisoning enough of them. "Crime has increased as the expected costs of committing crimes has fallen," writes Texas A&M economist Morgan Reynolds. "Today, for a burglary, for example, the chance of arrest is 7 percent. If you are unlucky enough to be one of the 7 percent arrested, relax; only 87 percent of arrestees are prosecuted. Of those, only 79 percent are convicted. Then only 25 percent of those convicted actually go to prison. Multiplying all these probabilities gives your would-be burglar a 1.2 percent chance of going to jail."

In response, many judges, even those not known for being especially soft, will argue that we can't afford to send every convicted felon to jail: There just wouldn't be enough space. "You know what's going to happen when you have sentencing provisions as draconian as this?" asked Bronx judge Burton Roberts (model for the judge in Tom Wolfe's *Bonfire of the Vanities*), in response to one plan to increase sentences for violent first-time offenders. "Our detention facilities are going to come apart at the seams." It's true that prisons are full: As of 1995, state prisons were at 103 percent of capacity. So aren't judges just being pragmatic in looking at alternatives to incarceration? This argument is wrong on two levels.

First, we don't really spend that much on jails and law enforcement in general—just 3.8 cents of every government dollar goes for the administration of justice, including all police, prisons, and courts. We spend twenty-seven times more on education and libraries than we do on prisons and jails, twelve times more on public welfare programs.

Jails are admittedly expensive—it costs about the same amount, roughly $15,000 to $25,000, to keep someone in prison for a year as it would to send the same person to an Ivy League college—but part of this cost is artificial; as we shall see in Chapter 5, judges mandate that prisoners have all sorts of expensive privileges like law libraries, larger cells, TV sets, and so forth. It's somewhat disingenuous for judges and their defenders to then complain that prisons cost too much.

Anyway, if judges just keep sending criminals to the slammer, legislators will be forced to find the extra funds needed to keep them away from the rest of society. The first duty of government is, after all, to protect the law-abiding against the lawbreaking.

The second and more important problem with the we-can't-afford-to-lock-'em-up argument is that it ignores the costs of *not* putting felons away. It is of course impossible to accurately calculate the cost of crime—what price tag do you put on the grief of a murdered child's mother?—but some academicians have tried. Several studies, including one conducted by researchers from the University of Pennsylvania and Harvard, have found that since the average felon commits twelve to twenty-one crimes a year, it costs about twice as much to let criminals roam the streets as it does to lock them up. Other studies suggest the benefits of incarceration are much higher.

To the question "Can we afford to get even tougher?" the proper answer is another question: "Can we afford not to?"

The Role of Judges in Reducing Crime

Who is responsible for making crime pay? Why aren't we locking up more violent criminals? Legislators deserve some of the blame, but for the last decade or so, they've been passing ever tougher laws—truth in sentencing, three strikes and you're out, and the like. Politicians are constantly competing to see who can introduce the most bills increasing jail sentences. The people clearly want to toss violent felons in jail and throw away the key. But standing in the way are many of the "experts" who run the criminal justice system—criminologists, parole boards, social workers, and others who insist on "rehabilitating" criminals instead of punishing them, on attacking the "root causes" of crime, rather than its consequences. The American people are clearly fed up with this attitude: In a 1996 nationwide Gallup poll, 85 percent of those surveyed said that courts in their area don't deal "harshly enough" with crime.

If there's one group that must be singled out for special opprobrium, it's soft-on-crime judges like Terry McDonald and others we'll meet in this chapter. Many of them genuinely, if wrongly, believe that jail isn't the answer; many others simply get tired of sending a long parade of defendants, most of them young black men, into the maw of the prison system. No matter how idealistic their motives, their actions can have terrible consequences, as the family of Kevin Roberson's murdered girlfriend can testify.

I am by no means suggesting that the majority of judges are motivated by a "root causes" mentality; most judges, in my experience, are determined to be as tough on criminals as they possibly can be, while staying within the law. But a few liberal judges, especially when they're concentrated in our major metropolises, can have a disproportionate impact on the criminal justice system, since virtually every criminal they release will usually go on to commit multiple crimes. In addition, these judges serve as propagandists for an ideology that trickles down to other benches.

The problem is multiplied when you factor in judges who are simply incompetent. These out-to-lunch jurists may have no particular ideological ax to grind but sometimes allow serious offenders to slip through the court system unpunished simply because they're not diligent enough to scrutinize the details of every case that comes before them. In Pennsylvania, for instance, a state judge known for copious consumption of Coors Light in his chambers was allegedly so inebriated during one preliminary arraignment that he freed an assault suspect by mistake.

Whatever the cause—whether it's devotion to the "root causes" view or sheer incompetence—there are plenty of judges across America who refuse to deal harshly with criminals during sentencing. This is no small concern because sentencing (except for the death penalty) is the one phase of a criminal trial where the judge has complete control over the outcome. Thus, when judges make a mistake in sentencing, the repercussions can be catastrophic. As criminologist John DiIulio writes, judges are "behind each of the most perverse failures of today's justice system: violent offenders serving barely 40 percent of their sentences; 3.5 million criminals, most of them repeat offenders, on the streets on probation and parole; 35 percent of all persons arrested for violent crime on probation, parole, or pretrial release at the time of their arrest."

Let's examine the causes of these "perverse failures"—and some others—one at a time, from the pretrial period to the death penalty phase.

Failure No. 1: Bail Bungling

IT WAS JUST a few minutes after noon on February 12, 1996, when Benito Oliver walked into a Volkswagen dealership in Queens. He tracked down his former girlfriend, Galina Komar, who worked there, and first killed her, then himself in a hail of bullets.

It soon emerged that Oliver, a convicted rapist, had a long history of battering his girlfriend. On their last night together, he'd slammed her around his apartment, held a butcher's knife to her throat, and threatened to kill her. He was arrested, but Judge Lorin Duckman of New York Criminal Court ignored Komar's pleas for protection and instead listened to Oliver's lawyer, who claimed that the entire dispute was over Komar keeping Oliver's "show dog." If the animal was returned, the lawyer assured the judge, everything would be fine. So Judge Duckman freed Oliver on just $2,000 bail.

The New York tabloids went into a feeding frenzy, with complete justification, after it emerged that during the bail hearing the judge was more concerned about Benito Oliver's dog than Galina Komar's injuries. "I am not suggesting that bruising is nice, but there is no disfigurement," the judge infamously intoned. "There are no broken bones."

Judge Duckman was similarly lenient with convicted batterer Maximo Peña. After he was found guilty by a jury of harassing and attacking his girlfriend, Peña was freed by Duckman, on the grounds that the forty-one days he'd already served in jail were sufficient punishment. Peña then showed up at his girlfriend's house at 2 A.M. one morning and dragged her down a flight of stairs and punched her in the face.

How Bail Became Such a Problem

Who was responsible for releasing Benito Oliver and Maximo Peña? The proximate cause was undoubtedly Judge Duckman, who displayed spectacularly bad judgment in both instances. But we may also attach some residual blame to two Anglo-Saxon kings named Hlothaere and Eadric. It was during their reigns in the seventh century that the first laws were passed providing that "persons accused of a crime pay bohr, a form of blood price, to the family of the victim, with the money being returned if the accused was proven innocent." This was the origin of the modern system of bail, which we inherited from our British forefathers.

Traditionally, judges set bail based on the nature of the crime the defendant was charged with and the strength of the prosecution's case. The Eighth Amendment stipulates that "excessive bail shall not be required," and most states hold that bail can only be denied in capital cases. The only legitimate aim of bail was to guarantee a defendant's appearance in court, not to punish the person for alleged crimes. However, there was no requirement that bail be set low enough for the defendant to pay, and since bail was based on the nature of the offense, not the background of the alleged perpetrator, poor defendants—the vast majority—often couldn't afford to spring themselves from the pokey, even if doing so only required paying 10 percent of the bail amount to a bondsman.

By the 1960s, liberal critics were assailing the bail system for discriminating against poor suspects and for locking up too many defendants ultimately judged innocent. Spurred by a reform project in New York, most state legislatures and Congress passed laws establishing "either a preference for, or a presumption of, pretrial release." The reforms of the 1960s also allowed defendants to be more readily released "on their own recognizance"—that is, without posting a bond or cash bail, the traditional methods of ensuring that they didn't flee. At the same time, new bail laws at the state and federal level gave judges the ability to impose nonfinancial conditions for pretrial release, such as the defendant's attending a drug treatment program or staying away from the scene of previous criminal activity.

The liberal reforms of the 1960s led to a backlash when it became apparent that violent criminals were being released prior to trial to prey on their victims once again. The 1984 federal Bail Reform Act, since emulated by at least twenty states, maintained the hope that, ideally, defendants should be released on their own recognizance. But at the same time, the act created a presumption that certain categories of defendants—principally drug dealers and those convicted of violent crimes in the past five years—would be incarcerated prior to trial. The law also gave federal judges the discretion to impose pretrial detention if the defendant posed a flight risk or a serious threat to the community—or even if it appeared that the bail would be paid with illicit funds (a provision designed to keep narco-traffickers from buying their release as the cost of doing business). Although many states still don't allow pretrial detention except in first-degree murder cases, judges can usually achieve this end simply by setting bail so high that the defendant can't afford to pay or by imposing onerous conditions on the defendant.

Law-and-order jurists can use this latitude to keep violent defendants in jail prior to trial. Judge John Sheldon of Maine, for instance, once presided over a bail hearing for a suspect accused of rape. The defendant was from Louisiana and had committed rape in the past, yet under the state constitution Judge Sheldon couldn't deny him bail. So, the judge recalled, "I said to him, 'OK, this is your reasonable financial obligation, but before you can be released on bail, you must first memorize *Hamlet*.' Since he was sitting on the extent of his IQ, he of course sat in jail."

Unfortunately, all too many judges use their discretion to release defendants, not to keep them locked up. The median bail for defendants charged with serious crimes is just $10,000—in other words, they can typically get out by paying $1,000 to a bondsman or to the state, an amount that no doubt represents a few minutes' work to an industrious drug peddler. Of course, that's only the median. One-fourth of all defendants are released on personal recognizance—no bail required. They just get to walk free.

Even more ominous, in 1992 *only about one-third of all felony defendants in America's 75 most populous counties were detained until their case was disposed of.* In other words, two-thirds of the most serious criminal suspects are on the streets after being arrested and charged. And these aren't "just" drug offenders. Even one-fourth of those charged with murder were released prior to trial, as were one-half the defendants facing rape, robbery, and burglary charges.

Sometimes judges will excuse their pretrial failures on the grounds that the defendant in question was a first-time offender or didn't have a history of violence, so it wasn't possible for the judge to predict that releasing the offender on bail would result in another atrocity being committed. But judges have no excuse when they release repeat offenders who are arrested again. This happens all the time: *Fifty-six percent of defendants already on pretrial release in 1992 were set free again after being rearrested.*

Judges often claim that releasing defendants is justified because there's no evidence they will fail to show up for their next court appearance. But what happens when the defendant goes out and commits fresh crimes? This is not at all unusual: *One-third of the urban defendants on pretrial release in 1992 were caught committing some kind of misconduct.* The victims of Kevin Roberson and Benito Oliver paid with their lives for this unfortunate statistic.

"Certain Things Are Just Cultural":
Explaining One Judge's Bail Lapses

What leads judges to make such lenient bail decisions? It's impossible to generalize, of course, but the example of Lorin Duckman is instructive.

We now know a great deal about Judge Duckman's motivation and conduct, thanks to an investigation by the New York State Commission on Judicial Conduct. A state referee wound up sustaining nearly 350 counts of misconduct, almost all of them unrelated to the Galina Komar case that thrust the judge into the public eye in the first place. The referee's report depicts a judge for whom defendants are heroes and cops are villains.

Judge Duckman, appointed by Democratic mayor David Dinkins in 1991 (and not subject to election), constantly berated, screamed at, and generally abused the young assistant district attorneys who had the temerity to prosecute defendants in his courtroom. When these prosecutors would follow their superiors' orders and refuse to agree to absurdly low bail amounts or to drop charges altogether, Judge Duckman would scold them for behaving "like such a Nazi" or a "good little soldier boy." There is no record of the judge acting uncivilly to defense lawyers.

The judge, you see, had a more sophisticated view of crime than those of us who naively think that the way to protect society is by locking the bad guys away. On one occasion, he informed a prosecutor, "You don't achieve anything by putting people in jail." Instead, he suggested we should provide "health care on demand" and jobs to ward off lawbreaking. (If only "Clintoncare" had passed, crime would now be nonexistent, right?)

Judge Duckman was particularly perturbed by the parade of black defendants in his court. "Don't you understand that all you're doing is putting poor black men in jail?" he demanded of one assistant district attorney. When she replied, "Judge, I have a lot of poor black victims," Duckman flew off the handle. On another occasion, the judge told a prosecutor that he didn't understand "these people"—presumably meaning black defendants—because of his "middle-class background." The prosecutor in question happened to be black—unlike the judge.

Duckman didn't just express opinions more appropriate for a social worker than a judge—he also acted on them. The referee who heard his case concluded that in seventeen instances the judge illegally dismissed charges against defendants because prosecutors wouldn't agree to generous plea bargains.

In short, the Galina Komar case was no aberration. Judge Duckman had inexhaustible wellsprings of sympathy for defendants, and he was willing to go to almost any lengths to come up with some justification—no matter how insulting—for their violent behavior. Referring to one assault cause involving two African-American women, the judge proclaimed, "You know, sometimes certain things are just cultural."

Indeed they are—but not in the way Duckman meant. The cultural problem here is not with criminals, it's with judges, in particular soft-hearted (and soft-headed) judges like Lorin Duckman who refuse to crack down on defendants who violate society's most basic rules. This outlook has been the "root cause" of countless bail tragedies—and will cause many more until we get more tough-minded jurists on the bench.

Failure No. 2: Probation, Not Punishment

Pretrial release is only the first opportunity that judges have to spring violent defendants from jail. They get another shot in the sentencing phase. Just as it would be simple to make sure that violent offenders don't get bail set too low, so it would be even easier for judges to send them to prison. But because judges have a lot of discretion, they often sentence criminals to probation, not to time behind bars.

Probation simply means releasing an offender back into the community. It is much like parole, the only difference being that parole is handed out by parole boards after a criminal has served at least the minimum prison time dictated by a judge, whereas probation is dispensed by the judge as part of the initial sentence. With both probation and parole, the released criminal is supposed to be supervised by a law enforcement officer, and if he violates the term of his release (such as staying away from former associates or going into drug treatment), the judge overseeing his case can send him to prison. But since probation and parole offices are invariably burdened with too heavy a caseload—parole officers in New York City handle up to one thousand cases each—criminals are essentially set loose on society with no check on their behavior.

Probation traces its roots to fourteenth-century England, where it emerged as a hallmark of efforts to show Christian charity to convicts. In America, the father of probation was John Augustus, a Boston boot maker, who in 1841 began petitioning judges to suspend convicts' sentences and release them into his custody for a period of supervised rehabilitation. In 1878, Massachusetts passed the first formal probation law and hired its first professional probation officer. By 1925, every state had some sort of probation for juveniles, and by 1967, every state had adult probation laws. "Probation was an alternative to prison," writes a legal historian. "Its success depended on sifting through the facts about a man or woman convicted of crime and deciding that some were sound enough human material to deserve another chance. It focused, in short, on the offender, rather than solely on the offense."

A commendable concept, but one prone to go dangerously awry when judges—whether out of sympathy with defendants or simply out of a desire to find a cheaper alternative to incarceration—hand out probation to the wrong people. Nowadays, judges have decided that an awful lot of convicts deserve a second chance. *Twenty-nine percent of all those convicted of a felony—including 2 percent of murderers—serve no time behind bars. Even one-third of those with prior felony convictions did not receive any prison time when convicted of a new felony.* Instead, these hardened felons receive probation.

In all, there are nearly 3.1 million adult lawbreakers on probation, or 58 percent of all adults under criminal justice supervision, walking America's streets. To give you some idea of how many criminals on the loose that represents, imagine the entire city of Chicago (as opposed to just its board of aldermen) populated entirely by crooks.

Guess Who's Loose

One of those probationers-on-the-loose is Lorenzia Wright, a seventy-something retired longshoreman. You may ask, How much harm can an old man do? Well, this particular septuagenarian shoved a thirty-one-year-old woman down a flight of stairs, hit her at least twice on the back of the head with a hammer, and then—prepare yourself—ripped out one of her eyes with the claw hammer. The reason for this gruesome attack is that Wright was convinced the woman—a crack addict with whom he'd been partying—had stolen one of his pills. A jury found Wright guilty of aggravated battery, a felony that normally carries a sentence of six to twenty years. But Wright was sentenced to only two years of home detention, followed by some probation.

Judge Paula Lopossa of the Marion County Superior Court in

Indianapolis, Indiana, tells me she decided against jail time for Wright in large measure because he'd successfully raised eleven children and didn't have any prior blemishes on his record. Those are both legitimate factors to take into account, but are they reason enough to set somebody free after such a heinous crime? "It is outrageous," said the prosecutor. "This sentence says that if you somehow get the sympathy of the judge, you can bash someone in the head with a hammer and be sentenced to stay home, put your feet up and watch Oprah for two years."

Equally outrageous was Judge Lopossa's treatment of Paul W. Stewart, age sixty-nine, convicted of raping a nineteen-year-old female army reservist in a hotel he owned. Stewart's sentence: two years of nights at a work-release center, two years of probation, and a $5,000 fine. Again Judge Lopossa seemed to display her weakness for geriatric thugs—and her disdain for the victims of crime. In explaining her decision to me, Lopossa all but suggested that the victim had asked for it: The judge said that the woman was "wearing short shorts and a tank top" and had agreed to visit the hotel's office with Stewart (where the rape occurred), so the geezer must have decided she was consenting to have sex with him. "I bet a lot of potential rapists look forward to being 'sentenced,' or should I say 'let off,' by Judge Lopossa," wrote one outraged Indianapolis resident.

It's a gross abuse of discretion for a judge to give such reprobates, no matter how advanced in years, nothing but probation. In all too many instances, judges' leniency in handing out probation only creates more victims of crime. *An estimated 43 percent of probationers are rearrested on a felony charge within three years of being placed on probation.* That's a staggering statistic. Almost one-half of all probationers are caught breaking the law again! Keep in mind that not all crimes lead to arrests, so the actual amount of lawbreaking by probationers is certain to be much higher.

The poster boy for probation—as for much else wrong with the criminal justice system—is none other than O. J. Simpson. Recall that five years before the murder in Brentwood, Simpson was convicted of battering his wife, Nicole. The prosecutors argued for jail time and mandatory counseling, but the judge was "unreceptive." Instead, Judge Ronald R. Schoenberg of Los Angeles County Municipal Court sentenced Simpson to two years' probation and ordered him to pay $970 in fines. We can only speculate whether a more severe sentence might have shocked Simpson enough to avoid the murderous path that he later chose.

Probation for Young Guns

Releasing adult criminals on probation is bad enough. Even worse, in many respects, is the lenience with which the criminal system deals with pint-size Al Capones. Juvenile crime is soaring across America: The number of youths under eighteen arrested for murder tripled between 1984 and 1994. Yet most of the young thugs who get arrested are promptly released again. More than half of all adjudicated juvenile cases (and 40 percent weren't even formally adjudicated) resulted in the juvenile being placed on probation, not being sent to a detention center.

Judges often say, in their own defense, that they want to "take a chance" on a juvenile, to see if the kid will turn out OK. "It drives me nuts when judge say that!" roars Peter Reinharz, chief juvenile prosecutor for New York City. "The judge isn't taking a chance on a kid. It's the community that's taking a chance. The kid will be taking chances with people's lives."

No judge in America has taken more chances on kids, and with worse consequences, than David Ramirez, who handles 80 percent of Denver's juvenile cases. One of those cases involved Adam Romero, a fourteen-year-old who allegedly got a gun from a locked cabinet and gave it to a boy who used it to kill a fourteen-year-old girl. Romero then helped drag the girl, still alive, to a field, where she died. Romero was convicted of being an accessory to manslaughter and juvenile possession of a gun. But Judge Ramirez handed Romero just two years' probation and forty-five days of juvenile detention over the strenuous objections of the prosecutor, who pointed out that Ramirez had blamed society for the crime, in fact had "blamed everybody but Adam Romero."

Judge Ramirez insisted to me that the sentence was justified because Romero "didn't actually do the shooting. His involvement at best was moving the body." Says the victim's stepfather: "Judge Ramirez is in the wrong profession. He should be a social worker, not a judge."

Offenders have often taken advantage of Ramirez's misplaced kindness. A fifteen-year-old thug shot a man in the leg at a McDonald's restaurant. Ramirez gave him probation and sent him to live with his grandmother in Oregon, who sent him back because she couldn't control him. He was next placed in a group home, and although prosecutors tried to revoke his probation because of gang-related activities, Ramirez refused to put him behind bars. Two weeks later, the fifteen-year-old shooter vanished.

Neither of these two cases were flukes. Judge Ramirez is widely known as "Uncle Dave" among Denver's juvenile miscreants for the lenience with which he treats their transgressions. Ramirez, who was a Legal Aid lawyer before his appointment to the juvenile bench in 1989, distilled his philosophy as follows: "Crime doesn't go down when you put a kid in jail. It's not working."

Actually, what's not working is Ramirez's approach. "He's trying to make guardian angels of these kids, but he's actually making them worse criminals," said a teacher at a local high school. This judgment was confirmed by a seventeen-year-old who had been paroled and acknowledged that Ramirez hadn't been tough enough on him: "Uncle Dave didn't do me any favors."

He certainly didn't. Giving youthful offenders nothing but probation only encourages them to keep on breaking the law, until they finally wind up in a facility that makes a juvenile detention center seem like the Waldorf-Astoria by comparison. Whether they're dealing with juveniles or adult criminals like O. J., judges shouldn't be so blinded by their impulse to be merciful that they overlook the fact that sometimes the greatest mercy of all is sending a first-time offender to jail, however briefly. That may, just may, shock miscreants enough to turn them into law-abiding citizens.

The Benefits of Supervised Probation

As we've seen in this section, far too many criminals receive probation. What makes it worse, as we've also seen, is that most probationers are virtually unsupervised. They may be required to get drug counseling or pay victims restitution, but a Justice Department study found that about half of them don't comply with the terms of their probation. The answer in most cases is for judges to be far more sparing in handing out probation. And when they do hand it out, they should make sure that felons are going to be released into programs where they'll be closely monitored.

Such programs do exist. In Boston, for instance, local probation officers have teamed up with cops and clergymen to make sure that fewer probationers break the law. In Philadelphia, the district attorney's office has recruited neighborhood volunteers to monitor probationers' compliance with the terms of their release. That effort boasts an 80 percent success rate.

Such programs give some hope, however scant, that probation doesn't have to be a one-way ticket back to a life of crime. But unless such programs are implemented elsewhere, judges need to sharply rein in their use of probation.

Failure No. 3: The Incarceration Gap

BY NOW, an optimistic reader might be thinking: OK, many felons get nothing but probation, but at least the ones who go upriver stay there for a long time, right? Wrong. Despite all the talk about getting tough on crime, *the average jail or prison sentence for a felony in 1994 was just six years*. Wait. It gets worse: *State inmates typically serve only about one-third of their sentence behind bars*. That means the typical felon will serve only about two years behind bars, and the typical violent felon, only four and one-half years.

It is important to stress that judges alone can't be held accountable in all these cases. Parole boards, especially, play a part in releasing dangerous felons into the population (though far more criminals are on probation than parole). But even when a parole board is the ultimate culprit, judges can't escape responsibility altogether. After all, they impose the initial sentence, often an indeterminate one (that is, X years to Y years), and if they don't impose a high enough floor, then a parole board is free to release the felon at any time. Parole and indeterminate sentences, like probation, first became popular in the late nineteenth century as part of an effort to rehabilitate criminals. Unfortunately, most of the criminals who are released early go right back to crime.

What else can most ex-cons do? With the notable exception of Michael Milken, not many of them start foundations to fight prostate cancer. Not many study aeronautical engineering either. Or even get burger-flipping jobs at McDonald's. They generally deal drugs, shoot people, and hold up liquor stores, which is to say, they return to the only life they know. *More than 60 percent of all former inmates are rear-rested within three years of getting out of prison, one-fourth within six months of winning their freedom.*

Or look at it from the other side: *Two-thirds of all urban criminal defendants have been arrested previously, with 36 percent having at least five prior arrests. Fifty-five percent—including a majority of murderers—have a felony arrest record, and 38 percent have previously been convicted of a felony.*

If they'd been put away the first time, they wouldn't have had an opportunity to commit another crime . . . and another . . . and another. The RAND Corporation, a California think tank, estimates that former inmates, while on the outside, commit a *median* of 15 serious crimes a year, excluding drug offenses. The *average*—skewed by a hard core of super criminals—is 187 to 278 crimes a year. Thus, the answer to dramatically reducing crime appears to be relatively straightforward: Take this group of sociopaths off the street. Close the incarceration gap—the amount of time that inmates should spend, but don't, behind bars. But judges, for one reason or another, often seem reluctant to take this simple step.

Through the Revolving Door

What's the worst that can happen when judges don't sentence harshly enough? Meet Conrad Jeffrey, occupation: pedophile. In 1993, Jeffrey kidnapped, raped, and killed seven-year-old Divina Genao in Passaic, New Jersey.

Jeffrey was a homicidal psychopath who had a decades-long history in the criminal justice system. In 1971, he was convicted of robbing Rutgers students with a straight razor. He was sentenced to seven years but was released in 1972. He committed several more crimes in the following year but was out of jail by 1974. Three months later, he was charged with stabbing a woman thirty-four times with a pair of scissors and throwing her off a building to her death. He confessed but was deemed mentally incompetent and was committed to a psychiatric hospital until 1983. Two years after his release, he sexually assaulted a twelve-year-old boy, pled guilty, and served only a year in jail. In 1990, he abducted a fourteen-year-old girl at knifepoint and tried to rape her. Bergen County Judge Frederick Keuchenmeister, apparently unaware of Jeffrey's violent history, approved a plea bargain under which Jeffrey wound up serving just two and one-half years in prison.

He got out in 1993 and immediately committed some offenses that could have led a judge to revoke his parole. But it wasn't revoked, and six weeks after leaving prison, Jeffrey lured Divina Genao to his seedy rooming house and suffocated her after first raping her.

Conrad Jeffrey, unlike other criminals discussed in this chapter, wasn't released because some "root causes" judge was ideologically predisposed toward giving criminals a break. Jeffrey just fell through the cracks of the criminal justice system. "At almost every step in Conrad Jeffrey's 20-year criminal career, an alert prosecutor, judge, or parole officer could have made the move that might have saved Divina Genao's life," wrote one reporter who covered the case. But no one did anything, and Divina paid the ultimate price.

This is almost more horrifying than the mishaps caused by "root causes" judges. At least with lenient judges, it's often possible to identify them and work to get them removed. But what do you do when judges, along with other people in the criminal justice system, are so inattentive, so slothful and sloppy, that they allow a sociopath like Conrad Jeffrey to skate through court? It's an invitation to disaster.

And indeed, less than a year after little Divina Genao's death, two similar tragedies occurred in New Jersey: six-year-old Amanda Wengert was raped and murdered by a neighbor with a long history of child-molestation arrests, and seven-year-old Megan Kanka was killed by a convicted child molester who hadn't served long enough in prison for his previous two offenses. (This is the case that spawned the adoption of "Megan's Law" throughout the country, requiring community notification whenever a pedophile is released from prison.) We obviously need not only more tough-minded judges but also judges who simply pay more careful attention to the cases they process.

How to Keep Criminals in Jail Longer

Part of the answer to preventing similar tragedies in the future is to pass legislation to lengthen prison terms. But we also need tougher judges willing to sentence convicts under the *existing* laws. Federal and state courts have approached the problem of lenient judges in different ways.

In the federal system, Congress essentially solved the problem in

1984 by creating sentencing guidelines. I've never met a judge, liberal or conservative, who likes the guidelines. Critics circulate exaggerated horror stories about how defendants are sent to prison for life just for having a few ounces of drugs in their possession. The common complaint is that the guidelines, especially mandatory minimums, take away judges' discretion and turn them into sentencing cyborgs.

Precisely. That's the point. And it's worked.

The Justice Department found that "offenders sentenced under the federal guidelines are more likely to go to prison and to stay there longer than were offenders sentenced for crimes committed before the guidelines took effect in November 1987." Specifically, 74 percent of defendants sentenced under the guidelines went to prison, compared to 52 percent of preguideline defendants. And convicts who receive prison terms in the federal system serve a longer proportion of their time than state prisoners.

Sentencing guidelines act as a check on judges like Leonie Brinkema, a Clinton appointee to the U.S. District Court in Arlington, Virginia. In one case, Judge Brinkema presided over the trial of Andrew Scott Morin, convicted of trying to hire a hit man (who, alas, turned out to be an FBI agent) to kill his martial arts instructor. The sentencing guidelines called for Morin to receive at least seven years in prison, but Judge Brinkema gave him less than two years, in part because she thought he was so "naive" in the way that he "interacted with the hit man" that he couldn't have really had murder in his heart. The U.S. Court of Appeals for the Fourth Circuit promptly reversed her decision.

In another case, Judge Brinkema refused to sentence a major drug dealer, convicted of selling crack cocaine, to a mandatory minimum of twenty-four years in prison; she gave him only twenty years because the longer sentence frustrated her sense of "symmetry and justice." The Fourth Circuit slapped her down for the tenth time in a sentencing case. "The district court was obligated to properly apply the Sentencing Guidelines," the appellate panel wrote. "Instead it chose to frustrate the Guidelines' goal of national sentencing uniformity by granting a downward departure based on its own 'sense of symmetry and justice.' We strongly disapprove of the district court's actions and exercise our discretion to correct this plain error."

While the sentencing guidelines have done a lot of good in these cases, they don't have a major impact on criminal justice in general, since only a tiny percentage of all criminal prosecutions occur in the federal courts. A few states, too, have adopted sentencing guidelines, but most have chosen other ways of restraining liberal judges or ameliorating the consequences of their behavior. Many states have passed statutes like "Megan's Law" (which, as already noted, requires a community be notified whenever a sex criminal is released), "three strikes and you're out" (which sends a criminal to prison for life after the third conviction), and "truth in sentencing" (which mandates that inmates must serve at least 85 percent of their prison time).

As with federal sentencing guidelines, these laws elicit howls of protest from judges who claim that their discretion is being unduly limited, that they're losing the ability to tailor a sentence to meet the facts of each individual case. This is a valid complaint, and in a better world, we *should* allow judges more discretion. But judges have nobody to blame for their loss of autonomy but themselves. If they'd been more consistent in handing out longer prison sentences in the first place, there wouldn't have been a groundswell of popular support for laws like "three strikes." The gavel-wielding guardians of justice shouldn't expect to get more of their discretion back until they inject a little of the spirit of Judge Roy Bean into their courtrooms.

Failure No. 4: The Death Penalty, R.I.P.

On SEPTEMBER 6, 1901, a young Polish immigrant named Leon Czolgosz fatally shot President William McKinley. After being captured and tried, the assassin was executed on October 29, roughly seven weeks after the commission of the crime. This is about the same amount of time it took to argue one motion in the O. J. Simpson trial. If Czolgosz had committed his crime today, he would probably have died of old age, not the hangman's noose.

That's the case because modern courts have thrown up so many procedural hurdles and roadblocks that it's virtually impossible to execute even the most vicious criminals. Most Americans seem to think that something is lost—call it deterrence, justice, or simply vengeance— when society can't express its abhorrence of the most heinous crimes by taking the life of the criminal. But liberal judges, motivated by deep-rooted antipathy to capital punishment, have frustrated the overwhelming will of the people. The failure to carry out the death penalty is the final sentencing failure examined in this chapter.

"Cruel and Unusual Punishment"?

The first and most formidable obstacle to carrying out capital punishment was the Supreme Court's 1972 decision in *Furman v. Georgia*. A bare majority of five supremes held that, in the immortal words of former Chief Justice Earl Warren, "the evolving standards of decency that mark the progress of a maturing society" had made the death penalty as then practiced a violation of the Eighth Amendment's ban on "cruel and unusual punishment." Two justices, William J. Brennan Jr. and Thurgood Marshall, even held that capital punishment was unconstitutional under all circumstances, a remarkable conclusion given that the Constitution itself mentions the death penalty no less than three times. (The Fifth Amendment states: "No person shall be held to answer for a capital or otherwise infamous crime, unless on presentment of indictment of a Grand Jury." Did Justices Brennan and Marshall think that capital in this context means "excellent"?)

The *Furman* ruling cleared the nation's death rows, guaranteeing that 629 of the most violent criminals would live longer than their victims had. Their penalties were commuted to life in prison. In California, 47 of the 174 convicts on death row in 1972 wound up being paroled (which gives the lie to the argument that it's just as efficacious to give killers life in prison as the death penalty; in fact, thanks to lenient parole policies, "life" sentences often last only a few years). Among these was Robert Lee Massie, given the death penalty in 1965 for shooting a woman during a robbery. He was released from prison in 1978. Eight months later, he shot a San Francisco market owner during a robbery and wound up back on death row. In all, the *Sacramento Bee* tracked down thirty-four of California's death row parolees and found that half of them were back in prison, including eight, like Massie, convicted of violent crimes. It is no exaggeration to say that the blood of their victims is on the hands of the five justices who voted to overturn the death penalty in 1972.

Public outcry was such that in 1976 the Supreme Court declared, "Oops, we didn't mean it." After thirty-five states had passed revised death penalty statutes, demonstrating that societal standards *hadn't* evolved to the point where the death penalty was "cruel and unusual," the high court ruled that Georgia's newly enacted law was constitutional.

But the Court in *Gregg v. Georgia*, and subsequent cases, mandated a confusing and often contradictory array of procedural safeguards to carry out the death penalty. "On the one hand there must be individual justice: there can be no mandatory death sentence, no matter how heinous the crime," summarizes Judge Alex Kozinski of the U.S. Court of Appeals for the Ninth Circuit. "On the other hand, there must be consistent justice: discretion to impose the death penalty must be tightly circumscribed."

The result: procedural gridlock. In most states, all death penalty verdicts are automatically appealed to the state supreme court (even if the inmate doesn't want to pursue the possible legal remedies), and if affirmed, appealed to the U.S. Supreme Court. If that doesn't avail, convicts get a second thwack at the piñata: They may petition the federal courts for a writ of habeas corpus, claiming their constitutional rights have been violated. These two sets of appeals routinely take a decade or more, in part because judges are so slow in ruling on motions, in part because there aren't enough defense lawyers willing and able to handle these convoluted cases.

Even though the Supreme Court in recent years has been trying to speed up the process, the death penalty is still carried out with notable infrequency—especially outside a handful of Southern states led by Texas. Between 1977 and 1994, 4,937 prisoners were sentenced to death, but some 40 percent of these sentences were overturned and only 257 convicts (5.2 percent) were executed. (By contrast, between 1940 and 1949, at a time when the nation's population was considerably smaller, 1,284 convicts were executed.) Death row is getting more crowded every year: In 1994, 304 prisoners were sentenced to death, but only 31 executions were carried out.

An overwhelming majority of the public—between 70 and 80 percent in most polls—supports the death penalty, but the will of the people is being frustrated by the men and women in black robes.

Staying Executions

The notorious case of Robert Alton Harris illustrates how far some judges are willing to go to throw a gavel into the gears of what Justice

Harry Blackmun described as the "machinery of death." In 1978, Harris killed two teenagers because he wanted to steal their car, then he finished off the hamburgers they'd been eating. There was never any doubt of his guilt; he confessed. Nevertheless, he appealed his death sentence six times before the California Supreme Court and six times before the U.S. Supreme Court. He lost every time. Finally, in April 1992 he appeared to be drawing close to death's door.

A week before his scheduled execution, the ACLU filed a civil suit on behalf of death row inmates, and U.S. district judge Marilyn Hall Patel—a former board member of the ACLU—granted a temporary restraining order to stop the execution on the grounds that California's gas chamber might constitute "cruel and unusual punishment." A panel of the Ninth Circuit vacated that restraining order.

With the execution scheduled for midnight on April 21, more activist judges swung into action. Judge Betty Fletcher, one of the most liberal members of the Ninth Circuit and a Carter appointee, issued a stay based on allegedly new evidence; the Supreme Court swiftly overrode her. Then a group of ten other judges issued stays based on the use of lethal gas; Judge William Norris, another Carter appointee, followed suit.

The Supreme Court lifted the second and third stays, and Harris was actually strapped into the chair at 4 A.M. Then the Ninth Circuit's Harry Pregerson, *another* Carter appointee, issued a fourth stay based on the lethal gas issue. Harris was led back to his cell to await the resolution of this appeal. It didn't take long. By this time, the Supreme Court was so exasperated that seven justices voted not only to overturn Pregerson's order but also, in an almost unprecedented move, to instruct all federal courts not to issue any more stays.

Finally, at 6:07 A.M. Harris was executed—thirteen years after beginning his legal battle. The cost to taxpayers of what Governor Pete Wilson described as this "macabre legal circus": at least $1.7 million. That's the price the public pays for the adamantly anti–capital punishment views of judges appointed by presidents like Jimmy Carter and, to a lesser extent, Bill Clinton.

Granting Death Penalty Appeals—Eventually

It's natural that judges would hesitate to kill another human being, even when the person forfeits the right to life by killing someone else.

There is always a chance, no matter how remote, that the convict will eventually be cleared of the crime. It's understandable that no judge wants to take the chance of sending an innocent person to death. But the death penalty is the law of the land, and judges violate their oath of office by not carrying out the law.

No judge has dishonored his oath more than John Nixon of the U.S. District Court in Tennessee. His chambers in Nashville have become a final resting place for five death penalty convictions. He's never approved a sentence of death. Almost as bad, he takes an average of eight years—*eight years!*—to decide each capital appeal, so there is no closure for victims' families.

Judge Nixon, appointed in 1980 by President Carter, overturned his first death penalty case in 1984. The inmate in question had actually refused to appeal his conviction, but a group of anti–death penalty groups petitioned the court on his behalf. In response, Nixon ruled that conditions on death row at Tennessee State Penitentiary were so unsanitary that they violated the Eighth Amendment. In the words of a former prosecutor, "three cockroaches running across the floor constitute cruel and unusual punishment." Nixon, according to one state senator, "is personally opposed to the death penalty and will use any technicality—the minutest detail—to overturn a conviction."

One of Judge Nixon's death penalty cases involved William Groseclose and Ronald Rickman, convicted in 1978 in a murder for hire. Groseclose hired Rickman to kill his twenty-four-year-old wife, a mother of two, in order to collect life insurance. She was raped twice, choked, stabbed, and left to die of heat exposure—she literally cooked to death—in the trunk of a car abandoned in a downtown Memphis parking lot. Rickman appealed his conviction on a habeas corpus petition to Judge Nixon in 1985.

Nixon finally resolved the case in 1994—only after prodding from the Sixth Circuit—by vacating Rickman's conviction. The next year, he overturned Groseclose's conviction, too. In both cases, he cited similar reasons—inadequacy of counsel (presumably any counsel who allows a client to be convicted is inadequate) and improper jury instructions (the trial judge told the jury, as per Tennessee law, that capital punishment is reserved for crimes that are "heinous, atrocious and cruel"; Judge Nixon thought that was "unconstitutionally vague").

Of course, when a case is more than a decade old, it is extremely difficult to have another fair trial for the defendants. "It's just crazy," said the victim's sister. "All the time and money spent on this case is sickening."

What are outraged citizens supposed to do when a judge like John Nixon flouts the law? Relatives of some victims tried complaining to the Sixth Circuit Court of Appeals. The chief judge of the circuit ruled that the delays in Nixon's death penalty cases were "excessive and should not have occurred," but the circuit's judicial council refused to punish Nixon; indeed, there wasn't much it *could* have done to punish him. In response, some 19,000 people signed petitions calling for Nixon's impeachment.

If Nixon were a state judge, all this pressure might avail. In the 1996 election, Tennessee voters—fed up that their state hadn't sent anyone to "Old Sparky" (the electric chair) since 1960—threw out of office state supreme court justice Penny White, who'd voted to overturn a number of death penalty convictions. But since Nixon is a federal judge appointed for life, the people of Tennessee won't be rid of him until he's ready to go. Meanwhile, opined the *Nashville Banner*, "Tennessee has no death-penalty law, thanks to this state's 'supreme executive legislator,' Nixon."

The Future of Capital Punishment

In light of the prevalence of judges like John Nixon, it's ironic that death penalty opponents, including many judges, claim that capital punishment is too costly. Yes, it does cost a lot to execute an inmate— usually more than keeping the person in prison for life (though, as we've seen, even life sentences often result in parole). But the expense isn't inherent. It doesn't cost much to shoot a few thousand volts of electricity through a chair or buy a few cyanide capsules for a gas chamber. The reason the death penalty costs so much is because judges allow so many time-consuming, money-wasting, nonsense-spouting appeals in each case.

All those appeals also help explain another argument frequently heard against the death penalty: It doesn't deter. There's evidence both ways on this point, but if capital punishment doesn't deter, that is hardly surprising, considering how rarely it's carried out. Deterrence would be greatly enhanced if the death penalty were *mandatory* for first-degree murder, but the Supreme Court won't allow this.

Congress tried to increase the death penalty's speed—and hence its presumed deterrence value—by passing limits on habeas corpus appeals in 1996. The Supreme Court acted swiftly to uphold the law, but it doesn't seem to have had much effect so far. In 1997, for instance, California saw a virtual replay of the Robert Alton Harris case. Sixteen years after raping and killing a young woman, Thomas M. Thompson was finally scheduled to be executed for the crime. But at the last minute, the Ninth Circuit Court of Appeals voted 7–4 (all seven in the majority were Democratic appointees, all four dissenters were Republicans) to reverse the rape conviction and halt the execution.

As this example demonstrates, a mere change in procedure won't deter some liberal judges from ignoring their oath of office to carry out the laws of the land. They'll simply invent other excuses to stop society from meting out a punishment they view as "cruel and unusual." These judges seem to follow an odd philosophy: A bruise for an eye, a scratch for a tooth. Most Americans want judges who will follow the more familiar biblical injunction for dealing with criminals.

Conclusion: Punish Guilty Judges

THROUGHOUT this chapter I've berated judges for refusing to put criminals where they belong. Remember one vital statistic, cited in "The Incarceration Gap" section: Two-thirds of all criminal defendants have been arrested previously. The criminal justice system has come to resemble one of those sleazy hot-sheet motels on L.A.'s Hollywood Boulevard, where guests come and go all the time, each spending only a few hours. To dramatically reduce crime, we have to turn the criminal justice system into the equivalent of a "roach motel": Serious offenders check in, but they don't check out. At least not for a good many years.

Whenever public attention focuses on this problem, it's usually to call for legislative tweaks like Megan's Law or "three strikes." As I've stated before, those are good ideas, but they would be unnecessary if we had better judges and without better judges, they'll probably not be very effective anyway. Given the amount of sentencing discretion judges retain, at least in state court, they're often able to frustrate the best-intentioned efforts of law-and-order legislators. For instance, an anonymous survey of Wisconsin judges revealed that a majority would simply trim sentences if convicts had to serve 100 percent of their time under a proposed truth-in-sentencing law.

The only legislative approach that would probably work would be to impose sentencing and bail guidelines, similar to those in the federal system, in state courts. Until that happens, we need to keep the heat on judges to set higher bail for dangerous defendants; not hand around probation like Snickers bars on Halloween; to make sure that serious felons receive the maximum possible prison term; and, lastly, to mete out the death penalty where appropriate. All this can be done under the existing laws.

To shame judges into doing their duty, we need to publicize instances when they fail, as in the examples discussed in this chapter involving Kevin Roberson (the Caller ID killer), Benito Oliver (the girlfriend slayer), and Conrad Jeffrey (the child murderer). Judges like to claim they're impervious to popular pressure, but that clearly isn't true. If judges take enough heat, they *do* change their behavior—witness Judge Terry McDonald finally giving a life sentence to Kevin Roberson. The problem today is that the vast majority of criminal cases, including homicides, are processed outside the public eye (the *Los Angeles Times*, for instance, covered only 15 percent of the homicides in Los Angeles County from 1990 to 1994), so judges are free not to punish criminals.

Judges who don't remove serious offenders from the streets should be removed from the bench. A good, although perhaps insufficient, precedent is found in the fate of Judge Lopossa, who gave probation to the elderly maniac who had ripped a woman's eye out with a claw hammer. The judge, after being lambasted in the local press, lost a race for the Marion County, Indiana, circuit court and instead wound up presiding part-time over a small claims court, where, presumably, she can do less damage. An even better precedent was set by the disciplinary case mounted against Judge Lorin Duckman, who released the two girlfriend abusers on bail. The New York Commission on Judicial Conduct eventually recommended that Duckman be kicked off the bench because of his disreputable conduct in a host of cases. Too bad so many other judges who don't deal with convicts harshly enough continue to sit on the bench.

"In the court of law the judge sits over the culprit," wrote Ralph Waldo Emerson, "but in the court of life in the same hour the judge also stands as culprit before a true tribunal." It's time we found more judges guilty in the court of life—and punished them accordingly.

CHAPTER 3

Criminal Exoneration

Judges Who Let

Lawbreakers

off the Hook

Our procedure has been always haunted by the ghost of the innocent man convicted. It is an unreal dream. What we need to fear is the archaic formalism and the watery sentiment that obstructs, delays, and defeats the prosecution of crime.
JUDGE LEARNED HAND, *United States v. Garrson*

ON THE morning of December 8, 1992, Luis Mujica, an unarmed security aide, was patrolling the corridors of William Howard Taft High School in the Bronx. Mujica knew he had to be vigilant. Taft had a reputation as the most dangerous school in New York City, which is sort of like having a reputation as the most dangerous street corner in Beirut. That year, some thirty-three assaults and twenty-five robberies would be reported on campus. A teacher would be shot in the head while waiting for a red light two blocks away from the school. Weapons ranging from box cutters to knives to guns were common on campus. (In 1997, Jonathan Levin, a Taft teacher, would be slain in his apartment, allegedly by a former student.)

As he later testified, Mujica sensed danger when he saw fifteen-year-old Juan C. walking toward him, tugging on the left side of his leather jacket. Mujica tried to grab Juan, but the student ran away. Mujica caught up with him and felt the bulge of a gun in his jacket. He then grabbed his walkie-talkie and announced a "code red," bringing another unarmed security aide running. The two of them removed a loaded .45 caliber semiautomatic from Juan's pocket, then turned him over to a police officer to be arrested.

This is exactly the kind of action we expect of those trying to ensure the safety of our students. But family court judge Stewart Weinstein thought otherwise: He threw out the criminal case against Juan. In Judge Weinstein's expert estimation, Juan's jacket was so bulky that "the outline of the gun was not visible, the slight bulge was not in any particular shape or form and was not remotely suspicious." Therefore, he ruled, the search was illegal and the evidence inadmissible in court.

After the criminal charges were dropped, the New York Board of Education held hearings and decided to suspend Juan for a year. A small enough punishment, you might think, for carrying a loaded weapon to school. A lower court judge agreed.

But then the case came before the First Department of the Appellate Division, New York's intermediate appeals court. The First Department is located in a marbled palace in midtown Manhattan. It hears cases in a rococo courtroom full of burnished wood and stained glass. The judges sit on an imposing wooden throne, much as medieval monarchs might, facing a mural in the back of the courtroom depicting *The Law*—a fierce-looking maiden in white—drawing "her sword on behalf of appeal." In this case, the First Department drew its sword of exclusion and decided that the Board of Education had no right to suspend Juan for a year.

The four justices decided to apply the exclusionary rule—which holds that illegally obtained evidence may not be used in court—against the actions of a security aide in a school disciplinary procedure. The exclusionary rule was originally intended to deter misconduct by police in criminal cases, and the U.S. Supreme Court has never decided whether the rule applies to schools, though the justices have exempted civil proceedings in general from the requirements of exclusion. New York's courts, however, have crafted a more defendant-friendly regime. The exclusionary rule in New York has been applied in proceedings involving a liquor license and a police disciplinary matter, among others. But never in a school discipline case. Until 1996.

The First Department judges simply decided, in a fit of gavelitis, that the benefit of radically expanding the exclusionary rule "far outweighs" the cost to the community.

"If security aides are to be deterred from engaging in unlawful conduct with respect to the Fourth Amendment rights of students," wrote Justice Joseph P. Sullivan, "they must understand that their methods of enforcing school safety rules are subject to scrutiny and that, if a student's rights have been violated, evidence illegally seized as a result of such violation will be excluded." There was no mention in this amazing opinion of the rights of students to be free of gun-wielding predators in their midst. The judges, ruling from the safety of their gilded palace, were more concerned with deterring *security guards* than armed teenagers.

The ruling caused an outcry as New York City contemplated the prospect that it would be unable to enforce even minimal standards of discipline in its already dangerous schools. The city appealed the Juan C. ruling, and under heavy pressure from everyone ranging from parents to the teachers' union, the court of appeals—the state's highest court—reversed the lower court judgment. The court of appeals ruled unanimously that Juan could be disciplined, but only because the New York City school board hadn't participated in the family court proceeding that concluded his gun had been unlawfully seized—a convenient skirting of a politically volatile issue, which drew appropriate hosannas from elected officials.

What the cheering section overlooked is that, in the first place, the court ruling doesn't change the fact that Juan C. can't be criminally prosecuted for his misconduct. And in the second place, the opinion says nothing to suggest that the exclusionary rule *does not* apply to school disciplinary cases. Quite the contrary. The opinion, written by Judge Joseph W. Bellacosa, unctuously suggested, "We should not lose sight of a seeming paradox that these same school authorities must simultaneously exemplify, honor and fulfill their constitutional and pedagogical obligations by respecting the rights of many thousands of law-abiding students, yearning to learn about school subjects and life in society." (*Life in society?* For this insight, Judge Bellacosa credited a lecture by . . . Joseph W. Bellacosa.)

Presumably, this means that school officials can ensure that the kid sitting at the next desk isn't holding a trigger instead of a pencil—but they must do so in a way that doesn't offend the sensibilities of enlightened judges.

Protecting Lawbreakers, Not the Law-Abiding

How did we come to this? How did we reach a stage in our nation's existence where school authorities in our largest city must tread carefully in order to take guns away from students? We have nobody to blame for this unfortunate development but judges. They created the exclusionary rule, and some of them apply it with fierce abandon, even if the result is to put teenage terrors like Juan C. back on the street.

This is only part of the procedural web judges have spun to prevent criminals from falling into the maw of the prison system. In the previous chapter, we saw how judges all too often refuse to sentence even hardened felons to enough time behind bars. In Chapter 4, as part of a broader examination of constitutional law, we'll see how judges have overturned laws—such as New York's anti-panhandling statute—that have long been one of the most reliable weapons in a policeman's arsenal. And in Chapter 5, we'll look at how judges have taken over the running of prisons and mandated in some instances that inmates, even dangerous ones, be released because of supposed overcrowding.

In this chapter, we'll examine perhaps the worst perversion of criminal justice: what happens when judges decide to let violent defendants off the hook altogether. Two of the leading causes of judge-mandated acquittal are the exclusionary rule, generally governing physical evidence, and the better-known Miranda rule governing confessions. Both hold that evidence obtained "illegally"—with illegality being defined by judges, not legislators, often in unpredictable ways—cannot be admitted in court proceedings.

These rules of criminal procedure were erected by idealistic judges attempting to enforce what they saw as the protections of the Constitution. Unfortunately, these illogical dictates not only confound society's desire to put felons behind bars but also do little to protect innocent citizens unjustly charged with crimes. Yet despite ample evidence about how these rules aren't working, judges continue enforcing them.

The problem is that the gavel wielders appear to have become so transfixed with their own elaborate philosophical constructs that they've lost sight of the primary duty of government: protecting the safety of its citizens.

The Making of a Monster: Origins of the Exclusionary Rule

JUDGES SAY that the exclusionary rule derives from the Fourth Amendment. But obviously they must be referring to a different copy of the Constitution than the one in my possession. In mine, the entire Fourth Amendment reads: "The right of the people to be secure in their persons, houses, papers, and effects, against unreasonable searches and seizures, shall not be violated, and no Warrants shall issue, but upon probable cause, supported by Oath or affirmation, and particularly describing the place to be searched, and the persons or things to be seized."

There's nothing in there about exclusion of evidence at trial. There's not even anything requiring that all searches be conducted pursuant to a warrant—a popular misconception of the Constitution that has taken root in many corners of the bench.

The history of the amendment suggests that the drafters weren't worried about limiting searches in general. What they wanted to limit were *search warrants*. This is curious to the modern sensibility because today we regard warrants as a check upon police power. That's not how the Founders saw it. In their time, warrants shielded the king's officials from civil actions by the victims of unjust searches; only warrantless searches could result in the award of damages against the offending officials. "Far from looking at the warrant as a protection against unreasonable searches," one scholar has written, the Founders "saw it as an authority for unreasonable and oppressive searches."

Thus, the Fourth Amendment mandated a fairly low burden of proof for most searches, prohibiting only those that were "unreasonable." By contrast, the amendment required a much higher burden for obtaining a search warrant—"probable cause." This was because the Founders expected that most searches would be warrantless, with the constables facing ruinous civil damages if their actions should later be judged "unreasonable."

This, then, was the history and purpose of the Fourth Amendment.

The Founders would no doubt be incredulous if they could be resurrected to discover that a twisted reading of this amendment has led to the exclusion of relevant evidence in a criminal trial. Indeed, this reading is of fairly modern vintage.

There was no exclusionary rule for most of the nineteenth century in America (as there still is not in Britain). U.S. Supreme Court justice Joseph Story summed up the law in an 1822 opinion: "[T]he evidence is admissible on charges for the highest crimes, even though it may have been obtained by a trespass upon the person, or by any other forcible and illegal means."

The exclusionary rule entered history only in 1886, invented by an activist Supreme Court bent on protecting private property rights against a nascent regulatory state. The mad scientists of the court mated two mismatched parts of the Constitution—the Fourth Amendment protection against "unreasonable searches and seizures" and the Fifth Amendment's protection against self-incrimination (the court reasoned that using a man's wrongly seized possessions as evidence against him would somehow be forcing him to be a "witness against himself")—and, voilà, created the Frankenstein monster known as the exclusionary rule. This strained justification has long since been repudiated by the court itself, but its mutant offspring has continued to march across the law ever since, leaving havoc and mayhem in its wake.

The exclusionary monster stomped into federal criminal law in 1914 by way of a Supreme Court ruling. But the villagers living in the states wielded their axes and pitchforks and held the beast off for decades. Benjamin Cardozo, when he was still chief justice in New York (before joining the U.S. Supreme Court), coined a famous epigram—"The criminal is to go free because the constable has blundered"—to protest against the introduction of the exclusionary rule in state proceedings.

Even the Supreme Court itself, in 1949, expressly refused to apply the exclusionary rule against the states. But just twelve years later, a bare majority of justices changed their minds and issued the infamous *Mapp v. Ohio* opinion, which has caused most of our current troubles with the exclusionary rule.

Mapp was supposed to be a First Amendment case: It involved police searching the house of Dollree Mapp to discover obscene books and pictures that violated a state antipornography statute. When the Court met to discuss its ruling, a majority agreed to overturn Mapp's conviction on the grounds that the law was unconstitutional. But in a "rump caucus" conducted later in an elevator, four of the supremes, led by Chief Justice Earl Warren, decided to throw caution to the winds and overrule *Wolf v. Colorado*, the 1949 case that held that the exclusionary rule didn't apply to the states. Justice Hugo Black reluctantly went along in a concurring opinion, and the result was a sweeping expansion of the exclusionary rule to every courtroom in the country. This was part of the Warren Court's pattern of adopting expansive readings of the Bill of Rights and then, using the club of the Fourteenth Amendment, applying those rights against the states.

Although Chief Justice Earl Warren and a handful of other radicals (the likes of Justices William O. Douglas and William Brennan) have held that the exclusionary rule is required by the Constitution, a majority of the Supreme Court has never adopted this fanciful view. Even in *Mapp*, Justice Black acknowledged that the exclusionary rule is "perhaps not required by the express language of the Constitution," but he decided to approve it on essentially policy grounds. Since then, the Court has consistently held that the exclusionary rule is "a judicially created remedy designed to safeguard Fourth Amendment rights generally through its deterrent effect, rather than a personal constitutional right of the party aggrieved."

In other words, the exclusionary rule is a product of judicial legislation. The Supreme Court noted that approximately half the state legislatures, in a regrettable oversight, had failed to provide adequate safeguards for the rights of criminals, so it decided to create some safeguards on its own.

Who's Protected by Exclusion?

ACCORDING TO the Supreme Court, the purpose of the exclusionary rule is "to compel respect for the constitutional guarantee in the only effectively available way—by removing the incentive to disregard it." This plausible-sounding rationale has garnered wide support for *Mapp*. And not just among liberals. The National Rifle Association, of all groups, joined not long ago with the ACLU to issue a letter urging Congress to "preserve, and indeed strengthen, the exclusionary rule to safeguard citizen rights and curb police misconduct."

Both the left and right are worried, as we all should be, about lawless behavior by the police, not only in events like Waco and Ruby Ridge but in other, less publicized incidents. In one case mentioned by the exclusionary rule's defenders, Drug Enforcement Administration agents burst into a house after midnight without identifying themselves. The owner came out to defend himself with a gun, and the DEA agents shot him three times. No drugs or anything else incriminating was ever found.

But what does *Mapp* or any other Warren Court invention do to restrain police in such a situation? Nothing. Dirty Harry isn't punished when his case is thrown out; most cops are promoted based on their "clearance" rate, meaning arrests, not convictions. In fact the proliferation of abusive police behavior in the post-*Mapp* age shows just how little the Court's decisions have accomplished. What deters officers from abusing the citizenry is not the prospect of a case getting thrown out but the threat that they will personally face punishment, as the cops who beat Rodney King did.

Indeed, far from deterring police misconduct, the exclusionary rule encourages senior police officers to overlook instances of misconduct if they know that punishing the officer will result in the case getting thrown out. In addition, *Mapp* actually encourages one form of police abuse: to wit, "testilying." Cops are loath to see manifestly guilty defendants let off the hook because of some procedural irregularity. So, in the course of doing their jobs, many are forced to shade the truth or even perjure themselves on the stand.

The public may have seen an example of "testilying" in the O. J. Simpson case. In the early morning hours of June 13, 1994, after the bodies of Nicole Simpson and Ron Goldman were discovered, police went to O. J. Simpson's compound, jumped over the wall, and conducted a warrantless search. On the witness stand later, Detective Philip Vannatter denied that at the time of the search, Simpson was a suspect in his wife's death. Instead, he testified, the cops jumped the wall because they wanted to notify Simpson about his wife's death and feared for his safety.

To Simpson's lawyers, this testimony strained credulity. Alan Dershowitz, one of the defense lawyers, believes that under *Mapp*, all the evidence subsequently recovered at the Rockingham estate—"the bloody glove found behind the house, the socks found in his bedroom, the blood found in his driveway"—should have been excluded. Judges Kathleen Kennedy-Powell and Lance Ito didn't do that, though Ito did admonish Vannatter about his "reckless" statements.

The point isn't that detectives like Vannatter are wrong to shade the truth (if, in fact, that's what he did). They have no choice if they want some semblance of justice to prevail. As former New York police commissioner William Bratton notes: "They are lying to get a guilty person, someone they've caught red-handed, into the [criminal justice] system. They are not faking evidence." The absurdity is that the Supreme Court has put cops in the untenable position of either perjuring themselves or letting the guilty go free.

OK, you may say, the exclusionary rule doesn't do much to deter police misconduct, but surely it must provide other benefits for the law-abiding public. What benefits? Well, that's hard to say.

A blameless victim of police misconduct—say, a black motorist unjustly pulled over or a homeowner whose privacy is illegally invaded—does not receive any recompense from the exclusionary rule, because there's no evidence to be excluded against such an innocent. By definition, only the *criminal* benefits from the exclusionary rule. And the greater the crime, the greater the benefit because there's more incriminating evidence to be excluded.

No wonder a veteran prosecutor I know has suggested that the exclusionary rule should be renamed the "exoneration rule." That's its effect.

Get Out of Jail Free:
The Consequences of Exclusion

IN CASES such as Juan C.'s, the Supreme Court has conceded, the exclusionary rule creates a "considerable cost to society as a whole, because it excludes evidence probative of guilt." The only question is: How much cost? There's no very good answer to that question.

The conventional wisdom among legal academics is that the cost is low to nonexistent. This assumption was buttressed by a 1988 American Bar Association (ABA) survey that found most prosecutors and police "do not believe that Fourth Amendment rights are a significant impediment to crime control." But it seems clear that the study was designed to reach that very conclusion. Consider one of the questions the ABA committee asked of a prosecutor at one of its field hearings: "Do you agree with the perception that constitutional rights are a leading cause of crime?"—a cartoonish oversimplification of law-and-order views that only Archie Bunker would defend. (The prosecutor answered, as expected, "I don't.") This bias should perhaps not be surprising, given that the ABA committee was chaired by liberal law professor Sam Dash, and the views of law enforcement were represented by a South Florida prosecutor named . . . Janet Reno.

Despite its obvious pro-*Mapp* outlook, the Dash Committee found that "prosecutors perceive that 5 percent or less of all cases are dismissed after filing because of the exclusionary rule." This is actually higher than the most commonly cited figure, which comes from a series of studies conducted by the National Institute of Justice (NIJ) and others in the late 1970s and early 1980s. These studies concluded that between 0.6 percent and 2.35 percent of all adult felony arrests are lost due to the exclusionary rule.

"Many of these researchers have concluded that the impact of the exclusionary rule is insubstantial," wrote Supreme Court justice Byron White, "but the small percentages with which they deal mask a large absolute number of felons who are released because the cases against them were based in part on illegal searches and seizures."

Let's have a look at the absolute numbers. In 1994, the most recent year for which statistics are available, approximately 14.6 million people were arrested in the United States. If 2.35 percent of those arrests are thrown out—using the lower NIJ figure, not the ABA's higher estimate, to avoid charges of exaggeration—that's approximately 343,100 criminals on the loose. Of course, not all those offenses are serious. Using just the FBI's *Index of Violent Crimes*, we find that 18,000 suspects arrested for violent offenses were sprung because of the exclusionary rule.

To see the effect of this jailbreak, consider just one category of serious offense: aggravated assault. In 1994, approximately 547,000 suspects were booked for aggravated assault. If the exclusionary rule applied at the expected 2.35 percent rate, that means almost 13,000 of these violent offenders were released. Remember what we learned in the last chapter: A criminal on the loose commits a median fifteen crimes a year. Therefore, those arrested and released for aggravated assault would be expected to attack another 195,000 people—enough, if gathered together in one place, to fill Yankee Stadium almost three times over. By the second year, the number of victims would climb to 390,000, and so on. That's a fearsome toll for the exclusionary rule—and of course it's a vast understatement of the rule's real impact.

This is only a count, a tentative one, of the number of cases thrown out. Yet many times the exclusionary rule doesn't result in cases being thrown out. Instead, it leads to a plea bargain and reduced jail time for malefactors (which of course means convicts get out sooner, and more than likely resume their reign of terror). And in countless other instances, the police don't even bother to investigate unlawful behavior or prosecutors refuse to file charges, because they know the case wouldn't survive the *Mapp* test.

The Biggest Beneficiaries: Drug Dealers

The exclusionary rule has a disproportionate impact on cases where the only way to convict is through physical evidence, which is to say drug and weapons-possession cases. The Dash Committee quoted one big-city prosecutor's comment that "because of search and seizure issues, he refuses to prosecute 50 percent of the gun and drug arrests in his jurisdiction." Overall, studies suggest that up to 7.1 percent of all felony drug arrests are lost due to *Mapp*.

For some defenders of the rule, this shows that exclusion has only "minor" effects. But as the recent experience in New York City shows—the police department slashed crime dramatically under Mayor Rudolph Giuliani—it's precisely by tackling "small" offenses like drug dealing that the cops can reduce the overall crime rate. It's not hard to see why: Somebody locked up for a small drug offense today is unable to commit a more serious violent crime tomorrow. Yet, thanks to overzealous judges, police departments are having trouble locking up some hardened drug offenders—as the follow example demonstrates.

On September 26, 1994, at around 7:25 P.M., two detectives with the Milwaukee County Sheriff's Department were on patrol for drug smugglers near the airport. The two detectives—one with twenty-six years' experience, the other with seven—were looking for "target vehicles": vans or two-door cars from "source states" such as Florida, Texas, Arizona, or California. They spotted such a vehicle, a Honda Prelude with Dade County, Florida, license plates and tinted windows, in the parking lot of a Quality Inn. They radioed in and discovered that the owner was Carlos Sollis of Miami; they further learned that Sollis's license had been suspended and he'd been arrested the previous month for smuggling contraband into the Dade County jail.

At 11 P.M., the cops returned and knocked repeatedly on the door of Room 161, where Sollis was registered, and yelled for him to open up, but he didn't answer the door. One of the detectives then went around to the window and shone his flashlight into the room, where he saw people moving around.

"We'd like to talk to you," he told Sollis, who was peering back at him. "Could you please open the door for us?"

Sollis nodded yes.

When they came in, they asked whether Sollis and the other man in the room—subsequently identified as Lenin Jerez—would speak with them.

"Sure, come on in," Sollis told them.

The cops observed a half-smoked marijuana cigarette on the bed. They then asked Sollis and Jerez where they were from. The two replied they were from Miami and were "on vacation" in Milwaukee. They also said they were visiting relatives but couldn't give the name or address of a single relation in the area. Becoming suspicious—*On vacation? In Milwaukee? Gimme a break!*—the cops asked whether they could look through the belongings in the room. Both Sollis and Jerez said to "go ahead."

After a search, the cops recovered three kilograms of cocaine and arrested both Sollis and Jerez, who admitted smuggling the drugs. They pled guilty, and federal judge Thomas J. Curran, after denying their motion to exclude the evidence, sentenced each of them to just under five years in prison.

Judge Curran's decision seems eminently reasonable. After all, the cops got the suspects' permission to search their property. Surely that can't be a Fourth Amendment violation. Yet a bitterly divided panel of the Seventh Circuit Court of Appeals decided, 2–1, that Sollis and Jerez's rights had indeed been violated. The problem, apparently, was that the cops didn't leave immediately after Sollis and Jerez refused to answer their knocks on the door.

"The officers' persistence," wrote Judge Kenneth F. Ripple, "destroyed any possibility that the occupants could return to sleep and ignore the officers." Well, yes. That's why they're cops, not chamber-maids. But Judge Ripple decided that the cops' persistence turned this incident from a "consensual encounter into an investigatory stop," which requires reasonable suspicion to be constitutional. And, the judges wrote, "the deputies simply cannot point to any facts which would give rise to a reasonable suspicion that Mr. Jerez and Mr. Sollis 'had committed or [were] about to commit a crime.'"

Therefore, the judges invoked the exclusionary rule—to the out-rage of Judge John L. Coffey, who filed a blistering dissent. He argued that the encounter was consensual, that the veteran cops did have plenty of reason to be suspicious, and that their actions were perfectly reasonable. "We must not wear blindfolds and disregard the ever-growing 'cancer of drugs on humanity,'" Judge Coffey wrote, "or ignore the potential impact our decisions have on the good-faith efforts of law enforcement officials to eradicate that cancer."

Small Transgressions, Major Consequences

All too often, though, judges do ignore the real-life impact of their decisions. This oversight can be especially glaring when the exclusion-ary rule is invoked because of tiny transgressions by cops in the course of capturing a truly heinous criminal.

At 2 A.M. on November 20, 1990, two New York state troopers were patrolling a desolate stretch of road about thirty miles north of New York City when they observed a U-Haul van whizzing along at 70 miles per hour. They were suspicious not only because of the early hour and the high rate of speed but also because deer hunting season had just started. Hunters often come up from New York City and sometimes try to poach animals.

So after pulling over the van, one of the troopers asked driver Leonardo Turriago, "Do you mind if we see what's in the back of the truck?"

He replied, "Sure, I'll show you."

When the trooper got into the trailer, he found several boxes and asked Turriago to open them. "Sure," he replied again.

The boxes contained clothes, a hammer, and some pillow cases. The trooper then asked Turriago to open a trunk, and Turriago eagerly replied, "Sure."

He seemed to have trouble opening the trunk. The trooper told him to keep trying, but "if it's broken, it's broken." Just then, the trunk clicked open and Turriago took off running. When the trooper lifted up the lid, out popped a pair of human legs.

After Turriago and two companions were apprehended, investigators discovered that Turriago had killed the victim over what he called "a drug thing," first shooting him in the face, then repeatedly striking his head with a hammer. Turriago and the others were transporting the corpse from New York City for disposal in the countryside. When police searched the apartment where the murder took place, they found numerous weapons and 11 pounds of cocaine. A police scuba team recovered a .25 caliber handgun, believed to be the murder weapon, from the Hudson River. Turriago admitted to committing the murder.

A slam-dunk case for the prosecution, right? Wrong. A 4–1 majority of the First Department of the Appellate Division—including Justice Joseph Sullivan, author of the Juan C. opinion discussed at the start of this chapter—decided that the evidence and the defendant's confession weren't admissible. They overturned Turriago's conviction.

Ah, but didn't Turriago give permission for the cops to search his van? In the judges' view, it didn't matter: "When a motorist, stopped for some minor traffic infraction on a lonely stretch of road in the dead of night, is approached by two imposing State Troopers—the very personification of State authority on the highway—one of whom leans over the car and asks, 'Mind if we look in the trunk?' can the forthcoming affirmative response truly be regarded as the product of free will?" An interesting metaphysical point, perhaps, but in this case, if upheld, it would have exonerated an admitted murderer.

Turriago, however, didn't place his faith in the appellate process. Just before the First Department issued its favorable ruling, he was arrested on charges of hiring a hit man to eliminate potential witnesses against him.

The *Turriago* decision, like the Juan C. case, generated intense political heat on the New York State Court of Appeals. The court therefore decided unanimously to send the case back to the trial judge to consider whether the "inevitable discovery" doctrine—which holds that evidence can be admitted if it would have been discovered notwithstanding the Fourth Amendment violation—might allow the body in the trunk to be admitted at trial.

As in the Juan C. case, the New York high court seems to be shying away from the disastrous consequences of the exoneration rule in one particularly controversial case, without seriously questioning the rule itself. And the basic thrust of the rule seems to be this: It doesn't matter how small the errors committed by the cops are; that's still enough to allow even the most cold-blooded murderer to go free.

No matter what is ultimately decided in the Turriago case, it's clear that not only does the exclusionary rule have the potential to release predators onto our streets (a fact not denied by even its most zealous defenders)—but in fact it *does* release quite a few. Remember the previously cited figure on how we could fill Yankee Stadium three times over with all the people who fall victim every year to aggravated assault suspects set loose because of the exclusionary rule.

Indeed, if it didn't wind up releasing all these criminals, *Mapp* wouldn't be doing its duty—which, in the view of its black-robed creators and defenders, is to deter police misconduct. This cockamamy view of criminal justice sends a dispiriting message to the public in general and police in particular; the message is that the courts think cops pose a bigger danger to society than crooks. No statistician can calculate the countless ways in which that attitude, which radiates out of the judicial system, casts a "chilling effect" on effective law enforcement.

This is a tragedy, because ultimately our safety depends not on the black line of jurists but on the thin blue line. To twist a 1960s slogan: The next time you get mugged, try calling a judge.

Just Shut Up: The Origins of the Miranda Rule

Y OU HAVE the right to remain silent. Anything you say can and will be used against you in a court of law. You have the right to an attorney. If you cannot afford an attorney, one will be provided for you. Do you understand these rights?"

Any American who's ever seen a TV show or movie, which is to say *any* American, is familiar with the Miranda warning, usually growled by glamorous cops as they take snarling suspects into custody. Whence does this warning derive? Not from the Constitution or common law. Like the exclusionary rule, it is wholly a product of the Supreme Court's fertile imagination.

Throughout most of our history the rule on confessions was: They'll be admitted into evidence if made voluntarily. The use of torture or threats of violence during interrogations has long been repugnant to English common law, both because this practice was considered to be barbaric and (the more practical reason) because confessions obtained under physical duress were viewed as unreliable. There is no clear ban in the Constitution itself against the use of torture to get a suspect's confession. But the Founders did appear to have this problem in mind when they drafted the Fifth Amendment guarantee that no one "shall be compelled in any criminal case to be a witness against himself, nor be deprived of life, liberty or property, without due process of law." The commonly accepted view among scholars is that "due process of law" essentially constitutionalized the age-old ban on the use of torture in confessions.

Justice Felix Frankfurter summed up the traditional view of confessions as late as 1961:

> The ultimate test remains that which has been the only clearly established test in Anglo-American courts for two hundred years: the test of voluntariness. Is the confession the product of an essentially free and unconstrained choice by its maker? If it is, if he has willed to confess, it may be used against him. If it is not, if his will has been overborne and his capacity for self-determination critically impaired, the use of his confession offends due process.

A classic example of the kind of confession—the only kind—that was traditionally tossed out by the courts occurred in a 1936 Mississippi case. A body was discovered in a farmhouse, horribly mutilated. That evening, a white deputy sheriff, accompanied by a lynch mob, seized a black suspect, strung him up in a tree, and whipped him. After this failed to produce a confession, the deputy two days later arrested the suspect and beat him again. He told the suspect that the whippings would continue until he confessed; the confession finally came. The deputy then arrested two other suspects, both black, and whipped their bare backs with a leather strap and buckle. They, too, confessed, after being told the beatings would continue until they did so. The confessions were admitted into evidence, and the defendants were sentenced to death. The case eventually reached the U.S. Supreme Court, where the justices unanimously threw out the convictions as a violation of the Due Process Clause, because the confession was clearly not voluntary.

Until the 1960s, even the Warren Court hewed to the traditional view of confessions. In two 1958 cases, the justices upheld the admission of confessions from suspects whose requests for a lawyer had been denied.

By 1964, however, the Court had become more radicalized, which led to the *Escobedo v. Illinois* decision, for the first time establishing a right to have counsel present during police interrogation. The justification for this newfound right was said to rest in the Sixth Amendment's guarantee: "In all criminal prosecutions, the accused shall . . . have the Assistance of Counsel for his defense."

It would have been news indeed to any court of the previous 175 years that suspects were entitled to a lawyer while being given the third degree in a police station. A New Jersey court summed up the traditional view in 1915: "The Constitution does not provide that the defendant shall have the right to have assistance of counsel from the time of his arrest, but for his defense. . . . Confession is a thing entirely apart from defense upon a trial."

By executing this old conception in *Escobedo*, the Warren Court set the stage for its most audacious expansion of criminals' rights. Having established that "voluntariness" was not the sole touchstone for confessions, the justices now proceeded to attach cumbersome new conditions to police interrogations.

Writing in the manner of a legislator, not a judge, Chief Justice Earl Warren used his opinion in *Miranda v. Arizona*—the name applied to the general opinion comes from one of four similar cases reviewed at the same time by the Court—to boldly lay out a new regime that all police everywhere would have to follow. In essence, the justices decided that the Fifth Amendment protection against self-incrimination could only be enforced if police informed suspects that they had a right not to talk and to have a lawyer present.

It wasn't immediately apparent why the justices thought the old voluntariness standard wasn't working. In the four cases under review—lumped together as "Miranda"—there was no evidence that the police had used any third-degree techniques, much less beaten the suspects. Warren admitted as much: "To be sure, the records do not evince overt physical coercion or patent psychological ploys."

But as Justice Byron White complained in dissent, the Court seemed to feel that because of the "compulsion inherent" in police custody of a suspect, no statement from a defendant could "truly be the product of free choice, absent the use of adequate protective devices as described by the Court." Unless a suspect "knowingly and intelligently" waives his rights, the Court held, all his statements—and any evidence that might subsequently be derived from them—would be excluded from evidence.

Warren acknowledged this result was not dictated by the Constitution: "We cannot say that the Constitution necessarily requires adherence to any particular solution for the inherent compulsions of the interrogation process as it is currently conducted." Indeed, virtually the Court's only bow to stare decisis, the doctrine of respecting precedent, was to declare that "we adhere to the principles of *Escobedo* today"—a two-year-old case that overturned decades of precedent.

Instead of constitutional principles, the *Miranda* opinion ruling was full of hand-wringing about the plight of suspects who don't know enough to clam up and holler for an attorney as soon as they are taken into police custody. "We cannot penalize a defendant who, not under-standing his constitutional rights, does not make the formal request, and, by such failure, demonstrates his helplessness," Chief Justice Warren wrote. "To require the request would be to favor the defen-dant whose sophistication or status had fortuitously prompted him to make it." In other words, all criminals, no matter how poorly edu-cated, should be given a sporting chance to escape conviction.

The justices, driven by what Justice White's dissent characterized as "deep-seated distrust of all confessions," ignored copious evidence that coming clean actually benefits many defendants, because it gives them "psychological relief" and enhances their "prospects for rehabil-itation." The majority also never addressed Justice John Marshall Harlan's dissent, which asked why "those who use third-degree tactics and deny them in court" won't be able to lie with equal facility about whether "warnings and waivers" were properly administered.

Such reservations were of no concern to a Supreme Court majority in the grip of gavelitis and determined to make the rest of the country pay the price for its devotion to misguided philosophical principles.

Bride of Frankenstein:
The Consequences of *Miranda*

IF THE exclusionary rule is a Frankenstein monster, then *Miranda* is the Bride of Frankenstein. By radically expanding the scope of the exclusionary rule, the decision ensured that many more criminals would get to thumb their nose at justice. As with *Mapp*, the beneficiary of *Miranda* isn't the law-abiding citizen unjustly accused—that person would be happy to talk to the police to clear up the confusion as soon as possible—but the suspect who really did it. The Miranda rule provides this criminal with yet another route to avoid punishment.

Justice White predicted the upshot of *Miranda*: "In some unknown number of cases, the Court's rule will return a killer, a rapist or other criminal to the streets and to the environment that produced him, to repeat his crimes whenever it pleases him."

University of Utah law professor Paul G. Cassell, an avowed critic of the Miranda rule, has attempted to quantify its cost. He found that the percentage of violent crimes solved remained stable from 1950 to 1965, at around 60 percent. But in 1966, the year of *Miranda*, the figure dropped to 55 percent, and by 1969, it was at 46 percent, roughly where it has stayed ever since. At around the same time, the confession rate among criminal suspects declined by about 16 percentage points, falling from 60 percent to 44 percent. Cassell ran a sophisticated multiple regression analysis to show that there is a statistically significant correlation between the drop-off in the "clearance rate" and the decrease in confessions in the post-*Miranda* age.

This finding is confirmed by the experience of Britain, where until 1986 police told suspects they had the right to remain silent but didn't follow the rest of the Miranda regime. Under those rules, British bobbies obtained confessions at a rate at least 20 percent higher than American cops. After Britain adopted a Miranda-style system in 1986, confession rates plummeted.

Cassell estimates that the decrease in confessions in America due to the *Miranda* ruling has led to almost 4 percent of all criminal cases being lost. Again, to understand what this percentage means, let's look at the absolute numbers: Cassell estimates that 28,000 cases against violent suspects and 79,000 cases against suspects in property crimes are lost every year because of Miranda. And many of those not actually set free receive reduced jail time: Cassell calculates that Miranda causes 24,000 pleas to reduced charges for violent crimes and 67,000 pleas for property crimes annually.

These are only estimates, of course. But they give some idea what the Warren Court has wrought, and they refute the popular academic view that Miranda has had no impact on law enforcement.

To understand the full human dimension of those statistics, consider an example of how Miranda works. In 1995, a sixty-five-year-old disabled man was stabbed twenty-seven times and killed in his house in Avon, Massachusetts. The case gained national notoriety when one of the alleged accomplices to the murder, eighteen-year-old Patrick Morse, bragged that he and two friends were "natural-born killers," inspired by Oliver Stone's eponymous movie. The killing was cited by presidential candidate Bob Dole as evidence of Hollywood's moral rot. Now the case also stands as evidence of the corrosive impact of the Supreme Court's rules of criminal procedure. Superior court judge Judith Cowin threw out Morse's confession on the grounds that he hadn't been properly "Mirandized."

Here's what happened: Morse went voluntarily to the police station and was initially interviewed as a witness, not a suspect. When police asked him about contradictions in his statement, he acknowledged that he knew his two friends were planning to break into "some old guy's house" in Avon. Realizing he was now a suspect, police immediately read him his Miranda rights. But he didn't confess at this time; he still insisted that all he had done was drive his friends to the Avon house and then later pick them up. The next time he was interviewed, six hours later, he was again read his Miranda rights, and this time he confessed. Morse said he participated in the break-in, handed a friend the knife used to kill the disabled man, threw away the knife after the crime, and participated in the cover-up of the murder.

Judge Cowin ruled that police had erred by not Mirandizing Morse *before* he admitted knowing that his friends were planning to commit a robbery—in other words, before he was a suspect. Prosecutors contended that this wasn't necessary because Morse wasn't in custody at that time. But since police failed to read him his rights at the beginning, the judge held, his confession was inadmissible as the "fruit of a poisonous tree." If the ruling is upheld on appeal (still pending, as of this writing), Morse will presumably walk out of jail.

Often, of course, Miranda rulings result not in a conviction being overturned but in a generous plea bargain being struck by desperate prosecutors. For instance, cab driver Patrick Crone picked up passenger Thomas Damiano at the Providence, Rhode Island, train station just before midnight on September 30, 1993. As they were driving along, Crone said he had to stop and get gas. Damiano—who, according to prosecutors, had been drinking and snorting cocaine—accused the driver of being in a conspiracy against him. Damiano told Crone he had a gun and to keep driving. As they were speeding along, Damiano pushed or threw Crone out of the cab and into a river, killing him. He then crashed the vehicle.

When police found him, Damiano had lost his shirt and shoes and was screaming about being robbed. The local police considered him a witness, but because he was acting "wild," they handcuffed him for his own protection. State police began talking to him as a witness, said the prosecutor, "but within two minutes they realized he was a suspect so they read him his rights." Damiano then revealed what had occurred in the cab, though he contended the driver jumped on his own "without warning."

In 1995, state judge Richard Chin ruled that everything Damiano said was inadmissible because he began talking before being Mirandized, a decision upheld by Rhode Island's highest court. Prosecutors had no choice but to let Damiano plead guilty to manslaughter and be sentenced to ten years' probation. In other words, this killer is now walking the streets because of the *Miranda* decision.

"We always had faith in the judicial system," said one of the victim's brothers. "We just lost faith," said the other brother. Such are the laments of *Miranda*'s victims.

Ironically, one of the victims of the *Miranda* opinion was Ernesto Miranda himself. The rapist, whose conviction was overturned by the famous Supreme Court case, was stabbed to death in 1976 in a Phoenix bar. The cops arrested a suspect in the killing, but after being read his Miranda rights, the alleged killer refused to talk. No one has ever been convicted in the slaying.

Grin and Baer It:
The *Mapp* and *Miranda* Mess Today

IF YOU LISTEN to some liberal law professors, you'd think that because of recent Supreme Court rulings, *Miranda* and *Mapp* have more holes in them than a corpse at the St. Valentine's Day Massacre. It's true that the Burger and Rehnquist Courts have narrowed the scope of both Warren Court decisions, but the justices, unfortunately, haven't come close to defenestrating either precedent.

Time and again, the Rehnquist Court has affirmed *Miranda*, though the justices have scaled it back a bit. The Supreme Court has created a "public safety" exception: For example, police don't have to read Miranda rights if they're asking a suspect questions about a gun left around where it could be picked up and used to hurt someone. Courts have also moved toward allowing into evidence the "fruit" of an illegal confession, often physical evidence that came to light as a result of the suspect's description.

Alas, judges are often loath to apply these exceptions in practice. On February 3, 1996, a New York City police officer heard a report of shots fired and arrested a suspect fitting the description of the shooter. The suspect, however, didn't have a gun on him. He said he'd dropped a BB gun and offered to show the cop and his partner where it was, but they couldn't find it. The cops questioned him repeatedly to find out where the gun was, but getting no answers, they took him down to the station. After he was Mirandized and questioned some more, the defendant finally admitted that he'd been carrying a 9 millimeter semiautomatic and told the cops where it was.

Prosecutors argued that the confession should be admitted because the pre-Miranda questioning was covered by the "public safety" exception. But a New York state judge decided that the public safety exception was so "narrow" that it could not encompass asking a suspect about a lost gun several hours earlier—so he threw out both the confession and the gun. Other judges may well interpret the public safety doctrine more broadly, but as this example shows, they're perfectly within the law to virtually read this exception out of existence.

The exclusionary rule has seen a broader retrenchment. Unwilling to let serious criminals go free, the Supreme Court has created all sorts of loopholes. Grand jury inquiries and civil proceedings, such as deportation hearings, among others, have been excluded from the exclusionary requirement. The Court has also created an "inevitable discovery" doctrine, which we've previously encountered in the Turriago body-in-the-trunk case.

When necessary, the Court has strained logic and semantics in order to avoid excluding evidence. The justices have decided, for instance, that neither a dog sniff nor traipsing through somebody's "open fields" constitutes a "search." This may be perfectly clear to the justices, but it leaves this observer, for one, scratching his head in befuddlement.

The biggest exception created by the Court is the "good faith" doctrine, which holds that evidence doesn't need to be excluded if the cops relied on a legitimate warrant or law that was subsequently invalidated. But the impact of the good faith exception has been blunted by the fact that many leading state courts, including those in New York and Pennsylvania, don't recognize it. (The Supreme Court only sets a "floor" for defendants' rights; individual states are free to exceed the mandated protections.)

One of the odder, and perhaps unintended, consequences of recent Supreme Court action is that the government has greater leeway in searching the general public than it does criminal suspects. The courts, for instance, have authorized metal detectors at airports, sobriety checkpoints on roadways, and random drug tests of federal workers, while blocking "no-knock" searches of drug dealers' safe houses. Where's the logic here?

I'm not suggesting that searches with a low probability of success, such as those administered by airport metal detectors, shouldn't be allowed. They obviously should be. But if they're legal, why not conduct searches with a much higher probability of nailing a crook?

Ruling by Ouija Board

What the Rehnquist Court is doing is akin to trying to shove a bunch of wire coat hangers into a small plastic trash bag: They'll fit, but only if you're willing to rip and tear the bag.

By squeezing all sorts of exceptions under the rubric of *Mapp* and *Miranda*, the Court has turned Fourth and Fifth Amendment law into what one leading commentator calls a "mess" and an "embarrassment." Criminal court judges are forced to spend an inordinate amount of time deciding *Mapp* and *Miranda* motions. (No wonder they complain about being overworked!) But judges have little guidance about how each case should come out. They might as well flip a coin or consult a Ouija board. Instead, what they wind up doing is substituting their own personal preferences for the rule of law.

Most of the time the result isn't bad; most judges don't want to let criminals go free, so they'll bend the rules as much as they can to avoid such a horrible outcome. Indeed, some law-and-order judges employ what's known informally as the "ax murderer exception"—they more or less waive rules like *Mapp* and *Miranda* when the effect of applying them would be to release a super-dangerous criminal. But liberal judges, who seem to be almost as plentiful as panhandlers in many of our metropolises, are able to selectively cite precedents to achieve the results they want—greater rights for criminals.

Cops and prosecutors have no way to predict which kind of judge will snare any given case, and that raises yet another major problem with *Mapp* and *Miranda*: the lack of predictability of outcome. The rule of law is supposed to mean the application of previously announced holdings. When they know what the law is, those subject to its dictates can conduct themselves accordingly. But if judges don't know how any given *Mapp* or *Miranda* case will turn out, then cops can't possibly know either. Thus, they have no idea what they're supposed to do to stay within the law. So much for the vaunted "deterrence" effect of those two rules.

There is no better illustration of the confusion plaguing our courts than the taxi searches in New York City, as the following example shows. On the night of July 2, 1996, three New York City police officers pulled over a livery cab in the Bronx. They were part of the Taxi/Livery Robbery Task Force, conducting safety checks of cabs in that crime-prone area. As one of the officers approached the cab, he saw passenger Jeffrey Santiago "dip" his shoulder. When he looked inside the cab, he saw the handle of a gun protruding from under the seat. The officers promptly arrested Santiago, a convicted felon who had no business carrying a weapon.

But U.S. district judge Shira Sheindlin, a Clinton appointee, decided that it was the cops who were the wrongdoers. "I find that the police officers had no probable cause or reasonable suspicion to stop the taxicab," she wrote in throwing out the case against Santiago.

The judge acknowledged that the Supreme Court has allowed police to pull over vehicles as part of a drunk-driving checkpoint or for some other good cause, as long as the stops are not "discretionary." The police testified that the taxi program met this test—the officers simply tried to pull over every occupied cab they saw. But Judge Sheindlin astutely noted that the cops "were not able to stop all such cabs." Thus, she held that because they couldn't stop all of them, they didn't have a right to stop any of them.

If her ruling holds up, the police department will be forced to stop a program credited with cutting crime against taxi drivers by two-thirds since 1993. However, three New York state judges, presented with almost identical fact patterns in other cases and interpreting essentially the same body of state and federal cases, approved the work of the taxi task force. It will now be up to appellate courts to straighten out this confusion. No one, including the judges (*especially* the judges), has any idea how all this will turn out. The outcome will depend, more than anything, on whether these cases draw liberal or conservative appeals judges.

The notion that exclusionary rule issues are governed by any binding precedent was resoundingly refuted by the example of U.S. district judge Harold Baer Jr. of New York. Judge Baer, recall, was the judge who earned himself an infamous place in legal annals by not allowing into evidence 80 pounds of cocaine and heroin worth $4 million.

The cops had confiscated the drugs after seeing four men loading duffel bags into the trunk of a car. The men ran away upon the approach of the officers, who then pulled the car over and busted an admitted drug courier from Detroit. Judge Baer ruled that in the poor Washington Heights neighborhood where the seizure occurred, residents viewed the police as "corrupt, abusive and violent," so there was nothing suspicious about the men running away. "Had the men not run away when the cops began to stare at them," the judge wrote, "it would have been unusual."

This ruling, issued during the 1996 presidential election, briefly made Baer the object of more scorn than any judge since Roger Taney, author of the *Dred Scott* opinion. Even President Clinton, who appointed Baer, suggested that he ought to quit. Judges rushed to his defense, proclaiming that he was only following precedent. The evidence was excluded, Baer's defenders proclaimed in all seriousness, not because of his whims, but because of the sacrosanct U.S. Constitution itself.

But after four months of shellacking—guess what?—Baer suddenly saw the precedents in a new way. He reversed his earlier ruling and allowed the drugs as evidence after all, though he insisted that he would continue "fearlessly" drawing the line between searches good and bad. The Constitution, presumably, had changed overnight.

Rulings like this one suggest that if you don't like the way an exclusionary rule issue has been decided, just grin and Baer it: Some other court, perhaps even this very court, may well reach a different conclusion before long. It does not enhance the reputation of the legal system when attorneys and even judges are reduced to flipping a coin to figure out how important criminal procedure cases will be decided.

Conclusion: Turn Back the Clock

IS THERE NO way out of this mess? The best bet for sweeping reform of *Mapp* and *Miranda* is probably legislation, though there's a big question about whether the Supreme Court justices, inflamed by gavelitis, would allow this. In 1968, Congress actually passed a law to override *Miranda;* the statute stated that the absence of constitutional warnings would not preclude a voluntary confession from being admitted into evidence. But this law, which remains on the books, has been "largely ignored," according to one commentator, because "everyone really understood that a constitutional amendment, not a mere statute, is required to overturn a decision based on the Constitution."

Now some legal scholars argue that Congress *can* override the exclusionary rule and *Miranda*, at least for cases argued in the federal courts, because the Supreme Court has acknowledged that both rulings are "prophylactic devices" created by the Court itself, and not compelled by the Constitution. It's certainly worth testing whether the Court is serious about this.

But what would happen if we could get rid of *Miranda* and *Mapp?* What then? Some scholars—principally Yale's Akhil Amar, a leading liberal critic of both rulings—suggest that we need to replace the exclusionary rule with greater civil damages against rogue cops and ditch *Miranda* only at the cost of getting rid of all unsupervised police interrogations of suspects. Amar and other scholars argue that we can't simply throw out these two rules because police power has grown immeasurably since the early days of the republic, when the law was enforced by a few disorganized constables. Americans, Amar argues, need enhanced protection from today's paramilitary-style police departments.

But would it really be so awful if we could simply click our heels three times and transport ourselves back to 1960? In that not-so-distant day, the Supreme Court did not compel any state to institute either an exclusionary rule or a Miranda rule. Police departments then were as well (or better) organized than they are today, and Americans could sue for damages from the police under rules not too dissimilar from those that exist today. Was America terrorized by brutes with badges in those benighted days? Were citizens' liberties routinely violated? Nope. Or, at least, there's no evidence that police misconduct was worse then than it is today. And perhaps coincidentally, violent crime was four times lower in 1960 than it is today.

Going back to the future would require admitting at trial all reliable physical evidence and all voluntarily obtained confessions. If we can make this leap, either judicially or legislatively, the benefits will extend beyond locking up more criminals and making the streets safer. The biggest benefit of all would be increased respect for the legal system and the judges who run it.

It sends a "demoralizing message," in the words of Harvard law professor Charles Nesson, when the courts let manifestly guilty defendants go because of some "evidentiary rule." By ditching *Miranda* and *Mapp*, the justice system could return to its rightful role: "a search for truth."

CHAPTER 4

Juristocracy

THE

UNELECTED

LEGISLATURE

[T]he judge *should never be* the Legislator: *Because, then, the Will of the Judge would be the Law; and this tends directly to a State of Slavery.*

GOVERNOR THOMAS HUTCHINSON,
Charge to the Grand Jury

ON NOVEMBER 5, 1996, 54 percent of California voters approved Proposition 209, prohibiting the use of racial or sexual preferences by the state government in public employment, education, and contracting. On November 27, the votes of 4.7 million Californians were overridden by one man—Thelton Henderson. As chief U.S. district judge in northern California, Henderson issued a temporary restraining order to block the implementation of 209 and then followed up, on December 23, with a preliminary injunction to prevent enforcement of the voter initiative until a trial was held. His actions provide as good an example as any of how activist judges are prone to become dictators in black robes—a trend that is increasingly abridging American democracy.

In this chapter, we'll see how judges have unfairly overridden polit-

ical decisions in such areas as term limits and panhandling—and have
done so most especially concerning a host of controversial issues, such
as single-sex education, gay rights, and abortion, that have fallen
under the ever-expanding domain of the Fourteenth Amendment. In
most cases, the judges' decisions have little basis in the law. Instead,
their decisions, like Thelton Henderson's ruling, represent an attempt
by the judiciary to impose its political preferences on the voters.

That Judge Henderson was hearing the 209 case at all was extraordinary. Under the random rules of case assignment, the suit filed
against 209 by various liberal groups the day after the election should
have been heard by Judge Vaughn Walker, a Bush appointee. At the
time, Henderson was hearing an unrelated case in which a contractor
was challenging San Francisco's racial set-aside program. Henderson
allowed the Coalition for Economic Equity, an activist group, to intervene in the contracting case and, over the protests of the plaintiffs, to
raise 209 as an issue. This gave Henderson an excuse to transfer the
209 case into his court. (The judge claimed that "issues concerning the
validity of Proposition 209 are inevitably implicated in the [other]
action.") Attempted forum shopping isn't at all unusual in American
courts, but it's not every day that judges do so much to aid this disreputable practice.

Supporters of 209 moved to recuse Henderson—who told his
Senate confirmation hearing, "I guess I have been pretty much identified with civil rights activities since graduating from law school"—
from the case. Federal law holds that judges shouldn't hear a case
when they have a personal bias for or against any party in the litigation
or when their "impartiality might reasonably be questioned." In this
case, there were questions aplenty.

Until his appointment to the bench in 1980 by Jimmy Carter,
Henderson had been a board member of the American Civil Liberties
Union of Northern California and a group called Equal Rights
Advocates—both plaintiffs in the 209 case. At his confirmation hearings, Henderson had pledged to resign from both boards and to recuse
himself from cases involving these groups "for some period of time."
But in 1986, he went ahead and joined the board of a Berkeley-based
outfit called the Meiklejohn Civil Liberties Institute, which describes
itself as a "unique center for peace, law and human rights." Henderson
finally left Meiklejohn's board of directors in 1992, around the time a

conservative group filed a motion with the Ninth Circuit claiming that his affiliation represented a conflict of interest. Meiklejohn, too, was a party in the 209 litigation; the group filed an amicus brief against the initiative. Despite all this, Henderson claimed with a straight face that he was impartial and refused to recuse himself.

Instead, the judge proceeded to issue an "anomalous and bizarre" decision—the words come from an appellate opinion—holding that in all "likelihood" 209 was unconstitutional. Henderson decided that 209—which merely restated, word for word, the ban on using race and sex classifications found in the 1964 Civil Rights Act—was a probable violation of the Fourteenth Amendment's Equal Protection Clause, which forbids a state to "deny to any person within its jurisdiction the equal protection of the laws."

In reaching this conclusion, Henderson noted that 209 would forbid women and minorities to seek preferential treatment, which would reduce the number of people from those favored groups being admitted to state colleges or receiving state contracts. Thus, he concluded, 209 imposes a "substantial burden on the interests of women and minorities."

In short, Henderson's opinion held that a law demanding that everyone be treated equally ran afoul of a constitutional provision demanding that . . . everyone be treated equally. "If merely stating this alleged equal protection violation does not suffice to refute it," a panel of the U.S. Court of Appeals for the Ninth Circuit later wrote, "the central tenet of the Equal Protection Clause teeters on the brink of incoherence."

Constitutional issues are seldom so clear-cut. The Ninth Circuit's decision gives some indication of how little Henderson's ruling was grounded in any reasonable interpretation of the Constitution or case law. What made Henderson's opinion even more startling was a long line of Supreme Court cases holding that any use of racial or gender classifications by government must pass "the most exacting judicial scrutiny" and can only be justified if the classifications are "narrowly tailored to serve a compelling government interest." Yet here was Henderson telling the voters of California that they couldn't get rid of these preferences that are inherently suspect. As the Ninth Circuit panel noted dryly: "The Fourteenth Amendment, lest we lose sight of the forest for the trees, does not require what it barely permits."

The Ninth Circuit panel, led by Judge Diarmuid O'Scannlain, came under fire from many journalistic and legal quarters for issuing an opinion so wide-ranging that it not only struck down Henderson's injunction but ruled on the merits of the case ("Proposition 209 does not violate the United States Constitution"). O'Scannlain and the two other judges happen to be Republican appointees who are among the most conservative members of the Ninth Circuit. Critics have accused 209's supporters of engaging in the same kind of judge shopping that opponents used to land Henderson on the case.

In fact, the three appellate judges were chosen by chance; they just happened to be the ones assigned to hear motions during January 1997. It is precisely for this reason that advocates of judicial restraint can take little heart from their action; if three other Ninth Circuit judges had been chosen at random, there's a good chance that 209 would never have gone into effect.

The California Civil Rights Initiative, as 209 was known, could easily have suffered the same fate as another initiative passed by California voters. In November 1994, 59 percent of the state's voters approved Proposition 187, cutting off state aid to illegal immigrants and their offspring. Federal judge Mariana Pfaelzer blocked the state from implementing key parts of the measure but, as of this writing, has refused to issue any final order that the initiative's supporters could appeal to the Ninth Circuit. As one of 187's authors put it, the judge left the initiative in "legal limbo," effectively frustrating the will of the voters. The same thing happens to virtually "every conservatively based initiative passed in California," according to Governor Pete Wilson.

Various commentators have ascribed the differences between judges like Thelton Henderson and Diarmuid O'Scannlain to politics. Henderson is a liberal Democrat, O'Scannlain a conservative Republican. True, but there's a more fundamental and pertinent dividing line that accounts for the differing outcomes of their decisions.

Henderson, while claiming that his personal philosophy doesn't influence his decisions, uses the bench as an instrument to achieve his conception of social justice. In the past, he has issued rulings to protect the "rights" of inmates in a maximum security state prison and to restrict the imports of yellowfin tuna caught with "dolphin-killer" nets. O'Scannlain, by contrast, advocates a philosophy of judicial restraint. He believes in acting in accordance with the text of a statute or the

Constitution rather than according to his own conception of social justice. "If the federal courts were to decide what the interests of the people are in the first place," he wrote, "judicial power would trump self-government as the general rule of our constitutional democracy."

"There Are No Gaps": Defining the Problem of Judicial Activism

WHAT Judge O'Scannlain fears has happened. America used to be a democracy, a government of, by, and for the people. Now it has all the earmarks of a *juristocracy*, a government of, by, and for people who have attended law school. Judges have assumed unprecedented authority over our lives, usurping the powers once delegated to elected lawmakers, based on no solid grounding in the text of either a statute or the Constitution itself.

Because plaints about activism from the bench have been heard so often in recent decades, it's important to be specific about what we're objecting to—to wit, judges who rule based on their own preferences, not on the law. We should avoid becoming beguiled by three myths that are common in conservative circles:

First, it is not the case that judicial legislation began with the Warren Court. Even *Marbury v. Madison*—the 1803 ruling in which the Supreme Court for the first time declared an act of Congress unconstitutional and thus established the right of judicial review of legislation—has no real foundation in the text of the Constitution itself. Judges, no matter what their personal views, have always been tempted to make law, not interpret it, and not always with negative consequences.

Second, judicial activism is not strictly a liberal phenomenon. In the early years of this century, the Supreme Court was dominated by laissez-faire activists, and there are still a few conservative activist judges around.

Witness U.S. district judge Michael Hogan's decision blocking the implementation of a 1994 Oregon initiative legalizing physician-assisted suicide on the grounds that it was unconstitutional; this is as wrong-headed as Judge Henderson's actions in California. Or there's U.S. district judge John E. Sprizzo's 1997 acquittal of two "pro-life" protesters on charges of blocking access to a Dobbs Ferry, New York, abortion clinic; the judge ruled that the men hadn't violated the law because they had acted out of religious, not criminal, motives. Good thing Judge Sprizzo didn't handle the trial of the World Trade Center bombers. Presumably, he would have let them go, too, because their terrorism had religious roots—in their case, radical Islamic views.

The third myth of the right is that judicial legislation is always wrong. Actually, in one area at least, legislating has always been the function of the judge, and so it should remain. This is the area of common law, the (state) law that today by and large governs contracts, torts, property, trusts, and estates. It would be extremely difficult, if not impossible, for a legislature to codify all the law in these areas; no legislature could anticipate every possible contingency in every case that may be filed. So judges, acting ostensibly on the basis of precedent but really on their own intuition, have to decide for themselves the rules in these areas on a case-by-case basis.

The classical commentators of the law, the Blackstones and Cokes, denied that judges legislated even in these areas. Their theory was that "a preexisting rule was there, imbedded, if concealed, in the body of the customary law. All that the judges did was to throw off the wrappings and expose the statue to our view." Since the advent of "legal realism" in the early twentieth century, hardly anybody hews to this view anymore. But legal realism—the realization that judges make up the law—is not an invitation to an open-ended legislative role. The judge, Cardozo argues, "legislates only between the gaps. He fills the open spaces in the law." Cardozo goes on to note: "In countless litigation, the law is so clear that judges have no discretion. They have the right to legislate within gaps, but often there are no gaps."

This distinction, as crisp as a freshly printed magazine in Cardozo's mind, has gotten as blurred as a crumpled-up old newspaper with the passage of time. Justice Antonin Scalia argues that many of his brethren on the bench apply common-law techniques when they should instead be guided by the text of a statute or the Constitution itself.

Every student's first year in law school, notes Scalia, is spent playing common-law judge, "devising out of the brilliance of one's own mind, those laws that ought to govern mankind." Indeed, all American law students are taught based on the "case method": In a course on constitutional law, the students study *only* judges' rulings interpreting the Constitution; incredible as this may sound to a nonlawyer, our budding

Blackstones *never* study the text of the Constitution itself. And many of these students don't lose the habit of common-law judging even when they join the Supreme Court, where their job is to interpret the law devised by legislators or the Founding Fathers, not to create their own.

"The [Supreme] Court," Scalia argues, "will distinguish its precedents, or narrow them, or if all else fails overrule them, in order that the Constitution might mean what it *ought* to mean." The rule, he suggests, is that "[i]f it is good, it must be so," which effectively reduces the Constitution to the level of common law. In short, judges, and especially the justices of the high court, feel free to ignore the laws passed by others and instead impose their own policy preferences in their decisions.

Deferring to Uncle Sam, Not the States

WHILE THE expansion of judicial power has infringed upon democracy at all levels, the intrusion has been especially great at the state level. "States' rights" have largely been replaced with more nebulous, judicially created and judicially protected individual "rights."

Today, alas, "states' rights" is a battle cry associated in many minds with the South's defense of slavery and segregation. It's high time to rescue this concept from the opprobrium into which it has sunk; states' rights lie at the very heart of the American system of governance. State governments, after all, are closer to the people than are the federal authorities in Washington. They can create laws better suited to local conditions, and by a political version of natural selection, the best solutions will wind up being replicated elsewhere. "It is one of the happy incidents of the federal system," Justice Brandeis famously noted, "that a single courageous State may, if its citizens choose, serve as a laboratory; and try novel social and economic experiments without risk to the rest of the country." To give only one example of many: Wisconsin pioneered welfare reform measures that, in 1996, were implemented nationwide by Congress.

Another fortunate feature of federalism is that it contains a natural check on any state's going too far and enacting policies that are either counterproductive or downright tyrannical: Unhappy residents can always vote with their feet. If you don't like the high taxes and large government of New York, you can move to Utah, and if you don't like Utah's lack of amenities and regulations, you can move to New York. It's more difficult, however, for you to leave the country to protest the intrusiveness of the national government.

Federalism not only offers an excellent approach to safeguarding liberty and good government but also holds the key to social peace. In all multiethnic, multicultural nations there is great danger of minorities feeling oppressed by the majority, whether it's the Quebeçois in Canada or the Bosnian Muslims in the old Yugoslavia. Under the federalist system, minority groups—the Mormons, say—can enjoy a high level of self-determination at the state level, thus dissipating separatist pressures. The success of the federalist model can be measured by the more than 130 years of internal peace we've enjoyed since the Civil War. No wonder federalism is being widely adopted around the globe, from the European Union to Russia.

Yet at the same time, federalism is under siege in America. Under our federalist blueprint, the Constitution spells out certain "limited and enumerated powers" for the federal government and reserves all the rest to the states via the Tenth Amendment: "The powers not delegated to the United States by the Constitution, nor prohibited by it to the States, are reserved to the States respectively, or to the people." If the juristocracy respected the Founders' intentions, it would rule along the lines suggested by one scholar: "Any truly new thing done by the federal government is unauthorized and therefore void," while "[a]ny truly new thing done by a state must be outside of those prohibitions, and must, therefore, be constitutional." Instead, the courts' tendency is nearly the opposite: to clamp the states in judicial irons, while giving Uncle Sam freedom to do anything he likes.

Federal Power: Almost Unlimited

When it comes to federal legislation, the juristocracy's activism—if it can be labeled as such—takes the form of *not* acting. Federal judges have always been more loath to override Congress—which, after all, pays their salaries and staffs—than the state legislatures. Indeed, after *Marbury v. Madison* in 1803, the Supreme Court apparently didn't overrule another act of Congress for fifty-four years (in the infamous *Dred Scott* case); but many more state statutes fell by the wayside.

This tendency to give great leeway to Washington, but not to Albany or Austin, grew more pronounced after 1937. President Franklin Roosevelt threatened to add new justices to the Supreme Court in order to stop the conservative court from overturning New Deal legislation, as it had done in the past. Although the court-packing scheme was defeated, the justices suddenly saw the light, and in the famous "switch in time that saved nine," began rubber-stamping all future New Deal legislation. In the blink of an eye, the justices had gone from overturning too many federal laws to approving too many—a trend that only now, six decades later, is starting to abate.

The Court effectively refused to enforce any constitutional limits on the central government's authority by shoehorning every possible expansion of federal fiat under the Commerce Clause ("The Congress shall have Power . . . To regulate Commerce with foreign nations, and among the several states, and with the Indian Tribes") or the Necessary and Proper Clause ("The Congress shall have Power . . . To make all Laws which should be necessary and proper for carrying into Execution the foregoing Powers, and all other Powers vested by this Constitution in the Government of the United States, or in any Department or Officer thereof").

It was only in 1995 that the Court finally suggested, however gingerly, that the federal government had exceeded its enumerated authority. That realization was confirmed in 1997, when the justices overturned the Brady Act and the Religious Freedom Restoration Act on the grounds that Congress didn't have the power to run roughshod over the states in those areas. (It is also only in the last few years that the high court has rediscovered traditional property rights—as opposed to newfangled rights such a "right" to welfare benefits or public housing—which had generally been written out of the Constitution since the 1930s.)

Ironically, these modest attempts to impose some limits on Congress' authority have led some critics to label *this* Supreme Court as "activist." But this is pure sophistry, coming, as this criticism usually does, from the biggest fans of liberal judicial activism. Is it really activism for the Rehnquist Court to respect the status quo ante, namely, to show more respect for states' rights than some of its recent predecessors have done? Is it really activism for the Court to strike down *any* statute at all, no matter how clearly unconstitutional? I think not.

When the Court has struck down acts of Congress in recent years, the justices have usually been on solid ground. In 1976, for instance, the Supreme Court struck down most of a draconian campaign finance law on the grounds that capping political spending would be akin to capping political speech, which clearly isn't permissible under the First Amendment. More recently in 1997, the Court overturned, also on First Amendment grounds, the Communications Decency Act, which would have regulated all Internet content in a futile attempt to keep "indecent" material from kids.

With both the campaign finance and Internet cases, it took a flagrant violation of the Constitution for the Supreme Court to overturn an act of Congress—and in both instances, the justices displayed a high degree of unanimity in their findings. These were not instances of the justices substituting their own policy preferences for those of the Founders. Indeed, the more conservative members of the Court who voted to strike down the Communications Decency Act in all likelihood would have voted to approve it had they sat in Congress. They must have overturned the law with reluctance, and only because it so clearly conflicted with the Constitution. Had the justices *not* overturned those statutes, they would have been guilty of activism— ruling based on politics, not the law.

Term Limits: A Rorschach Test of States' Rights

Unfortunately, as we saw with Proposition 209, federal judges are less reluctant to strike down the actions of state voters than those of the national legislature. In all too many instances, judges have substituted their own judgment for that of state voters and lawmakers. The most striking instance of the federal courts' willingness to overturn state laws on flimsy grounds came in the term limits controversy.

By 1995, twenty-three states had enacted term limits on their members of Congress, all but one of them by direct vote of the people. Congressman Ray Thornton of Arkansas challenged his state's law, which didn't even bar incumbents from running. All it required was that after three terms in the House or two terms in the Senate, an incumbent could seek reelection only by write-in vote; the incumbent's name couldn't appear on the ballot.

This case served as a sort of Rorschach test of the Supreme Court's attitude toward the states. There was nothing in either the Constitution or the Court's own precedents to suggest which way the case should be decided. Since the Court could interpret the inkblots of the law any way it wanted, the resulting decision offers a window onto the justices' thinking.

The only touchstones in the Constitution for deciding this controversy were the Qualifications Clauses of Article 1. The one for the House holds: "No person shall be a Representative who shall not have attained to the age of twenty five Years, and been seven Years a citizen of the United States, and who shall, when elected, be an inhabitant of the State in which he shall be chosen." The clause is similar for the Senate, except that the minimum age is thirty years and the minimum citizenship requirement is nine years. That's it. Nothing about term limits, and virtually no case law interpreting these clauses.

The closest case on point was *Powell v. McCormack*, a 1969 decision holding that Congress didn't have the power to expel Representative Adam Clayton Powell for alleged embezzlement. But *Powell* dealt with the power of Congress, not the states, to set qualifications for members, and it principally turned on an interpretation of Section 5 of Article 1, which holds that Congress may "punish its Members for disorderly Behavior," and not on an interpretation of the Qualifications Clauses.

Thus, it was with a tabula rasa that the Court confronted the essential question: Is the Qualifications Clause exclusive or not? That is, may the states impose additional requirements on their senators and representatives beyond those spelled out in the Constitution? The Court split 5–4 on this question. Both sides cited endless, inconclusive evidence from the constitutional debates to support their claims. But in the end, the case came down to presumptions.

Justice Clarence Thomas, writing eloquently for the minority, cited the Tenth Amendment and declared: "The Constitution is silent on this question. And where the Constitution is silent, it raises no bar to action by the States or the people."

Justice John Paul Stevens, writing for the majority, held, to the contrary, that under the Tenth Amendment the states retain authority "only to the extent that the Constitution has not divested them of their original powers and transferred those powers to the Federal government." Since no states limited the service of their members of

Congress in the early days of the republic, the Supreme Court held, they had in essence forfeited their right to impose term limits.

Leave aside the silly implications of the Stevens view. (Does this mean that the Court will strike down the Florida law disqualifying congressional candidates who are mentally ill or the Georgia law disqualifying jailbirds?) The larger point here is that the Supreme Court seems to be acting on a presumption that whatever the states do is inherently suspicious—the very opposite of what the Founders intended.

Outlawing State Puritanism

The term limits case, alas, is much more representative of the Supreme Court's jurisprudence of the last several decades than the handful of recent cases asserting state power at the expense of the federal government. The courts have been especially eager to strike down state laws on social and cultural issues—issues where there is a great chasm between the opinions of the chattering classes (the so-called opinion leaders who spout off in leading newspapers and on Sunday television talk shows) and the Bible Belt traditionalists. Guess whose side judges take in this culture war?

H. L. Mencken defined "Puritanism" as "the haunting fear that someone, somewhere might be happy." The Supreme Court seems to be animated at times by the haunting fear that someone, somewhere might be puritanical. Hence its diktats that nowhere, nohow, under no circumstances must any state restrict the availability of contraceptives or abortion before the point of "viability." So, too, the high court's prohibition of the time-honored practice of prayer in public schools, or even the invocation of God at public school graduations. (It's a sign of how the courts defer to the federal government that the justices allow official prayers every day on the floor of Congress.) And then, of course, there are the Court's pornography cases, which allow communities to ban only material deemed "obscene," not stuff that excites "normal, healthy sexual desires."

Virtually the only bow the Court has made in recent years to benighted notions of morality was upholding a Georgia antisodomy law, but in light of the justices' 1996 decision overturning a Colorado anti–gay rights initiative, even antisodomy laws may soon be relegated to the courts' trash bin.

We have a federalist Constitution precisely in order to allow conservative states to enact puritanical ordinances, whereas liberal states may take a more libertine path. This allows Americans of differing viewpoints—some traditional, others cosmopolitan—to live in whatever area makes them most comfortable. By striking down so many state laws, the courts are upsetting this delicate balance and undermining the foundations of American democracy.

Minority Rights Never Go Begging

The justification for all these intrusions into state sovereignty is to protect the rights of minorities who have supposedly been oppressed by a state's majority. This is a legitimate function of the federal judiciary, one envisioned by the Founders. But those eighteenth-century gentlemen would be startled to discover that the juristocracy has expanded this role out of all proportion. Judges seem to delight in recognizing ever-expanding "rights" for an ever-expanding array of minority groups, the cumulative effect of which is to trample on the traditional rights—the pursuit of life, liberty, and happiness—enjoyed by all Americans. This conflict comes into stark relief when we look at the latest minority group to win judicial protection—beggars.

Wander through the streets of New York City, or virtually any other major city, and you're sure to find sleeping on grates or huddled in doorways rag-covered individuals known as homeless people. Often they accost passersby and demand money with fanciful tales of woe, and if they don't get it, they become rude and downright menacing and, sometimes, violent. It has become virtually a rite of passage for a big-city resident to be bawled out in colorful, if obscene, language by some abusive derelict. This can easily create a coercive and intimidating environment that makes the city streets a hazard to be avoided at all costs by law-abiding citizens.

Cops have traditionally dealt with such problems by telling the offending beggars to "move on," citing them for loitering if they don't comply. But in 1993, the U.S. Court of Appeals for the Second Circuit decided in its august wisdom that this ancient police practice had suddenly become a violation of the Constitution. The Second Circuit held that begging now fell within the protection of the First Amendment because it "implicates expressive conduct or communicative activity." Judge Roger Miner wrote: "Begging frequently is accompanied by speech indicating the need for food, shelter, clothing, medical care or transportation." (So is mugging. Does that make robbery an activity protected by the First Amendment, too?) "Even without particularized speech, however," the judge went on, "the presence of an unkempt and disheveled person holding out his or her hand or a cup to receive a donation itself conveys a message of need for support and assistance." One can only marvel at the judge's powers of perception, which can detect such profound messages where the average person can hear only, "Spare change?"

Indeed, the judge showed greater perspicacity than his colleagues on the Second Circuit, who just three years before had upheld a ban on panhandling in the subway. "It seems fair to say that most individuals who beg are not doing so to convey any social or political message," Second Circuit judge Frank Altimari had written in overruling District Judge Leonard Sand's decision to allow subway panhandling. "Rather they beg to collect money. . . . Speech simply is not inherent to the act; it is not the essence of the conduct."

But this view is clearly too old-fashioned to carry much weight in advanced legal circles. A whole literature of begging rights has sprung up in the academy and is beginning to be implemented by our gavel-wielding guardians.

This development should not be unexpected, since the Burger Court had long ago struck down most vagrancy laws—allowing the police to crack down on troublemakers for simply standing at a street corner—as unconstitutional. Justice William O. Douglas, in a 1972 decision redolent of the ardors of the Vietnam era, held that "poor people, nonconformists, dissenters, idlers" may not be "required to comport themselves according to the lifestyle deemed appropriate" by police and the courts—a ruling that seemed to suggest that all panhandlers (many of them drug- and alcohol-addled, some mentally ill) are budding Thoreaus.

Such rampant moral relativism (or perhaps it's simply obtuseness) helped inspire Federal District Judge H. Lee Sarokin, a Carter appointee, to issue a decision, many years later, barring the Morristown, New Jersey, public library from evicting a smelly, offensive homeless man. "One person's hay fever," the judge wrote in a fit of lyricism, "is another person's ambrosia." The residents and readers of

Morristown can be grateful that the U.S. Court of Appeals for the Third Circuit turned thumbs down on Sarokin's poetic sally. But nobody's overturned a more recent decision by Federal Judge Constance Motley, a Lyndon Johnson appointee, to stop Amtrak police from evicting bums from New York City's Pennsylvania Station, one of the busiest commuter terminals in the country.

The panhandling and loitering cases demonstrate the dire practical consequences of federal judges' flights of fancy. These judges intent on protecting the rights of a minority—beggars—instead violate the right of everyone else to use city streets, transportation, and libraries unaccosted. These cases also display the utter lack of foundation in text or precedent for many of the juristocracy's most "progressive" decisions. Federal judges need rely on little more than their personal whims when they want to expand newfangled individual "rights" that infringe upon the traditional freedoms of the states. In the process, the juristocracy forecloses popular action on a host of controversial issues, ranging from term limits to panhandling—with dire consequences for our system of government.

"The virtue of a democratic system with a First Amendment is that it readily enables the people, over time, to be persuaded that what they took for granted is not so, and to change their laws accordingly," writes Justice Scalia. Thus, if the voters decide that racial preferences are desirable, that term limits aren't working, or that begging shouldn't be regulated, they are free to change the laws accordingly. That's democracy in action. But as Scalia notes, "That system is destroyed if the smug assurances of each generation are removed from the democratic process and written into the Constitution." With its activist jurisprudence, Scalia suggests, that is just what "this most illiberal Court" has wrought.

Expanding Egalitarianism:
The Equal Protection Clause

I CAN'T GET out of my head a commercial jingle: "More Americans get their news from ABC News than from any other source." In the field of constitutional law, the slogan could well be: More judicial legislation has come from the Fourteenth Amendment than from any other source. Indeed, so often is the Fourteenth cited in important Supreme Court cases that at times it's easy to forget that there are other parts of the Constitution, too.

The modern era of judicial activism springs from one clause of the Fourteenth Amendment, the Equal Protection Clause, which holds that no state may "deny to any person within its jurisdiction the equal protection of its laws." This has become the excuse today for the juristocracy to enact a host of controversial policies in areas ranging from single-sex education to gay marriage.

The Brown *Mystique*

The soaring generality of the Equal Protection Clause became the basis for 1954's *Brown v. Board of Education. Brown*, which abolished the separate but equal doctrine and outlawed school segregation, has become the Magna Carta of judicial activism. Indeed, one recent book ranks it as the second-greatest Supreme Court decision of all time, behind only *Marbury. Brown*'s reputation is so towering on all sides of the political spectrum that the Supreme Court continues to draw from its moral capital to justify its interventions in the political process.

This public esteem has tended to obscure the puzzlement, then as now, among many scholars about what "neutral principle" could possibly justify the conclusion reached in *Brown:* that is, how could the Fourteenth Amendment, which had existed for almost a century by that point, suddenly be interpreted to outlaw school segregation? Had some new clause been discovered? Or was the Court simply legislating in the guise of constitutional interpretation?

Chief Justice Earl Warren's brief opinion does not inspire confidence in this regard. He freely admitted that the intentions of the Fourteenth Amendment's ratifiers regarding segregated education were "inconclusive." Most scholars who have studied the history—starting with Herbert Wechsler and Alexander Bickel—think Warren was being disingenuous. Far from being inconclusive, the ratifiers' intentions were clear—they didn't intend to outlaw segregation.

The record seems fairly clear that the amendment, when ratified in 1868, was intended only to guarantee the "civil" rights of Southern blacks, a term that in those days was limited to the rights of contract, property, and court access. The Fourteenth Amendment was intended to stop blacks from being slaughtered or reenslaved. It wasn't meant to guarantee their "political" rights—that was why the Fifteenth Amendment was passed to give blacks the vote—or their "social" rights, which included education. It's hard to believe that Congress and the state legislatures intended to abolish segregated education since twenty-four of the thirty-seven states then in the Union either required or permitted racially segregated schools. Congress actually maintained segregated schools in the District of Columbia throughout Reconstruction.

"In the fractured discipline of constitutional law," writes one law professor, "there is something very close to a consensus that *Brown* was inconsistent with the original understanding of the Fourteenth Amendment, except perhaps at a very high and indeterminate level of abstraction." Various legal commentators, on both the left and right, have attempted to provide an after-the-fact justification for *Brown*, with varying degrees of success. But regardless of this academic debate, *Brown* remains sacrosanct in the minds of most Americans, which is why its legacy is so vulnerable to judicial manipulation.

At least with *Brown*, no matter how tangled its reasoning, the result is one we can all applaud—the end of government discrimination against blacks. Another revolution taking place under the name of the Equal Protection Clause, a revolution seeking to erase all legal distinctions between men and women, remains more controversial.

Enacting the ERA:
More Equal Protection Legislation

The fundamental problem confronted by judges in interpreting the Equal Protection Clause is that it is so broad—in that it forbids unequal treatment of anyone—that it's hard to know what specific practice it outlaws. Giving veterans' benefits only to veterans and reserving women's public rest rooms only for women are both examples of unequal treatment, but no court has (yet) held that either is illegal. Why not? Because for most of its history the interpretation of the Equal Protection Clause, racial cases aside, was governed by a simple test—if a state policy had any "basis in reason," then it was legal. This expansive standard began to change in the 1970s, at least in some areas, as the Burger Court acceded to the demands of the women's liberation movement to give females a special place in the constitutional pantheon, much as had already been won by African Americans.

At the time, a feminist litigator named Ruth Bader Ginsburg argued a series of Supreme Court cases that steadily elevated the level of protection women could expect to receive under the Equal Protection Clause. At Ginsburg's urging, the Court invalidated:

- An Idaho law holding that if two equally qualified candidates wanted to administer an estate, the male should be preferred (the state argued this arbitrary rule was the easiest way to avoid a costly court battle).

- A military rule that required men, but not women, to show that they actually depended on their spouse to qualify for dependent's benefits (the Court decided this money-saving arrangement wasn't rational).

- And, finally, an Oklahoma law prohibiting the sale of beer to males under twenty-one and females under eighteen (the state presented convincing evidence that teenage boys are more likely than teenage girls to drink, drive, and get into trouble).

This last case replaced the old "rational basis" test with a new standard of "intermediate scrutiny"—meaning that to differentiate between men and women, government would now have to prove that those classifications were "substantially related to the achievement of an important government objective." This accomplished part of the legal agenda of the women's liberation movement—but not all of it.

Once Attorney Ginsburg was magically transmogrified into Justice Ginsburg, the high court, as might be expected, was ready to go even further. And so it did in the landmark 1996 case involving the Virginia Military Institute.

VMI had existed for 187 years—128 of those years under the Equal Protection Clause—as an all-male public college that trained students under a harsh "adversarial model" akin to marine boot camp. Not a fun education (and not one I would ever volunteer for), but one that has produced a distinguished alumni corps, ranging from generals to congressmen.

Then in 1990, the Justice Department sued VMI, claiming its policy of excluding women was a violation of the Equal Protection

Clause. Although the Supreme Court in 1982 had invalidated an all-female nursing college in Mississippi, U.S. District Judge Jackson L. Kiser upheld VMI's single-sex policy under the intermediate scrutiny standard. The judge ruled that single-sex education yields tremendous benefits and that integrating women into VMI would destroy the adversarial model of education. The U.S. Court of Appeals for the Fourth Circuit disagreed with Kiser's interpretation of the law but agreed that at least "three aspects of VMI's program—physical training, the absence of privacy, and the adversarial approach—would be materially affected by coeducation." The appeals court gave Virginia a chance to correct the "problem" of VMI without coeducation.

Virginia thereupon set up a VMI-style training program for women at Mary Baldwin College, a neighboring all-female school. Virginia promised to give Mary Baldwin generous financial support and provide its graduates access to VMI's alumni network. The district court and appeals courts held that Virginia had satisfied its burden. Although Mary Baldwin was different in many ways from VMI—instead of the adversarial method, it was designed on "a cooperative method which reinforces self-esteem"—Judge Kiser ruled, "If VMI marches to the beat of a drum, then Mary Baldwin marches to the melody of a fife and when the march is over, both will have arrived at the same destination."

But the Supreme Court halted the march after only a few steps. The Court ruled 7–1 (Justice Thomas, whose son attends the Citadel, another all-male college, abstained) that Mary Baldwin was not "sufficiently comparable" to VMI. Justice Ginsburg, writing for the majority, held that VMI must now admit women. The outcome seemed, to some extent, predetermined because of the Supreme Court precedent outlawing the all-female Mississippi nursing school; it was for this reason presumably that some of the more moderate justices joined in the outcome. Nevertheless, the tone of Justice Ginsburg's opinion is striking for its arrogance; it's no wonder that Chief Justice Rehnquist, while concurring in the result, felt compelled to write his own opinion, distancing himself from his feminist colleague's more extreme position.

Justice Ginsburg's opinion cavalierly swept aside all the expert testimony developed during trial that showed that VMI's traditional approach to education could not survive in a coed environment. This judgment, she wrote, "is hardly proved"—grounds enough, apparently, for sweeping aside almost two centuries of tradition. Justice Ginsburg didn't even bother to mention whether the ratifiers of the Fourteenth Amendment in 1868 meant to abolish single-sex education. The reason for her omission is obvious: They had nothing of the kind in mind; indeed *most* schooling back then was single-sex. "This is not the interpretation of the Constitution," Justice Scalia protested in a lonely, bitter dissent, "but the creation of one."

The Constitution created by the VMI decision seems to include the Equal Rights Amendment (ERA). This proposed constitutional amendment, designed to enhance the status of women, wasn't ratified by the states in the late 1970s; many Americans feared that it was part of a radical feminist agenda. But one of the ERA's foremost proponents, Ruth Bader Ginsburg, has managed to smuggle it into the Constitution. In the VMI decision, she wrote that any sex-based state action requires "exceedingly persuasive justification"—a higher standard than the Court had previously employed. "There is no practical difference between what has evolved and the ERA," Ginsburg cheerfully acknowledged in a speech at the University of Virginia Law School.

Give Ginsburg credit for candor. But her amazing admission raises a pressing question: Why do we bother to have democratic debates when the juristocracy can simply rewrite the Constitution at will?

It is instructive to imagine what would have happened if the Supreme Courts of earlier eras had behaved like this one. Throughout the early years of the twentieth century, suffragettes pushed a constitutional amendment to give women the vote, a campaign that finally succeeded with the ratification of the Nineteenth Amendment in 1920. Almost everyone today can agree this was a good outcome. But why did the suffragettes need to go through the political process at all? Why didn't the Supreme Court simply give them what they wanted? After all, what's more a denial of equal protection than denying women the vote? Presumably, today's justices would have issued a decision giving women the vote under the Fourteenth Amendment, and suffragettes would have been spared the tiresome necessity of convincing Congress and two-thirds of the state legislatures of the rightness of their cause.

Yet no matter how glorious the results, it's always a mistake to let the Supreme Court short-circuit the political process. In the first place, decisions made via judicial fiat necessarily have less public legitimacy than those implemented through the democratic process. And in the second place, when the courts get into the business of legislating, the fallout can be pretty messy.

Consider the implications of the VMI ruling. Is it constitutional to keep women out of combat? Out of men's bathrooms? Nobody knows. It's not even clear whether the VMI decision is the death knell for all single-sex schooling. Justice Scalia thinks it may be: "Under the constitutional principles announced and applied [in the VMI case]," he warned, "single sex public education is unconstitutional." And it's not just public colleges like VMI and the Citadel that should watch out. The courts have previously ruled that any college, public or private, that accepts government money is bound not to discriminate on the basis of race. If sexual discrimination is also verboten now, it stands to reason that private, all-women's colleges like Mills and Mt. Holyoke—which accept some government grants—may also be unconstitutional.

This wouldn't sit well even with many feminists. One of the hottest trends in pedagogy these days is single-sex education for girls. Indeed, just after the VMI decision, an all-girls public school opened in East Harlem. The ACLU promptly sued on equal protection grounds. Defenders of the school hope, however, that it will somehow meet the test of constitutionality promulgated by Ginsburg's opinion. Wrote one feminist author: "Anyone who has seriously thought about the sorry results of public education—and any parent who is trying to find the best school match for a child—ought to be hoping that those loopholes [in the VMI decision] are wide enough to permit the continued existence of some taxpayer-funded single-sex schools, especially at the middle school and high school level."

Parents of girls need not worry unduly. There's reason to believe that Justice Ginsburg's opinion was guided more by results—getting rid of all-male bastions—than by any neutral constitutional principle. While striking down sex classifications that "create and perpetuate . . . the inferiority of women," Ginsburg specifically praised classifications that "compensate women for particular economic disabilities [they have] suffered" and "promot[e] equal employment opportunity."

This raises the specter, as Justice Scalia noted, that the Court will not consistently apply the principles of the VMI case. So while all-male public schools are already history, all-female schools may yet survive under the Court's peculiar jurisprudence. Or maybe not. It'll take years of litigation to flesh out the law in these areas and to reveal the full import of the VMI ruling. At least when legislators legislate, it's clear—usually—what they've done. Not so with the courts. And that is yet another reason judges should stay out of the legislating business.

Toward Gay Marriage: The Further Reaches of Equal Protection

All-male education isn't the only relic of the past the Supreme Court has decided to sweep away with its Fourteenth Amendment broom. Also unconstitutional now, it seems, is "animus" against homosexuals— a prejudice that, like sexual inequality, has been commonplace in the law for most of the period since the Fourteenth's adoption.

In 1992, 53 percent of Colorado's voters passed Amendment 2 to overturn some municipal ordinances that had declared homosexuals to be a protected class that, like racial minorities and women, couldn't be discriminated against in employment, housing, and so on. The title of Amendment 2 declared: "No Protected Status Based on Homosexual, Lesbian, or Bisexual Orientation." The state supreme court quickly overturned the amendment as an infringement of gays' political rights. The U.S. Supreme Court went along in 1996.

The State of Colorado argued that Amendment 2 did nothing more than deny homosexuals "special rights." The state rejected the arguments of critics who asserted that Amendment 2 would allow police to ignore crimes against gays or allow the government to deny pension benefits to gay employees. Justice Anthony Kennedy of the Supreme Court, writing for a 6–3 majority, did not dispute the state's contentions. Nevertheless, he held that "the amendment imposes a special disability" on gays alone. What disability? "They can obtain specific protection against discrimination only by enlisting the citizenry of Colorado to amend the state constitution." In short, Kennedy held, it was illegitimate for Colorado to preempt cities like Aspen—where gay voters might be a more powerful force than in the rest of the state—from passing local gay-rights ordinances. By this reasoning, state constitutional amendments in Utah, Idaho, and other states prohibiting polygamy must also be a violation of the Equal Protection Clause because polygamists can only "obtain specific protection" by amending the state constitution.

This isn't an argument against Amendment 2; it's an argument against democracy. The only way to characterize this reasoning is with Justice Scalia's phrase: "terminal silliness."

The real nub of the Court's ruling in *Romer v. Evans*, as the Amendment 2 case was styled, was that Colorado had no "rational basis" for passing the ordinance. Justice Kennedy wrote: "[T]he amendment seems inexplicable by anything but animus toward the class that if affects; it lacks a rational relationship to legitimate state interests." So there you have it: Disapproval of homosexuality—or at least refusing to express approval—is no longer a legitimate aim of state law. This may be a fine moral sentiment, but where can it be found in the Constitution?

It doesn't even square with the Court's own precedents in this area. In 1986, the justices in *Bowers v. Hardwick* upheld a Georgia statute illegalizing sodomy. "If it is constitutionally permissible for a State to make homosexual conduct criminal," wrote Justice Scalia, "surely it is constitutionally permissible for a State to enact other laws merely disfavoring homosexual conduct."

Apparently not. Somehow Justice Kennedy's majority opinion in *Romer* managed to avoid any mention of *Bowers*—an omission that underlines the logical incoherence of this decision. Clearly the *Romer* court was determined to override a controversial decision made by Colorado voters—and the justices weren't too scrupulous in how they reached their goal.

As with the VMI case, so with *Romer*: Legislating by the courts can often have sweeping, and perhaps unintended, consequences. In this case, the implication is that gays are now becoming a special class that, like women and minorities, enjoys an extra level of judicial protection under the Equal Protection Clause. Reading a Gay Rights Amendment into the Constitution has even more far-reaching implications than enacting the ERA. It's easy to imagine a day in the future when the courts will make homosexual marriage the law of the land. It's already almost happened.

Hawaii's supreme court ruled in 1993 that prohibiting people of the same sex from marrying constitutes sex discrimination. Only a state constitutional amendment appears to have stopped the Hawaii courts, for now, from legalizing gay marriage. But some other state court (or even the U.S. Supreme Court itself) could easily reach the same conclusion, and under the Full Faith and Credit Clause of the Constitution, other states would probably be forced to honor those gay marriages. To prevent this from happening, Congress passed the Defense of Marriage Act in 1996. But given *Romer v. Evans*, the Supreme Court could easily find that this law is animated by unacceptable "animus" toward homosexuals and therefore is unconstitutional.

Now, it's perfectly possible to construct persuasive arguments for gay marriage. But if we're going to abandon a six-thousand-year-old conception of marriage as a union between a man and a woman, perhaps the voters of America, or at least their elected representatives, should have a say in the matter.

Equal Protection and Reverse Discrimination

Most of the Supreme Court's equal protection jurisprudence has won cheers from the left and jeers from the right. But the positions are reversed in one area: appropriately enough, reverse discrimination.

At least four, and possibly five, Supreme Court justices are committed to the view that the Fourteenth Amendment forbids all racial preferences unless they are "narrowly tailored" to achieving a "compelling government interest," which is to say, "remedying the effects of racial discrimination." This has produced a series of cases striking down business set-asides, racially gerrymandered congressional districts, and other programs designed to benefit minorities. The U.S. Court of Appeals for the Fifth Circuit has even banned the use of race in the admissions process at the University of Texas Law School.

Jeffrey Rosen of the *New Republic*, among others, argues that these decisions are "flamboyantly inconsistent" with the intentions of those who ratified the Fourteenth Amendment. As we've seen, the Fourteenth Amendment was meant to protect "civil," not political or social, rights. It was only designed to guarantee equality in contracts, property, and court access; neither voting nor public employment should be governed by the Equal Protection Clause. Therefore, Rosen concludes, it is the conservative judges who are guilty of judicial activism by applying equal protection principles in these areas.

In their own defense, conservative jurists can point to the doctrine of stare decisis (abide by precedent). The Supreme Court's activists have created a lot of precedent in this area. The Warren Court summarily outlawed discrimination against blacks not only in schools but also in airport restaurants, public golf courses, public beaches, and a whole host of other areas not contemplated by the Fourteenth Amendment's ratifiers. Some of the more liberal justices, led by William J. Brennan Jr., went further. They argued that government may take race into account "to remedy disadvantages cast on minorities by past racial prejudices." In short, the Brennanist position was to follow the original understanding of the Equal Protection Clause for whites (allow them to be discriminated against), but not for blacks (no discrimination allowed).

Faced with this double standard, conservative judges have reacted by saying, in essence, that if we're going to read into the Fourteenth Amendment a generalized antidiscrimination ban—admittedly a strained interpretation, but the one we're stuck with—then that ban should apply equally, whether the discrimination hurts blacks or whites. In rejecting the Brennanist caste system, the conservative judges argue that they're being faithful to the larger intent of the Fourteenth Amendment: "to do away with all governmentally imposed discrimination," not just that against blacks.

But does the Brennanists' activism justify activism by conservative judges to right the scales? Not if you believe that two wrongs don't make—well, you know what. If conservatives are going to return the courts to the original intentions of the Founders, then it's pure hypocrisy for them to praise judicial activism when the results are pleasing to them. Certain affirmative action policies may well run afoul of color-blind civil rights statutes, but there's no call for invoking the Constitution to strike down these laws. It's a cop-out, an abdication of responsibility, for conservatives to expect judges with life tenure to abolish preferences that Republican legislators aren't willing to touch. Racial spoils systems, such as the one at the University of Texas, may be odious, but it should be up to voters, not judges, to eliminate them. It's important that the voice of the people not be drowned out by the bang of a gavel—whether that gavel is wielded by Judge Thelton Henderson or by the conservative judges of the Fifth Circuit.

Privacy Unbound:
The Perversion of the Due Process Clause

THE ARGUMENT is often heard that the Rehnquist Court has made policy-oriented judging a thing of the past. "The era of liberal judicial activism," a noted professor assures us in the pages of the *New York Times*, "is long gone." Meanwhile, other commentators are accusing these justices of being activists of the right. What, then of the VMI, term limits, and Amendment 2 decisions? Are these signs of judicial restraint? Or *conservative* activism?

At best, the Rehnquist Court has done to constitutional law what Ronald Reagan did to federal spending: slowed its growth. Granted, the Court has given those on the right a fair amount to cheer about—from the property rights and reverse discrimination cases to, most famously, its refusal to recognize a right to assisted suicide. But in the last instance, at least, I can offer no more than a cheer and a half for the justices' action. The result is a good one—but that's about the best that can be said for the assisted suicide decisions. The reasoning—or lack thereof—behind the rulings leaves less room for optimism.

To understand how the assisted suicide cases came about, and why the Supreme Court's rulings in this area are so troubling, we need to briefly review the history of the Due Process Clause.

The high court has a long history of twisting the Fourteenth Amendment's Due Process Clause ("No state shall . . . deprive any person of life, liberty or property without due process of law") beyond all recognition. On its face, the clause appears to simply guarantee that life, liberty, and property cannot be taken away without a fair trial. But through the dubious doctrine of "substantive due process"—an idea not fully endorsed even by Harvard law professor Laurence Tribe, today's leading proponent of judicial activism—this empty vessel has been filled with whatever watery sentiments animated the Supreme Court of the day.

Substantive due process apparently first made its appearance in the infamous *Dred Scott* case. The Fourteenth Amendment had not yet been passed, but Chief Justice Roger Taney interpreted the comparable due process provision of the Fifth Amendment to enshrine a right to slavery. Since that decision helped light the long fuse that detonated at Fort Sumter, one would think that substantive due process would have been somewhat discredited.

Yet by the early twentieth century, this doctrine was again being invoked, this time by an activist conservative Supreme Court bent on invalidating state regulation of business during the Progressive Era. Justice Oliver Wendell Holmes famously dissented in *Lochner v. New York* (the 1905 case that generated the term "Lochner era"), in which the Supreme Court struck down state regulations limiting how many hours bakery employees could work. "I strongly believe that my agreement or disagreement has nothing to do with the right of a majority to embody their opinions in law," wrote Justice Holmes. "It is settled by various decisions of this court that state constitutions and state laws may regulate life in many ways which we, as legislators, might think as injudicious, or, if you like, as tyrannical, as this, and, which, equally with this, interfere with the liberty to contract."

Sad to say, the Supreme Court majority wasn't listening—then or later. The *Lochner* line of cases ended in 1937, but the Due Process Clause again became a font of activism in the 1960s—this time from the left, not the right.

The "Right" to Contraception and Abortion

In the 1965 case of *Griswold v. Connecticut*, the Warren Court held that an archaic Connecticut law banning contraceptives was unconstitutional. There was no question that, as Justice Potter Stewart put it in his dissent, the Connecticut statute was "uncommonly silly," but it wasn't immediately clear why it violated the Constitution.

Justice William O. Douglas, who wrote the majority opinion, suggested that the right to privacy was to be found somewhere in the Bill of Rights, which, using the Due Process Clause, the Court then applied against the states (the Bill of Rights originally limited only the federal government). "[S]pecific guarantees in the Bill of Rights have penumbras, formed by emanations from those guarantees that help give them life and substance," Douglas wrote, rather obscurely, adding: "Various guarantees create zones of privacy."

This nebulous explanation became the basis for the Court's famous ruling in *Roe v. Wade* and its companion case, *Doe v. Bolton*, which turned abortion into a constitutional right on a par with free speech and the right of assembly. The seven-justice majority in *Roe* was not greatly troubled by the fact that at the time the Fourteenth Amendment was enacted, thirty-six states and territories either prohibited or limited abortion and that twenty-one of those laws still remained on the books in 1973. Justice Harry Blackmun, writing for the majority, nevertheless decided that the Due Process Clause protected abortion, though he conceded that other parts of the Constitution, such as the Ninth Amendment, might just as well accomplish the same ends; he wasn't picky, as long as the results were correct.

After many long hours of diligent study at that famous law library located at ... the Mayo Clinic (that's really where the opinion was written), Justice Blackmun even unearthed in the Constitution a three-part scheme for the regulation of abortion: During the first trimester, the state may not regulate abortion at all; during the second trimester, the state may regulate only to protect "maternal health"; and during the third trimester, the state may ban abortion except where it's necessary to protect the "health of the mother," broadly defined.

No matter what your view on abortion (my own position, incidentally, is closer to the National Organization for Women's than to the Christian Coalition's), it should strike any disinterested observer as preposterous to suggest that the Constitution not only guarantees the right to abortion but also gives the juristocracy leave to micromanage its application down to the trimester. Indeed, *Roe* has been criticized not only by right-to-lifers, but by scholars with impeccable liberal credentials, such as Archibald Cox, John Hart Ely, and Benno Schmidt.

Blackmun's regulatory framework essentially stood unchanged until 1992. That year, in *Planned Parenthood of Southeastern Pennsylvania v. Casey*, a three-justice bloc—Anthony Kennedy, Sandra Day O'Connor, and David Souter—issued an opinion piously praising stare decisis while substantially modifying Blackmun's handiwork. "*Roe* continues to exist," wrote Chief Justice Rehnquist in dissent, "but only in the way a storefront on a western movie set exists: a mere facade to give the illusion of reality."

The three justices, whose plurality opinion spoke for the Court, chucked out the three-trimester framework. Indeed, they had little choice, since, rather embarrassingly, medical science had moved the point of "viability" into the second trimester, so Justice Blackmun's carefully wrought *Roe* opinion allowed the abortion of babies that could live outside the womb.

Along the way, the three justices in *Casey* appeared to expand the right of privacy to almost boundless proportions:

> These matters, involving the most intimate and personal choices a person may make in a lifetime, choices central to personal dignity and autonomy, are central to the liberty protected by the Fourteenth Amendment. At the heart of liberty is the right to define one's own concept of existence, of meaning, of the universe, and of the mystery of human life. Beliefs about these matters could not define the attributes of personhood were they formed under compulsion of the State.

It's hard to see how such a soaring conception can possibly be confined to abortion or contraceptives. Why not the right to sell one's own body? Or the right to inject any drug imaginable to alter one's concept of the universe? Or, more to the point, the right to kill that body whenever you please, even if it requires the assistance of somebody else?

Physician-Assisted Suicide: The Limits of Due Process

Carrying this logic to its natural conclusion, two federal appeals courts decided in 1996 that assisted suicide should enjoy constitutional protection. The Ninth Circuit, in San Francisco, unearthed this "right" in the Due Process Clause; ill patients, the court decided, have a liberty interest in killing themselves. The Second Circuit, in New York, discovered this right in the Equal Protection Clause; New York laws prohibiting assisted suicide but not suicide itself, the court held, discriminated against those seriously ill patients who couldn't kill themselves.

The U.S. Supreme Court has now repudiated these holdings unanimously (although five of the justices left the door open to enshrining a right to assisted suicide sometime in the future). To achieve this outcome, Chief Justice Rehnquist's majority opinion had to labor mightily—and, to my mind, not very convincingly—to distinguish the assisted suicide controversy from the Court's prior due process rulings.

Judge Stephen Reinhardt, who wrote the Ninth Circuit's sweeping assisted suicide opinion, anchored this newfound right, first, in the long line of abortion precedents. Quoting *Casey*, he declared, "Like the decision of whether or not to have an abortion, the decision how and when to die is one of 'the most intimate and personal choices a person may make in a lifetime,' a choice 'central to personal dignity and autonomy.'" Indeed, the argument for assisted suicide as a constitutional right is arguably stronger than the claim of abortion. After all, in the case of abortion, the rights of a third party—a fetus—are infringed upon, whereas assisted suicide is (at least in theory) purely voluntary.

How does Rehnquist's majority opinion refute this logic? It doesn't. Here is the chief justice's key statement on this crucial subject: "That many of the rights and liberties protected by the Due Process Clause sound in personal autonomy does not warrant the sweeping conclusion that any and all important, intimate, and personal decisions are so protected, and *Casey* does not suggest otherwise." This, of course, entirely begs the question of why the right of abortion should be recognized, but not the right of assisted suicide. In Rehnquist's defense, it may be said that he has always voted against recognizing a "right" to abortion, but the Court majority—which favors abortion, but not assisted suicide—is clearly gripped by schizophrenia.

The Court's position is all the more difficult to justify in light of another of its recent cases that is cited prominently by proponents of assisted suicide. In the 1990 case *Cruzan v. Director, Missouri Department of Health*, Chief Justice Rehnquist wrote for a Supreme Court majority that "we assume that the United States Constitution would grant a competent person a constitutionally protected right to refuse lifesaving hydration and nutrition." In this case, if Nancy Cruzan—who was in a vegetative state—had had her feeding tubes taken away, she would have starved to death in short order, which would make her death appear to be virtually indistinguishable from physician-assisted suicide.

Judge Reinhardt leaped on this case as the Supreme Court's recognizing a "right to die" and, further, the right to a physician's assistance in that endeavor. This isn't much of a stretch, actually. Just imagine if the Court proclaimed a right to abortion but *didn't* add that there was a right to a physician's aid in killing the fetus. This would clearly be nonsensical.

There are in fact plenty of good *policy* reasons for drawing a distinction between removing lifesaving devices and administering a fatal dose of drugs. The latter—but not the former—has long been illegal in virtually every state, indeed in virtually the entire Western world (Oregon, as we saw earlier, not long ago became the first state to legalize euthanasia). But this is not a distinction rooted in the *Constitution*. Again, Rehnquist labors with only middling success to explain why the right to assisted suicide doesn't flow from *Cruzan*. The best he can do is to interpret the *Cruzan* holding in the narrowest possible terms, arguing that it didn't recognize a general "right to die," only a specific right to refuse unwanted medical care. The *Cruzan* court, Rehnquist claims, was doing little more than ratifying the traditional practice of the states in this area.

But in the first place, this wasn't how Justice John Paul Stevens and other members of the *Cruzan* court viewed the ruling. And in the second place, if *Cruzan* only ratified state practice, why was it necessary at all? By constitutionalizing what can be interpreted, fairly or not, as a "right to die," *Cruzan* opened a Pandora's box that the 1997 assisted suicide cases may close only temporarily.

The Greenhouse Effect

What's the real difference between *Roe* and *Casey*, on the one hand, and the assisted suicide cases, on the other? Why did the Supreme Court recognize a newfangled "right" in the former instances but not the latter? It can't be that the Constitution has different things to say about assisted suicide and abortion, since this document is conspicuously, thunderously silent on both topics.

The main difference between the Supreme Court's decisions on abortion and assisted suicide appears to be the differing climates of elite opinion surrounding those two issues. In 1973, the American Medical Association (AMA) was on record as favoring a right to abort—the fact of which Justice Blackmun took slavishly respectful note in *Roe*. In 1997, by contrast, the AMA opposed the right to physician-assisted suicide. In both instances, the views of the AMA were out of step with the attitudes of many ordinary Americans: A substantial minority, possibly even a majority, then as now, opposed abortion on demand, while it appears that most Americans (if the opinion polls cited by Judge Reinhardt's decision are to be believed) today favor a right to physician-assisted suicide. But in both cases it was the AMA, not the hoi polloi, that won the day.

It is easy to draw the cynical conclusion that the justices follow not the election returns but the parlor talk in Georgetown. Judge Laurence H. Silberman of the D.C. Circuit U.S. Court of Appeals has come up with a pithy term for this phenomenon—the Greenhouse Effect, named in honor of the *New York Times*'s Supreme Court correspondent, Linda Greenhouse. It is Judge Silberman's contention that the desire to curry favor with elite journalists, law professors, and other pillars of the establishment distorts judicial decisionmaking. The Supreme Court's abortion and assisted-suicide jurisprudence certainly lends credence to this thesis.

Conclusion: Return to Restraint

THE PROBLEM with the Supreme Court today is that Justices O'Connor and Kennedy—who hold the balance of power on most important issues—are every bit as much results-oriented as the Earl Warrens and William Brennans of earlier days. The only difference is that O'Connor and Kennedy are results-oriented justices of the center, whereas the others were results-oriented toward the left. That is, I suppose, an improvement of sorts, though not one likely to increase the public's respect for Court decisions.

It is doubtful that the Court will grow in public esteem as long as it appears to reach its decisions for political, not constitutional, reasons. The justices may insist, as Hugo Black once did in a TV interview, that their decisions are dictated by the Constitution itself and not by their own personal preferences, but that explanation can only be greeted with derisive smiles in light of the Court's open legislating in cases ranging from *Mapp* to *Miranda*, from *Brown* to *Casey*.

Yet the czars of the Court continue issuing ukases to the states, often decisions, as in *Casey*, that substantially modify the policy pronouncements of earlier days. The justices are pursuing a chimera—the notion that the Court can craft policy outcomes that will please the whole nation. But if the years since *Roe* have taught us anything, it is that the Court cannot, in Justice Scalia's phrase, impose a "jurisprudential Peace of Westphalia" on such emotional issues as abortion and the right to die. And the side spurned is likely to be all the more vehement in its protests because it realizes that it has no forum of appeal. The losers of the Court's policy battles are left to stew in their own venom while pondering the finality of the judges' diktats, instead of devoting their energies to convincing legislators of the rightness of their views.

What the juristocracy should do is simply pull back and recognize that where the Constitution and the law are silent, it has no business intruding. Let the process of democracy step into the breach on a state-by-state basis.

> [T]he division of sentiment within each State was not as closely balanced as it was among the population of the Nation as a whole, meaning not only that more people would be satisfied with the results of state-by-state resolution, but also that those results would be more stable.

So Justice Scalia wrote of abortion in his *Casey* dissent. The same logic holds for the questions of physician-assisted suicide, single-sex education, term limits, gay marriage, panhandling, and other divisive matters. These are all issues best resolved through the political process, however unpleasing to the chattering class the outcome may be in a few instances. The greatest good for the greatest number can be achieved through state-level democracy.

On the great questions of the day, judges, both conservative and liberal, should return to implementing the laws made by others; they should not create their own. The juristocracy would be wise to heed the admonition of the great judge Learned Hand: "For myself it would be most irksome to be ruled by a bevy of Platonic Guardians, even if I know how to choose them, which I assuredly do not."

CHAPTER 5

Juristocracy II

They [the judges] are then in fact the corps of sappers and miners, steadily working to undermine the independent rights of the States, and to consolidate all power in the hands of that government in which they have so important a freehold estate.

THOMAS JEFFERSON, *Autobiography*

A T 2:40 A.M. on February 4, 1991, police officer Daniel Boyle was patrolling a high-crime area in Philadelphia. He observed a car traveling the wrong way on a one-way street. He stopped the car, which had been stolen earlier in the evening. The driver, subsequently identified as Edward Bracey, jumped out of the vehicle and immediately began firing a 9 millimeter semiautomatic at Officer Boyle. One of the shots struck Boyle in the temple. Before dying at the hospital, Danny Boyle helped other officers by giving them a description of the suspect and his escape route. Boyle was only twenty-one years old, a rookie with just one year's experience. His father, a twenty-eight-year veteran of the Philadelphia force, lost his only son.

Later, after Bracey had been convicted and sentenced to death for killing Officer Boyle, the state judge presiding over his trial delivered an extraordinary courtroom declaration. Officer Boyle didn't have to die, this judge pointed out. Bracey had been arrested twice before for car theft, and twice he'd been released without bail or supervision. Twice he'd failed to show up for trial; in fact, he was a fugitive at the time he gunned down Boyle. Bracey, like so many other Philadelphia criminals, was released because of a "consent decree" supervised by federal judge Norma L. Shapiro. Officer Boyle, the state judge suggested, might still be alive, were it not for Judge Shapiro's order.

This was a powerful, and unexpected, indictment of one judge by another—but entirely deserved. Judge Shapiro has been responsible for as much crime in the City of Brotherly Love as any street gang. The story of her consent decree vividly illustrates how federal judges misuse their remedial powers during so-called public interest litigation.

Norma Shapiro's involvement with the Philadelphia prisons began in 1986, when inmates of a decrepit prison filed suit against the city. They complained of inadequate medical care, vermin infestation, and a host of other problems. The mayor at the time, W. Wilson Goode, decided to settle the case without going to trial, so he entered into a consent decree that did nothing to address any of the deplorable conditions in the jails. Instead, the decree tried to reduce the prison population by freeing prisoners. Judge Shapiro accepted the decree and took over the job of implementing its broad mandate. Mind you, there was never a finding that the city had violated the Constitution in any way. But using the authority of the consent decree, Judge Shapiro virtually decriminalized a wide range of offenses in Philadelphia. Under her orders, defendants charged with crimes such as drug dealing, stalking, manslaughter, weaponless robberies, burglary, car theft, vehicular homicide, and drunk driving could not be held in jail prior to trial. Local judges were forbidden to set bail using such traditional criteria as whether the suspect was a flight risk or a danger to the community.

Drug dealers soon learned to take advantage of this policy, making Philadelphia a major narcotics smuggling port for the first time. And why not? Under Judge Shapiro's law, any criminal caught with less than 50 grams of heroin (street value $33,000), 50 grams of cocaine (street value $5,000), or 50 pounds of marijuana (street value $225,000) went free. A study found that 76 percent of all drug dealers in Philadelphia became fugitives within ninety days of their arrest, compared to only 26 percent nationally. Overall, the total number of fugitives in Philadelphia nearly tripled, rising from 18,000 to almost 50,000, the equivalent of an entire year's worth of prosecutions.

Many of these thugs went on to commit fresh atrocities. According to former Philadelphia deputy district attorney Sarah Vandenbraak:

> During one 18-month period (1993 and the first six months of 1994), Philadelphia police rearrested 9,732 defendants released because of the consent decree. These defendants were charged with 79 murders, 959 robberies, 2,215 drug dealing crimes, 701 burglaries, 2,748 thefts, 90 rapes, 14 kidnapping charges, 1,113 assaults, 264 gun-law violations and 127 drunk driving incidents.

Researchers estimate that half or more of these crimes wouldn't have happened without the prison cap.

But unless these criminals were rearrested for crimes that didn't fall within Judge Shapiro's consent decree, they were right back on the streets again. Detective Patrick Boyle, father of slain officer Daniel, remembers that in late March 1994 he arrested a man for burglary: "He had been arrested in early March for the same crime at the same location. This individual had ten outstanding bench warrants. He had been released nine times without posting bond, because of the prison cap."

Philadelphia's Democratic mayor, Ed Rendell, and District Attorney Lynne Abraham petitioned Judge Shapiro numerous times to vacate her decree. The judge finally relaxed the prison cap as part of an "experiment" in late 1995. But by early 1996, the city prison population once again soared, so Judge Shapiro started releasing more prisoners, at a rate of about fifty inmates a week. "The same criminals are just returned to the streets to commit yet more crimes and ignore judicial proceedings," summed up Detective Boyle.

JDs Acting like M.B.A.'s

THE PHILADELPHIA story is part of a national trend. Other judges have personally taken the reins not only of prisons but also of schools, mental institutions, public housing, welfare agencies, unions, even large corporations. The ubiquity of judicial interventions in our governmental, and even private, institutions may surprise the nonlawyer:

- Federal judge David Edelstein supervised IBM's compliance with an antitrust consent decree from 1956 to 1995, at least two decades after anyone could plausibly assert that IBM was in danger of monopolizing anything (if indeed, such a danger ever existed).

- Since 1984, federal judge Richard Matsch (he of Timothy McVeigh fame) has been overseeing a twenty-seven-page consent decree governing bilingual education in Denver's public schools.

- State judge James R. Giddings has been governing Michigan prisons since 1988; his orders have included hiring a "press agent" to get out the inmates' side of the story in their ongoing litigation against the state.

Usually these decrees are entered in response to sweeping class-action suits filed by lawyers claiming to represent some large and amorphous group of plaintiffs, such as schoolchildren or mental patients, most of whom aren't even aware that a suit is being pursued in their names. The judge will hold a trial and, assuming the defendant loses, issue a court order, or the plaintiffs and the governmental defendant will negotiate a settlement.

While the original dispute may have been over some noble constitutional principle, the resulting decree leaves the judge free to issue public policy diktats of the most mundane variety, laying out in intricate and mind-numbing detail the steps that an agency will have to take to come into compliance with the law. To help carry out these decrees, judges often appoint special masters or other advisers, who wind up forming a "shadow" government.

This is how judges enforce the amorphous individual "rights" discussed in the previous chapter, such as the "right" of women to attend formerly all-male colleges. In principle, these decrees are supposed to be lifted when the problem that resulted in the suit being filed is resolved. But in practice, the goals of this type of litigation are usually so broad—creating great schools or wonderful prisons—that the results are never achieved, the decree is never lifted, and the judge gets to keep control indefinitely.

In short, judges often wind up performing work that might better be left to educated and experienced professionals. Since judges are so ill-suited to this role, the results of government by juristocracy are often farcical and occasionally—as in Officer Boyle's case—tragic.

The Flowering of Judicial Power

H ow DID judges go from deciding how to instruct a jury to deciding what kind of pretrial detention policies a city must implement? How did judges get the power to tell elected officials, "I'm
going to implement this policy whether you like it or not"? Good
question. As with all modern judicial activism, the answer comes back,
ineluctably, to *Brown v. Board of Education*.

Prior to 1954, judges rarely used decrees to implement controversial policies. They were forced either to rely on the executive branch
to implement their decisions or not see them implemented at all.

Even *Marbury v. Madison*, the 1803 case that established the principle of judicial review of legislation, supports a limited understanding
of judges' remedial powers. Although the Supreme Court decided that
the Jefferson administration had violated William Marbury's right to
his commission as justice of the peace for the District of Columbia,
Chief Justice John Marshall's opinion held that Marbury could receive
no remedy. The Court apparently realized it didn't have the power to
impose its solutions on another branch of government, a realization
shared by President Andrew Jackson when he uttered a famous—
though probably apocryphal—challenge: "John Marshall has made his
decision: now let him try to enforce it!"

The first flowering of injunctions occurred during the *Lochner* era,
early in the twentieth century, when an activist Court bent on protecting property rights used decrees to strike down state economic regulations and to block labor protests. This provoked such strong opposition that Congress in 1932 passed the Norris-LaGuardia Act to
prohibit courts from issuing injunctions in most labor disputes. But
even the injunctions of the *Lochner* era were relatively limited in scope.
They were negative injunctions, designed to prevent actions such as
strikes. They followed in the footsteps of long-standing precedent,
which held that a federal court "may enjoin a State officer from executing a state law in conflict with the Constitution or a statute of the
United States, when such execution will violate the rights of the com-
plainant." Unlike the court decrees of the future, the *Lochner*-era ones
did not command elected officials to take certain affirmative steps.

All that changed with *Brown v. Board of Education II*, the 1955

Supreme Court decision that authorized federal courts to enforce the desegregation mandate of *Brown v. Board of Education I*, issued a year earlier. Chief Justice Earl Warren made a bow toward local sensibilities, declaring that "school authorities have the primary responsibility for elucidating, assessing, and solving" the problems of desegregation. But he added: "During this period of transition, the courts will retain jurisdiction of these cases."

Warren gave federal district judges carte blanche to meddle in virtually every aspect of local school operations:

> [T]he courts may consider problems related to administration, arising from the physical condition of the school plant, the school transportation system, personnel, revision of school districts and attendance areas into compact units to achieve a system of determining admission to the public schools on a nonracial basis, and revision of local laws and regulations which may be necessary in solving the foregoing problems.

There's no question that all this judicial power was directed at a genuine evil—Jim Crow—but it didn't take long before federal judges were imposing their authority on a hitherto unimagined scale.

In 1969, U.S. district judge James B. McMillan, overseeing the desegregation of the Charlotte-Mecklenburg School District, which encompassed Charlotte, North Carolina, hired a special master, an "expert in education administration," to come up with a "pupil assignment plan." The plan went far beyond striking down the remnants of segregation. Instead, it aimed to create integration, according to precise mathematical formulas. As adopted by Judge McMillan in 1970, the plan called for busing blacks to nine of the school district's ten high schools, "producing 17 percent to 36 percent Negro population in each." A similarly ambitious target was set for elementary schools, which would be achieved "by transporting black students from grades one through four to the outlying white schools; and by transporting white students from the fifth and sixth grades from the outlying white schools to the inner city black school." In all, 13,000 students would be bused, whether their parents liked it or not.

Even though the Civil Rights Act of 1964 had expressly abjured court-mandated busing in order to achieve desegregation, the Supreme Court approved the Charlotte-Mecklenburg plan. After all, the justices weren't enforcing a mere statute. They were enforcing the Constitution itself—or at least what they took to be the Constitution. Chief Justice Warren Burger, writing for a unanimous Court, declared, "a district court has broad power to fashion a remedy that will assure a unitary [that is, integrated] school system."

The Court even pronounced that a district court's remedy could be "administratively awkward, inconvenient, and even bizarre in some situations, and may impose burdens on some." In this case, the inconveniences included forcing tiny tots, black and white, to board school buses for up to an hour each day and forcing the school board to purchase an additional 138 buses to transport all the students. But such problems didn't concern the high court. The buses "could easily be obtained," Chief Justice Burger declared. Easy for him to say.

A Never-Ending Mission: Judges as Schoolmasters

Brown I had been concerned with overturning the legal barriers to desegregation. But by 1970, those de jure (legal) barriers had largely fallen. So the courts embarked on a quixotic quest to end de facto, nonlegal barriers to segregation that had been caused primarily by the voluntary housing choices made by individuals. Many judges seemed to believe that all-black schools are inherently inferior, a theory buttressed by the dubious social science research cited in *Brown I* about the "psychological" harm suffered by black schoolkids under segregation. "Under this theory," writes Justice Clarence Thomas, "segregation injures blacks because blacks, when left on their own, cannot achieve. To my way of thinking, that conclusion is the result of a jurisprudence based upon a theory of black inferiority."

Justice Thomas also aptly summed up the other error being committed by the courts: " 'Racial isolation' itself is not a harm; only state enforced segregation is." But this distinction faded to nothingness by the mid-1970s, in a development dramatically illustrated by the school-busing battles of Boston, chronicled in J. Anthony Lukas's epic *Common Ground*.

Federal judge W. Arthur Garrity caused a virtual civil insurrection—recall the famous photo of a protester wielding an American flag like a spear—by imposing mandatory busing on the working-class Irish and black children of Boston in 1973. The judge's intervention was doubly intolerable to most Bostonians—first, because Garrity lived in tony Wellesley, where he and his circle would be immune from the effects of his social engineering; and, second, because Boston had formally outlawed segregation in *1855*. Judge Garrity's diktats were issued, Canute-like, to reverse the course of Boston history, which had led all ethnic groups to live in their own enclaves.

The judge's futile quest only resulted in accelerating "white flight" out of the Boston public schools. In 1972, when the National Association for the Advancement of Colored People (NAACP) filed suit, Boston had 90,000 students enrolled in its public schools, 60 percent of them white. By 1976, only 71,000 students were left in the system; less than 44 percent were white.

Screening Rooms and Swimming Pools

The disastrous experience of Boston and other cities in the North where desegregation plans were imposed did remarkably little to dampen the enthusiasm of the federal judiciary for this type of social engineering. The courts' desegregation movement reached its apotheosis in Kansas City, Missouri.

In 1977, a group of Kansas City parents and the Kansas City Missouri School District sued the state and surrounding areas, alleging that they had allowed a segregated school system to operate in Kansas City. After a trial that last seven and one-half months, U.S. district judge Russell Clark found that twenty-four schools were "racially isolated," that is, more than 90 percent black. This was hardly surprising, given that the school district's overall enrollment was 67.7 percent black. Yet Judge Clark adduced that this racial isolation was somehow due to state action, so in 1986, he launched what an appeals judge later described as "the most ambitious and expensive remedial program in the history of school desegregation." We might describe it, more simply, as a fit of gavelitis.

Judge Clark's goal was to "reverse white flight by offering superior educational opportunities." He declared virtually every school in the district a "magnet school." The schools were supposed to be magnets for students; instead, they became magnets for money. Here's a partial list of what Judge Clark ordered:

[H]igh schools in every classroom will have air conditioning, an alarm system and 15 microcomputers; a 2,000-square-foot planetarium; greenhouses and vivariums; a 25-acre farm with an air conditioned meeting room for 104 people; a Model United Nations wired for language translation; broadcast capable radio and television studios with an editing and animation lab; a temperature controlled art gallery; movie editing and screening rooms; a 3,500-square-foot dust-free diesel mechanics room; 1,875-square-foot elementary school animal rooms for use in a Zoo Project; swimming pools; and numerous other facilities.

Obviously, Judge Clark in his wisdom had discerned that the requirements of the Constitution couldn't be satisfied with a mere 12-acre farm or a 1,000-square-foot planetarium.

No area of school management was too small to evade Judge Clark's gimlet eyes. He objected, for instance, to a plan put forward by the State of Missouri to improve the appearance of school buildings: "This 'patch and repair' approach proposed by the State," Judge Clark wrote, "would not achieve suburban comparability or the visual attractiveness sought by the Court, as it would result in floor coverings with unsightly sections of mismatched carpeting and tile, and individual walls possessing different shades of paint." It's as if Martha Stewart had been given dictatorial authority to implement her decorating ideas.

The judge's orders, as might be expected, required the wealth of Croesus to carry out. The annual bill was hundreds of millions of dollars—far beyond the power of Kansas City to finance. The state constitution strictly limited property taxes, requiring two-thirds agreement from a school district's voters in order to raise the levy beyond $3.25 per $100 of assessed home value. State voters also passed an initiative designed to roll back property taxes. The Kansas City schools failed to convince the voters to raise taxes to pay for Judge Clark's grandiose plans. Therefore, as a first measure, Judge Clark issued an injunction to stop the popularly enacted property tax rollback from taking place. When that didn't bring in enough money, Judge Clark nearly doubled the property tax from $2.05 to $4.00 per $100 of assessed value and ordered the state to issue $150 million in capital improvement bonds—all this via fiat. The judge's actions had tremendous symbolic importance in a country born of a revolt against "taxation without representation."

Four justices of the U.S. Supreme Court thought Judge Clark was guilty of overweening hubris. "The power of taxation is one that the federal judiciary does not possess," wrote Justice Anthony Kennedy, adding, "Ill-considered entry into the volatile field of taxation is a step that may place at risk the legitimacy that justifies judicial independence."

But a majority of the Supreme Court thought Clark was doing a fine job. To be sure, the majority was troubled by the appearance of an unelected judge personally levying taxes. But the Court decided that a mere cosmetic change would fix the problem. "The District Court should not set the property tax rate itself," wrote Justice Byron White, "but should authorize KCMSD [the Kansas City Missouri School District] to submit a levy to the state tax collection authorities and should enjoin the operation of state laws hindering KCMSD from adequately funding the remedy." This is a distinction whose import would not have been obvious to taxpayers who saw their property taxes nearly double anyway.

The Supreme Court opinion approving judicial taxation was issued in 1990. Five years later, the case of *Missouri v. Jenkins* once again made its way—for the third time—to the Supreme Court. The issue this time was a court-ordered salary increase for all Kansas City school employees. Judge Clark, in essence, had allowed the school district and the teacher's union to bypass the normal collective bargaining process and produce a costly accord, with the bill being sent to the taxpayers, whose interests, of course, weren't represented in the court. With Clarence Thomas having replaced Thurgood Marshall, the Supreme Court mustered a bare five-justice majority to tell Judge Clark that he'd finally gone too far, that he was engaging in "pedagogical sociology, not constitutional adjudication."

Judge Clark, apparently slow to take the hint, didn't end his control of the Kansas City consent decree until some two years after the Supreme Court ruling. In 1997, almost twenty years after first taking the case, he generously allowed the state to phase out its support of the Kansas City school district with a promise to spend only $320 million more over the next three years.

The schools had already spent $1.8 billion as part of the desegregation plan. Kansas City was spending more per pupil than any other district in the country and had the lowest teacher-pupil ratios in the country. Still, when Judge Clark looked around and assessed the results of his actions, what did he find? While the school districts buildings looked great, there wasn't much learning taking place inside. The gap between whites' and blacks' test scores had remained constant. African Americans' test scores were still below the national average. And there had been no significant decrease in white flight. As the judge summed up, ruefully: "large expenses and inadequate school performance in many areas."

Yet the juristocracy's role in Kansas City continues. Another judge has taken over Clark's role in running the consent decree, and he has vowed to appoint "monitors" to manage the downsizing process that must take place because of the phaseout of state support. One judicial intervention, it seems, begets another.

Short-Circuiting Democracy:
The Lure of Government by Decree

IN THE 1990s, the Supreme Court has made it easier to phase out court oversight of schools. Some desegregation plans are indeed disappearing. In Baton Rouge, for instance, federal judge John Parker ended court-ordered busing in 1996 after fifteen years. At the same time, Judge Kenneth Ryskamp ended a decree in Broward County, Florida, after ten years. But plenty of other desegregation plans, affecting hundreds of school districts, many of them mandating busing, remain in effect.

After years of being spoon-fed by a judge, school officials aren't eager to go foraging for their own vittles. Education administrators have discovered that a judge—who doesn't have to pay much, if anything, out of pocket—is a lot more generous in funding bloated bureaucracies than voters, who are understandably reluctant to part with their hard-earned money. Why would the school board ever want to give up such a convenient excuse—*the judge made us do it*—for its own inefficiency?

Many officials also discover that it's only through a judge's intervention that they can make decisions, such as busing students, that might be ideologically alluring to them but unpopular with the community. As a result, says a former Justice Department official, "Many school boards are content—for either financial or ideological reasons—to have their school districts supervised by a federal judge rather than by themselves."

So the school officials are happy. The judges are happy. The only loser here is the democratic process. But who worries about that?

Certainly, this is of no concern to some of the deep thinkers of legal academia. Emboldened by the experience of desegregation—Oh, righteous cause!—some of these theorizers crafted an entire philosophy based on the assumption that judges (who stomped out Jim Crow) are to be trusted more than mere politicians (who propped up Jim Crow).

Courts shouldn't just be deciding cases, according to this line of argument: They should be guardians of our public morality. As one learned Yale professor put it: "Adjudication is the social process by which judges give meaning to our public values." Adjudication, in this view, is no longer about deciding specific cases; it's about ameliorating a "social condition." Judges are enforcing not the law but a "distinctive public morality" that requires them to impose their own values upon bureaucrats and, by extension, their bosses, the elected officials. This is a long and seemingly never-ending task: "A long-term supervisory relationship develops between the judge and the institution, for performance must be monitored, and new strategies devised for making certain that the operation of the organization is kept within constitutional bounds."

But why should judges, cloistered in their chambers, be better at reflecting public sentiments than elected officials, who regularly go out among the hoi polloi? It's hard to escape the suspicion that much of the professoriate favors judicial interventions precisely because they often deliver policy results that are at *odds* with the public's sentiments, which tend to be more conservative. Indeed, judges will often allow political activists to short-circuit the democratic process with astonishing boldness.

Trapped in the Sandbox

U.S. district judge Leonard Sand of New York, a Carter appointee, offers perhaps the best, though hardly the only, example of this phenomenon. In 1985, Judge Sand decided that the City of Yonkers, New York, was guilty of unconstitutional discrimination by locating public housing in a poor part of town bordering the Bronx and primarily inhabited by minorities. Of course, as a consultant to Judge Sand acknowledged, "The pattern of housing discrimination that occurred in Yonkers occurred, I would say, in most of the suburban communities of the nation." Nevertheless, Judge Sand tried to coerce the city into accepting a remedial plan that called for building hundreds of units of low-income housing in middle-class neighborhoods.

Sand, naturally, lived in the tony suburb of Chappaqua, so he wasn't affected by his actions. Homeowners in blue-collar Yonkers, however, stood to lose tens of thousands of dollars in property values if housing projects, with their attendant drugs and crime, moved into the neighborhood.

The Yonkers City Council at first resisted Sand's entreaties but finally wound up signing a consent decree. The council agreed to build two hundred public housing units but still balked at the judge's orders for eight hundred more, which would have entailed a 30 percent tax increase. Judge Sand declared that if the council didn't pass his "legislative package" by August 1, 1988, the city would be fined $100 for the first day, with the fines doubling every day, which would quickly make them reach $1 billion. Sand also let it be known that individual council members who refused to vote for his plans would be fined $500 per day and would be subject to jail for contempt of court.

Despite this Sword of Damocles hanging over their heads, the council members voted 4–3 to reject the judge's legislative package, so he began fining both the city and the recalcitrant councilmen. Finally, with the city facing sanctions of $1 million per day, which would have quickly bankrupted the municipality, the council decided to accede to the judge's demands.

The Supreme Court voted 5–4 in 1990 to overturn Judge Sand's sanctions against the individual council members, who were, after all, penalized for voting their consciences. The Supreme Court majority held that the "question of imposing contempt sanctions" against the councilmen should only have been considered if the sanctions against the city had failed to produce the desired result "within a reasonable time." In the dissent, Justice Brennan apocalyptically suggested that the majority's decision countenanced the defiance of court orders, "and if that situation is tolerated, then our constitutional system of government fails." In fact, however, the Court pointedly did not rule out sanctioning elected public officials who refuse to do a judge's bidding; the justices only held that this option wasn't called for yet in this particular circumstance.

Spallone v. U.S., as the Yonkers case was known, provided no real check on the power of federal judges. Thus, it is not surprising to find, years later, Judge Sand still in the grip of gavelitis and still trying to coerce Yonkers into building more public housing. In 1996, he finally got the city to agree to build six hundred low-income units, but the Westchester County legislature balked at releasing park land needed for the development. Perhaps it's time for the judge to throw the Westchester legislators into the hoosegow.

Unworkable and Inflexible: The Practical Problems of Decrees

THE UNDEMOCRATIC nature of the process is far from the only problem with the juristocracy's attempts to run government. The more practical problem is that people like Leonard Sand and Russell Clark are ill-suited to managing large institutions like school districts. "[A]sking courts to be the engine of fundamental social change in our complex society," notes a law professor, "makes as little sense as using a word processor to cook dinner, or a hair dryer to spray paint a house: It is simply not the job the machine was designed to do."

1. Running sprawling organizations, private or public, requires give and take, a willingness to compromise, that is entirely alien to the world of right and wrong, legal and illegal, that judges inhabit most of the time.
2. Judges usually don't have any management experience beyond bossing around a handful of clerks and secretaries.
3. Judges don't possess sufficient staff to create or carry out their policies.
4. Judges have no way to get information from the public about their decisions, receiving it only from the litigants before them.
5. Judges have no ability to marshal political support for controversial solutions.

Thus, when judges do get into the management business, the results are usually less than encouraging, as we've seen. Yet once a judge makes his ruling, that's it. You're stuck. Even if underlying conditions change, court orders seldom do.

Providence, Rhode Island, discovered that the hard way. In 1989 the union-run Retirement Board, which manages the pension plan of all city employees except teachers, increased cost of living adjustments (COLAs) for retirees. The city, which couldn't afford to pay, sued. After a judge ruled that the city had to pay up, the two sides signed a consent decree in 1991 that called for retirees to receive COLAs at a compounded rate of between 3 percent and 5 percent annually.

At the time, Mayor Vincent A. Cianci Jr. thought that this was the best deal he could get. But in subsequent years, the city council refused to raise taxes, and the city found itself unable to pay the agreed-upon COLAs. The city withheld the extra funds from retirees while it asked the state supreme court to vacate the consent decree. The justices refused in 1995, writing, with less than perfect grammar, "It appears to us that the City of Providence in its pending action is simply attempting to have the . . . Court pull it out of what it now believes was not too good a bargain when it entered into the consent decree."

The city is thus stuck with a $20 million bill for retroactive COLAs—a bill it can't pay, even as new costs mount. Much of the blame for this mess must rest with the mayor himself, though he felt forced into the decree because of the previous court ruling. But Providence's plight demonstrates yet another problem with running public policy through court orders: They're too inflexible.

And that inflexibility doesn't just extend to the area under court control. Court decrees wind up distorting all of public policy, much as a star's gravitational pull distorts the orbits of neighboring planets. The area being run by the judge isn't subject to normal legislative give and take; all decisions are made by a dictator in black robes. Thus, if the judge decides to spend money on, say, public housing or mental institutions, that's money not available for policing or libraries.

The District of Columbia, probably the biggest basket case in American municipal governance, is acutely aware of this problem because it's operating under dozens of court orders (nobody seems to know the exact number). Court-appointed monitors directly run the city's foster-care system, medical services at the D.C. jail, and the housing authority. Other court-appointed officials monitor services for Medicaid recipients, the mentally retarded, the mentally ill, and inmates in the city prison system. And plaintiffs in a class action filed in 1974 on behalf of the mentally ill were arguing in 1997 that it's time for a federal judge to appoint masters to run St. Elizabeth's Hospital and the city's Commission on Mental Health.

Mayor Marion Barry, never exactly a whiz himself at city governance, claims that the court orders make his job impossible. He complains that thirteen court orders at the Corrections Department alone cost $108 million and that they demand service levels far above those of most states' prisons. At the city's Department of Health and Human Services, sixteen court orders cost $346 million. In all, Mayor Barry says, D.C. spends $454 million a year complying with court orders.

In fairness to the judges, it's obvious that some of the court orders in D.C. are the result of the inability of the city government, and specifically Mayor Barry, to run anything properly. But is it really the job of the courts to step in and protect city residents from the consequences of their elected leaders' poor decisions? And do judges do a better job of running agencies than Mayor Barry's cronies? As a nineteenth-century Supreme Court justice wrote: "For protection against abuses by legislatures the people must resort to the polls, not to the courts."

Judges as Prison Wardens: The Comic Consequences of Decrees

SINCE JUDGES are the last people most of us would pick to manage anything, it should be no surprise that they've made quite a hash of prison litigation, second only to schools as an area of judicial activism.

As of 1995, 378 state and 113 federal prisons were operating under court order. Some of these decrees have ended genuinely inhumane conditions, such as the beating of inmates in the Texas prisons or the generally squalid conditions depicted in the film *Cool Hand Luke*. But most of those decrees were issued in the 1970s and have not been reevaluated since. Nowadays, judges are routinely holding wardens in violation of various constitutional "rights" granted to inmates, which range from having access to a prison law library to not being forced to share a cell with a smoker. Most of these judicially created rights are of recent vintage and were routinely violated throughout almost all of the nation's history. But violating these rights today gives a judge freedom to step in and administer an entire prison system.

New York's experience provides a good example of how pervasive judicial control of prisons can become. Federal judge Morris Lasker and a bevy of "special masters" began running New York City's jails in 1978 after Mayor Ed Koch signed a decree settling a suit brought on behalf of prisoners by the Legal Aid Society. There was never a finding that the city's jails were unconstitutional, but over the years, Judge Lasker's oversight of the 52-page decree spawned more than 1,500 pages of court orders governing virtually every aspect of prison operations.

For starters, the order guaranteed every inmate *free* access every day to newspapers, telephones, and television sets. But it went much further than that. The "Sanitation Order" prescribed that certain areas of the jails must be cleaned with a particular type of detergent, Boraxo, in a specified strength (half a cup per gallon of water). New York faced fines if it didn't follow this order's "floor care procedures"—for instance, if prison janitors failed to stay six inches away from baseboards and corners when applying the first two coats of floor finish.

Another order from the late 1980s mandated that prison officials use the "cook-chill" method of food preparation, the same one used aboard airplanes, where food is partially cooked and chilled at a production center and then reheated just before service. Making inmates eat airplane food—talk about cruel and unusual punishment!

Since the cost of implementing this technology was so high—$400 million—Mayor Rudolph Giuliani petitioned the court in 1994 to change this costly requirement. After six months of litigation, the court generously allowed the city to substitute a $200 million plan to improve existing jail kitchens, but only by entering into a new "food service" order governing operations until the year 2001 that specified, among other things, the number of forks, spoons, and "spoondles" (a spoon with tines used generally by those incarcerated in elementary schools and prisons") to be stocked in each jail kitchen.

An attorney for the city notes that the litigation over this food service order never once determined that the city's previous method of serving food was unconstitutional. Indeed, the special master overseeing the prisons certified that the city "routinely serves nutritious meals at proper temperatures." But that wasn't enough to satisfy the juristocracy's demands.

Every change to the New York prison consent decree involved moving a bureaucratic or judicial mountain. The consent decree allowed inmates to wear jewelry. In an effort to decrease violence, the city tried to prohibit gang-related jewelry. This was allowed only after another six-month litigation process during which the city had to turn over 1,500 pages of documents to the Legal Aid Society.

Yet another provision guaranteed all inmates access to the library, even those in the Central Punitive Segregation Unit, where 350 of the most violent and disruptive offenders were housed. These inmates would commit violent acts in the library, preventing other, less violent inmates from exercising their "right" to use the library. But in order to convince the court to allow guards to deliver law books to the violent convicts' cells, the city had to submit 5,000 pages of paperwork.

Just monitoring compliance with all these decrees cost the city more than $2 million annually. Federal judge Harold Baer, who took over from Judge Lasker, finally vacated the New York consent decree in 1996, a mere eighteen years after its inception. But a year later, a panel of the Second Circuit held that the state courts could continue to enforce the consent decree. Thus, judicial micromanagement of the New York jails seems destined to continue.

The consent orders are obviously enormously wasteful. Worse, the decrees force officials to concentrate all their attention and energy not on the question "How can we better manage the prisons today?" but on "How can we please the judge today?" This has a hidden, corrosive effect on city workers. "Such consent decrees," said an attorney for New York City, "stifle individual initiative and prevent managers from making salutary changes. And the excruciating detail governing ordinary procedures demeans and demoralizes managers and workers alike."

Hot Pots

For more evidence of how judicial decrees can have daft consequences, we must shift our attention from the concrete canyons of New York to the sandstone canyons of Arizona, where U.S. district judge Carl Muecke, a Johnson appointee, has been overseeing a consent decree governing the state's prisons since 1973.

Judge Muecke decided that the First and Fourth Amendments required the state to allow inmates generous access to gift packages and mail from the outside. When the state's corrections director tried

in 1994 to ban pornographic magazines from prisons, Muecke held
him in contempt of court and ordered him to pay $10,000 in attorney's
fees out of his own pocket.

The judge, a practicing Catholic, also insisted on generous provision
for inmates at Christmas time, ruling that they should be able to receive
up to three 25-pound gift packages. That's a lot of holiday ham! Since
the judge issued his original order in 1973, the number of inmates in
the state prison system has multiplied thirteenfold, making the costs of
screening all those packages for contraband prohibitive. The state
spent $124,000 to inspect 24,500 packages annually between 1990 and
1993. Arizona began petitioning in 1990 to delete the Christmas-package requirement, but Muecke rejected the request. Meanwhile, the
judge ruled that inmates should be given access to electric hot pots,
which they could use to cook in their cells. "This order is a mockery to
prison staff, and dangerous not only for them but also for inmates,"
declared the state's corrections director in disgust.

In 1996, after more than six years of protests by the state, the U.S.
Court of Appeals for the Ninth Circuit overturned Muecke's
Christmas-package and hot-pot diktats, holding that neither one was
within the scope of the original consent decree. The Ninth Circuit,
however, upheld another of Muecke's gems, a twenty-five-page order
governing prison law libraries.

Not only did Muecke spell out exactly how long each library must be
kept open each day and the minimum educational requirements for the
law librarians, he also held that all inmates, even those known to be violent, must be allowed access to the library. "The order," noted Justice
Clarence Thomas, "goes so far as to dictate permissible noise levels in
law library reading rooms and requires the State to 'take all necessary'
steps to correct any structural or acoustical problems.'" The U.S.
Supreme Court overturned this decree on the grounds that Muecke
had become too "enmeshed in the minutiae of prison operations."

Arizona governor Fife Symington thought that wasn't enough: He
called for Judge Muecke's impeachment. That may be too strong a punishment, but it's clear that Muecke and other judges have to be removed
from prison litigation—perhaps they can be locked in solitary confinement in their plush chambers—before they do much more harm.

Often, the consequences of their decrees are pure comedy—the
"cook-chill" order in the New York jails, for example, or the library-

noise order in Arizona. Only a judge with plenty of spare time could think of such trivialities as constitutional issues. But remember that lurking behind this silliness are very serious concerns. We're dealing, after all, with criminals, many of them violent. When judges decide that these hardened convicts should gain access to hot pots or be allowed to congregate in prison libraries at will, they frustrate wardens' attempts to keep order behind bars. Lives are at stake here, and judges have no right endangering either inmates or guards with their featherbrained schemes.

Jailbreak: The Tragic Consequences of Decrees

MOST OF the prison consent decrees are costly and counterproductive. However, some are downright deadly, not only to prisoners and guards, but to the world at large.

Hundreds of judges, such as Philadelphia's Norma Shapiro, have decided that prison overcrowding violates the Eighth Amendment ban on "cruel and unusual punishment," and to correct this violation, they've instituted caps on prison populations that automatically release prisoners under certain conditions. As of 1995, 228 state prisons were operating under court mandates to limit their population. These caps frustrate laws, such as mandatory minimum sentences, designed to keep inmates behind bars longer.

Even if prison conditions were far from perfect, that wouldn't justify releasing criminals so that they could prey on innocent citizens, not just fellow cons. Especially since there is no compelling evidence that prison overcrowding—the justification for all these population caps—is dangerous.

Texas's prisons were among the most crowded in the nation in the late 1970s, yet the state had a lower rate of inmate violence than comparable states. As Texas built more prisons in the 1980s, inmate violence soared. Based on such evidence, some leading penologists have concluded that what counts is how well prisoners are managed, not how many are housed in one facility. That isn't the message the public gets, of course, because prisoners' rights attorneys, wardens, prison-guard unions, and the jail-building industry all have a mutual interest in conjuring up horror stories about prison overcrowding—that's how they shake more money out of taxpayers. But the evidence is clear: While a population cap does nothing to improve the management of a prison, it can do a lot to increase crime outside the jailhouse walls.

The experience of Florida is instructive in showing the destructive consequences of judicially imposed prison caps. In 1975, federal judge Charles Scott decided that Florida's prisons were unconstitutionally overcrowded. As part of a consent decree, the state passed a law that would reduce inmates' sentences across the board every time the state prison system hit 98 or 99 percent capacity. This resulted in Florida inmates serving an average of only one-third of their sentences. To imagine the consequences of this policy, remember the statistics cited in Chapter 2 about the high recidivism rate among released prisoners (more than 60 percent of all former inmates are rearrested within three years of getting out of prison) and the large number of crimes each felon is likely to commit on the outside (former inmates commit a median of fifteen serious crimes a year, excluding drug offenses).

Among those eligible for release under Florida's prison cap was Donald McDougall, who accumulated enough credits to serve only ten years for torturing and murdering a five-year-old girl. A public outcry over McDougall's pending release (which never happened; he was eventually beaten to death in the prison yard) led the Florida legislature in 1992 to pass a law exempting violent criminals from getting overcrowding credits. In 1995, the legislature mandated that convicts serve at least 85 percent of their sentences.

The state attorney general, Democrat Robert Butterworth, issued formal opinions holding that the new laws had retroactively revoked credits already given out to inmates. So the state rearrested a number of recently released convicts. But one of those rearrested, Kenneth Lynce, who had been locked up for trying to kill his girlfriend, filed a habeas corpus appeal, an ancient remedy available under the Constitution to all convicts who believe they have been unjustly imprisoned.

A federal district court and an appeals court ruled against Lynce. The lower court held that the overcrowding credits had been given out in the first place for administrative reasons, not to decrease anyone's punishment, and therefore revoking the credits didn't violate the prohibition against ex post facto punishments in Article 1 of the Constitution. A unanimous Supreme Court disagreed. In 1997's *Lynce v. Mathis*, Justice John Paul Stevens wrote that whatever Florida's motivations, "the cancellation of 1,860 days of accumulated provisional credits had the effect of lengthening petitioner's period of incarceration" and therefore was unconstitutional. In a separate case, the Court blocked Florida from retroactively revoking "good time" credits for inmates.

Florida had no choice but to follow the justices' ruling and free thousands of violent felons who had accumulated overcrowding credits. In March 1997, the state Corrections Department released some 500 felons guilty of murder and other violent crimes, including one man who had beaten a two-year-old to death for vomiting in his Corvette and another who had led a gang of teens that killed a homeless man with a baseball bat. Up to 2,000 more inmates were scheduled for release in the following year.

John E. Armstrong was among the first batch of released cons. He had a criminal record stretching back almost two decades. But the Supreme Court ruling meant that he had to serve only one-and-a-half years of a twelve-year sentence for robbery. Armstrong took advantage of his freedom to go on a cocaine-fueled crime spree: He robbed two banks and two convenience stores and allegedly killed a man in a dispute.

When police tried to question him about the murder in early December 1997, Armstrong led them on a high-speed chase that ended with him breaking into an Orlando house and taking two small children hostage. For three days Armstrong held the toddlers at gun point until a police SWAT team finally crashed into the house and killed him in a gun battle. None of that would have been necessary if the Supreme Court hadn't freed this sociopath in the first place.

Now, the *Lynce* decision is certainly defensible as a matter of law; even conservative justices Thomas and Scalia joined in the result through a concurring opinion, and nobody has ever accused them of being soft on criminals. But rulings like this only feed growing public frustration with the judicial process. First, the courts in effect force Florida to release violent felons, then they prevent the state from correcting the worst consequences of that disastrous policy. Whose side are the judges on, anyway?

Incidentally, the consent decree that started this whole mess was finally vacated in 1993, after a twenty-one-year legal battle. This marathon litigation, which long outlived Judge Scott, cost taxpayers some $20 million, including up to $7 million in legal fees—money that could have been better spent on law enforcement.

It's possible, of course, that the suit achieved its stated aim: improving conditions for inmates. But it sure didn't do anything to improve life for the vast majority of the population outside prison walls. Every time a thug like John E. Armstrong commits fresh atrocities, the people of Florida will pay another heavy price for judicial activism.

Conclusion: Omniscient Courts?

JUDGES raising taxes. Fining elected officials for voting their consciences. Busing school students. Opening prison doors. Even supervising the preparation of jail grub.

It's hard to believe this is what the Founders had in mind when in Article 3 of the Constitution they vested the "judicial Power of the United States" in "one supreme Court, and in such inferior Courts as the Congress may from time to time ordain and establish." As Alexander Hamilton made quite clear in *Federalist No. 78*, the Constitution's drafters saw judicial power as quite limited: "The interpretation of the laws is the proper and peculiar province of the courts." Article 2 vested executive responsibility in the president, including the duty to "take Care that the Laws be faithfully executed," while Article 1 gave all legislative powers, including the "Power To lay and collect Taxes," to Congress. These functions were expressly not reserved for the courts. As *Federalist No. 78* further explained:

> The executive not only dispenses the honors, but holds the sword of the community. The legislature not only commands the purse, but prescribes the rules by which the duties and rights of every citizen are to be regulated. The judiciary on the contrary has no influence over either the sword or the purse, no direction either of the strength or the wealth of the society, and can take no active resolution whatever.

Can take no active resolution? Try telling that to Judges Russell Clark (the Kansas City school administrator) and Leonard Sand (the Yonkers housing boss) and Morris Lasker (the supervisor of the New York prisons) and Carl Muecke (the Arizona prison warden).

The Supreme Court has taken a small step toward returning to the original understanding of judicial power by overruling decrees in the

Kansas City school and Arizona prison cases. But never has the Court held that judges simply don't have the power to impose their will on local elected officials in such a flagrant manner. "The Court," writes one legal scholar, "does not appear to have ever invalidated a structural remedy on the ground that it improperly intruded upon the proper authority of state and local institutions." Yet it's hard to reconcile federal judges' cavalier preemption of local mores with the limits of the Tenth Amendment.

The courts have certainly not done a good job of limiting their own Article 3 powers, so Congress has stepped into the breach. The Prison Litigation Reform Act of 1996 limits judicial remedies in prison cases. The law calls for decrees to be "narrowly drawn," to extend "no further than necessary to correct the violation of the Federal right," and to use "the least intrusive means necessary to correct the violation of the Federal right." The act also limits the worst abuses, such as prisoner release orders, by mandating that they only be issued by three-judge panels, not by lone jurists like Norma Shapiro. Finally, the act makes it easier to challenge existing decrees and forces courts to give a speedy hearing to requests to terminate an order. Using the authority of this law, numerous elected officials have already challenged prison consent decrees, and some, such as the one in New York City, have been lifted.

This act can serve as a model for others. Congress can pass legislation to limit consent decrees in school desegregation and other cases. Decrees should only be allowed to remedy actual, ongoing violations of the Constitution, and they should be terminated as soon as the original problem is remedied.

Of course, activist judges may try to impede these reforms; indeed, some lower courts have already struck down provisions of the Prison Litigation Reform Act. But the Supreme Court—so far, at least—appears to be receptive to congressional attempts to limit the reach of Article 3. "At some point," writes Justice Thomas, "we must recognize that the judiciary is not omniscient, and that all problems do not require a remedy of constitutional proportions."

CHAPTER 6

The Civil Injustice System

[C]ourts do not sit to compensate the luckless; this is not Sherwood Forest.
JUDGE ALEX KOZINSKI, *Kern v. Levolor Lorentzen, Inc.*

A CASE THAT'S FOR THE BIRDS.

Ruby Campagna, a grandmother living in an apartment complex in Roanoke, Virginia, discovered some wrens nesting on her patio in 1993. She knew about the owners' policy banning birds—they apparently caused damage to the buildings—but she let them stay anyway. When building manager Judy Wood discovered the nest, she stomped the nest and the tiny birds, killing them. Campagna was so traumatized by this wrenicide that she sued Wood and the apartment complex—and won $135,000 from a jury.

Her lawyer claimed that Campagna's "whole worldview was shattered" by the incident: She "used to be a very happy, vivacious, sociable person. And then she became very sad and reclusive." A psychiatrist even testified that she suffered from post-traumatic stress disorder. Circuit court judge Richard Pattisall eventually threw out

$100,000 in compensatory damages but let stand $35,000 in punitive damages. The two sides wound up settling out of court.

WOMAN BITES LANDLORD.

Carol Roland had four or five drinks at a party in 1991, then went over to the apartment of her friend and neighbor Karen Shortell. One of Shortell's two pit bulls attacked Roland, who wound up suffering twenty-seven dog bites, many of them deep. Naturally, Roland sued— not Shortell (she didn't want to take a friend to court), but the owners of the apartment building.

In the wren-stomping case, a building manager was held liable for getting rid of animals on her property. In this case, the owner was socked with a $2.14 million jury award for *not* getting rid of the pit bulls. Under New Hampshire law, it seems, landlords can be held liable for dangerous conditions on their property. The two sides agreed to settle for $1.1 million, before the judge ruled on the defendant's motion to set aside the verdict.

AN ELECTRIFYING VERDICT.

Sang Yeul Lee, a Korean immigrant living in Chicago, was returning home from a party one night in 1977 when he wandered onto some rapid-transit tracks. He unzipped his pants and began urinating, when—zap!—he was electrocuted on the third rail, which carried 600 volts of electricity.

Tests subsequently revealed that he had a sky-high blood alcohol level of .341. The transit authority had put up warning signs, right-of-way fencing, access barriers, and chain-link fences to keep out intruders, but in his inebriated condition, Lee, who had limited English proficiency, had apparently ignored all obstacles.

His widow sued the Chicago Transit Authority and won $1.5 million, in no small measure because the trial judge gave the jury instructions favorable to the plaintiff. After a lengthy appeals process, the U.S. Supreme Court allowed the verdict to stand in 1993.

A JUDICIAL MUGGING.

One evening in 1984, Bernard McCummings, a twenty-three-year-old professional criminal, and two friends were looking for a likely mugging victim on a subway station on the Upper West Side of

Manhattan. They found seventy-one-year-old Jerome Sandusky and began choking and beating him. A couple of transit cops heard the old man's screams and came running. As McCummings was running away, one of the cops shot him in the back.

The mugger was paralyzed and wound up going to prison for three years. After getting out, McCummings sued the cops for using excessive force and won $4.3 million from a jury. The state court of appeals upheld the award, and in 1993 the U.S. Supreme Court refused to consider the case. "It is just unbelievable," commented Jerome Sandusky, "that someone who engaged in robbery and whose friends were trying to kill me should be given millions of dollars."

The Litigation Tide

THESE ARE all cases where judges allowed verdicts that boggle the imagination. It's hard to deny, when confronted with such claims, that we have a serious problem with frivolous lawsuits in this country. During the past several decades, judges have presided over a tidal wave of litigation that has drenched the courts, at heavy cost to society at large.

This is obvious to anyone who's ever looked at the legal system—except, oddly enough, for lawyers, law professors, and assorted camp followers. One of the subheads in attorney Ralph Nader's latest book boldly proclaims: "There Is No Litigation Explosion." Many in the legal industry seems to be in denial about the effect of their activities—much as the tobacco industry has been in denial for so long about whether smoking causes cancer.

One is entitled to doubt whether the arguments of Nader and Company are made in good faith. I've yet to meet anybody willing to defend the current civil justice system who doesn't benefit from it, either directly (as is the case with all practicing lawyers, even those who never enter a courtroom) or indirectly (Naderites get donations to their nonprofit groups from trial lawyers; law professors receive fat consulting fees from litigants).

And even as lawyers claim in public to be blissfully unaware of any increase in lawsuits, in private they worry as much as any doctor about malpractice suits. A 1996 article on legal malpractice suits in the *American Bar Association Journal* warns: "Expanding theories of liability, disregard for precedent by judges and juries, and unpredictable damage awards all conspire to promote the pursuit of claims that would not have been considered 10 years ago." The article counsels lawyers to shelter their own assets in places like the Cook Islands, which apparently offer more attractive laws than the United States.

But for the sake of argument, let's assume that the *lawyerati* are serious in claiming that there's nothing wrong with the civil justice system. In this chapter, we'll see why everything *isn't* OK—punitive damages are out of control, plaintiffs are winning huge awards without proving that the defendants caused their injuries, and various class-action scams are proliferating. And as we'll see, judges should be held accountable for many of these failures.

Are There Too Many Suits?

Let's begin by examining the argument that the civil justice system is functioning just fine right now—an argument that usually proceeds through several phases, which taken together are about as coherent and convincing as O. J.'s alibis.

First, lawyers will argue that examples such as those cited above are untrustworthy. They're "mere" anecdotes (or as one professor has it, "tendentious macro-anecdotes"), and they really tell us nothing about the legal system. Coming from lawyers, this is an odd argument, since the whole basis of the common law is the compiling of individual cases, a.k.a. anecdotes, to reach a general conclusion. Of course, lawyers are perfectly willing to turn around and cite their own anecdotes—usually about minorities and others who saw their rights vindicated—to demonstrate how great the legal system is.

The next argument usually made by defenders of the system is that we don't really know what's going on, and until we do, we can't possibly reach any conclusions. "What we think we know," writes one leading commentator, is "untrue, unknown, or unknowable." It's true that statistics about the civil justice system, especially at the state level, are fragmentary and incomplete. But it's impossible to wait until 100 percent of the evidence is in before reaching a conclusion; by that standard, we'd still be debating whether Galileo was right. Lawyers undercut this argument anyway when they trot out their own statistics in an attempt to prove that the number of suits isn't increasing.

The American Bar Association published a booklet called *Facts About the Civil Justice System* that asks: "Has there been an explosion of personal injury litigation in this country in recent years?" The ABA's answer: "No. In fact the volume of tort filings in state courts has declined since 1990." That's misleading at best. What the pamphlet doesn't mention is that the National Center for State Courts calculates that tort filings nearly doubled between 1984 and 1994.

Meanwhile, look at what's happening in the federal courts (where the statistics are more complete):

- The number of civil filings in federal courts increased 280 percent from 1960 to 1995—from 89,112 in 1960 to 248,335 in 1995.

- The number of federal tort cases—a subset of civil filings— briefly dipped in the late 1980s and early 1990s but then rose again, soaring 50 percent between 1992 and 1996.

- While this was happening, numerous other suits were flooding U.S. courts; for instance, the number of workplace bias cases filed in federal courts more than doubled between 1992 and 1996.

But defenders of the system don't want you to see the rabbit they're concealing behind their back. Instead, they attempt to distract you by waving a different argument in front of your face—they claim that far from having too many suits, we don't have enough. Lots of people are injured, they argue, yet few ever sue. (Note the assumption here: Every injury must be actionable.)

In support of this startling conclusion, defenders of the system will usually cite a Harvard study of New York hospitals published in 1990. This study found that for every 10,000 patients, 100 of them suffered iatrogenic (doctor-induced) injuries. Yet only 12.5 percent of these "victims" sued. "One of the most remarkable features of the tort system is how few plaintiffs there are," writes a leading academic defender of the current system.

This conclusion conveniently overlooks some other findings from the Harvard study: "[I]n the vast majority of cases the medically caused injuries are minor and their effects brief; in more than 80 percent of the cases where patients sued, no negligence was found; and in 67 percent of the suits the investigators found no evidence of any injury whatsoever." The author of the Harvard study says that there are seven to eight false claims of medical malpractice for every genuine claim. In other words, the Harvard study demonstrates not that there are too few suits but rather that there are too many frivolous, and possibly fraudulent, claims.

Defenders of the system will offer a few other equivocations and justifications as to why no litigation explosion exists, but the jig is basically up. The numbers we've examined confirm the evidence of our own eyes: There are lots of suits, many of them frivolous, and the number is growing.

The Costs of Litigation

So what's the cost of all this court activity? Ralph Nader and Wesley J. Smith belittle the impact of litigation: They write that product liability verdicts and settlements in 1993 cost less than what Americans spend on dog food, a product that must be risible in their eyes. But, to extend the analogy, just as dog food is only one category of pet food, so product liability cases are only a subset of litigation.

Overall, the consulting firm Tillinghast-Towers Perrin found that the civil justice system imposed direct costs of $152 billion in 1994, including everything from the cost of payouts to plaintiffs to the attorneys' fees incurred by both sides. The indirect cost—including attempts to calculate how much manufacturers, insurers, physicians, and others raise their prices in response to litigation—has been estimated at up to $300 billion. Even at the lower estimate, we spend 270 percent more on litigation than on police and fire protection combined. The direct cost of the civil justice system consumes 2.2 percent of America's gross domestic product, compared to an average of 0.9 percent for eleven other major industrialized countries. Americans pay about $900 more per household for their legal system than the residents of any other Western country.

The tort tax (meaning the cost of verdicts, lawyers' fees, insurance, and so on) accounts for approximately 70 percent of the cost of childhood vaccines, 20 percent of a stepladder, 16 percent of a pacemaker, and one-half the cost of a football helmet—if, that is, you can find one. Dozens of companies, including Wilson and Rawlings, stopped making football helmets because of the high cost of liability. Medicine has also been affected by the tort tax; a Stanford University study estimates that litigation adds $50 billion annually in unnecessary expenses to the cost of health care.

The cost of litigation can't be described in numbers alone. Litigation has altered the way Americans live their lives. In some cases, litigation has undoubtedly had a positive impact—removing from the market such dangerous products as diethylstilbestrol (DES), a drug designed to prevent miscarriages that wound up causing birth defects—but in many other instances, court cases have had unintended and damaging consequences:

- Metal slides, swings, merry-go-rounds, and other fixtures of childhood are disappearing from playgrounds, in large measure because of the fear of litigation. In some cases, these structures are being replaced with safer, rubber-padded alternatives, but elsewhere they're simply gone. "We removed all the playground equipment at our schools in 1995 to block any potential suits," says the business manager of the Millbrae California School District. "The loss from [lawsuits] against school districts for playgrounds is astronomical."

- Intrauterine contraceptive devices (IUDs) used to be a popular option for American women. Then along came the Dalkon Shield, which was found to cause pelvic inflammation and infertility. A. H. Robins, maker of the device, was driven into bankruptcy, and the Dalkon Shield was taken off the market. Having killed the Dalkon Shield, lawyers targeted other IUD makers. It didn't matter that the other IUDs, unlike the Dalkon Shield, were judged to be safe by the Food and Drug Administration (FDA) and doctors. The costs of fighting the suits were so high that their manufacturers pulled them from the market.

  Now, more than 90 million women around the globe use IUDs, while fewer than 1.4 million American women—just 1.4 percent of those using some form of birth control—employ them. A new generation of IUDs has been found to be safer and more effective than most other contraceptive methods, but no manufacturers are willing to sell the new-generation IUDs in the United States. Most obstetricians are too scared of liability to tell their patients about IUDs, anyway.

- Two Oregon men led a Boy Scout troop on a camping trip in 1991. A boy was paralyzed during a touch football game, and the scout leaders were judged negligent by a jury. The Boy Scouts had to pay a $7 million judgment. Howard Ryburn, one of the scout leaders, told the *New York Times* he won't volunteer again for a while: "Once I have my own kids, I will volunteer. Until then I wouldn't touch it." Other worthwhile organizations also face a loss of volunteers—and mounting costs for liability insurance. The Girl Scout Council of the Nation's Capital has to sell 87,000 boxes of cookies annually just to pay its liability premiums.

Who's to Blame?

Qui bono (who benefits)? Lawyers, who else? The RAND Corporation, a respected California think tank (and one often cited by the lawyers' side), found that plaintiffs collect less than half of every dollar spent on the civil justice system; the proportion is even lower for major cases. Lester Brickman, a professor at Cardozo Law School, estimates that contingency-fee lawyers have earned the equivalent of $5,000 per hour to handle routine asbestos claims. Nice work if you can get it. No wonder the number of lawyers in America grew by 130 percent from 1960 to 1985, while the general population increased by just 30 percent.

Because lawyers derive most of the benefits from the current system, the public naturally tends to blame them for the litigation epidemic. Naturally, but not logically. Lawyers, like any other businessmen, pretty much react to incentives. They wouldn't file outlandish claims if they didn't think they had a good chance of profiting from them. So who creates the incentives? Who's responsible for the litigation mess?

Legislators deserve part of the blame for passing laws—for example, the 1991 Civil Rights Act and the 1990 Americans with Disabilities Act—that spark countless lawsuits. But that's only part of the problem. "The fundamental problem in Texas tort cases is that judges don't do their jobs," writes *Texas Monthly*. "They don't toss meritless lawsuits out of court. They don't stop lawyers from using delaying tactics to drive up fees. They don't use their power to reduce absurdly high jury awards."

As in Texas, so in the rest of the nation. Let's look at what judges are—or aren't—doing about the litigation tide.

Making Doctors Pay for *Saving* Patients:
How Judges Expand Liability

L IABILITY IS by and large governed by judge-made common law, the accretion of countless cases spelling out duties and defenses. As law professor William Prosser once proclaimed, with no false modesty: "There is a duty if the court says there is a duty; the law, like the Constitution, is what we make it." The field of torts, or personal injury law, shows what a big impact judges have had. As we'll see, the tort tax is every bit as much judicially imposed as the property taxes Judge Russell Clark levied to fund the Kansas City schools.

Until the post–World War II era, the common law of torts was tilted against plaintiffs and in favor of defendants—or, if you prefer, in favor of individuals taking responsibility for their own conduct and its consequences. The basic rule was caveat emptor—let the buyer beware. But along came a generation of judicial revolutionaries, led by California Supreme Court justice Roger Traynor, to concoct new theories of liability designed to help plaintiffs. They asked, as one commentator summed it up: "How can society best allocate the cost of accidents to minimize those costs (and the cost of guarding against them), and to provide potential victims with the accident insurance that not all of them currently buy or can afford? The answer, by and large, was to make producers of goods and services pay the costs of accidents."

The more ambitious of these thinkers were attempting to do nothing less than to introduce European-style health insurance—in which every injured person can expect to be treated at society's expense— into America through the back door of litigation. Of course, turning to the legal system is probably the worst possible way to create a social safety net, since lawyers, not the intended beneficiaries, wind up taking the lion's share of the proceeds.

But such concerns did not greatly trouble the tort revolutionaries, so in the 1960s and 1970s, judges transformed personal injury law. Out went, among other safeguards, the old theory of contributory negligence, which held that if the plaintiff contributed in any way to his mishap, the defendant couldn't be held accountable. A judge in 1854 called this "a rule from time immemorial" and ventured that it was "not likely to be changed for all time to come." If only he'd lived to see the 1970s, when judges in most states began adopting the theory of comparative negligence, which holds that even plaintiffs who brought on much of their own misfortune could still collect from defendants. This helps explain why the Chicago Transit Authority was on the hook for the mishap of the inebriated urinator.

For some more examples of judicial lawmaking in action, consider the fate of the immunities that traditionally shielded many defendants from tort actions. "We used to have immunities like people had mice—57 varieties," says a trial lawyer apologist. Many of these pesky rules—pesky, that is, to plaintiffs' lawyers—were exterminated by the judicial pest-control squad.

- There was sovereign immunity, which shielded the government against most suits. The curbing of sovereign immunity is a major reason that local governments are removing their playground equipment.

- Charitable immunity protected nonprofit institutions. If this immunity still existed, the Boy Scouts probably wouldn't have been held liable because a boy got paralyzed playing football.

- Immunity for psychological injuries meant that plaintiffs couldn't collect for pain and suffering. The grandmother who was traumatized by the wrenicide would have been out of luck.

- Immunity of a product supplier meant that a manufacturer was only liable for damages to the immediate buyer, often an intermediary such as a store or wholesale supplier, and not to the ultimate consumer of the product. If this immunity still existed, the makers of IUDs or football helmets wouldn't have to worry about so many suits.

Along with some other changes—such as the Supreme Court deciding in 1977 to allow lawyer advertising—these judge-driven innovations are in large measure responsible for drenching America in a litigation tide.

New Theories of Liability

It's hard to realize just how radical the redefinition of tort law has been because it's happened so slowly over a long period of time; by the time most of us were aware of its consequences, it was a fait accompli. But in fact, the revolution never stops; liability is constantly expanding. A legal newspaper explains how the process works: An attorney or law professor comes up with a new cause of action, which must then undergo a "long and arduous process" of "gaining the willingness of judges to allow the causes to proceed."

Among the new theories striving for acceptance is medical battery, holding doctors liable for the sin of trying to *save* patients. Brenda Young of Flint, Michigan, had a massive seizure and was rushed to the hospital, where, a newspaper account informs us, doctors "made heroic efforts to save her." They succeeded, but she was left in a near-vegetative state. Her mother sued because Brenda had signed a "living will" authorizing her, the mother, to decline treatment. For treating Brenda, the doctors got socked in 1996 with a $16.58 million verdict, reduced by the judge to $1.4 million. In another medical battery case, however, the doctors were held not liable by a jury for giving a patient antibiotics despite the "patient advocate's" refusal of treatment.

Another innovative (a polite way of saying "far-fetched") plaintiff's theory is that guns don't kill people, gun manufacturers do. U.S. district judge Jack Weinstein, who has pioneered many torts, ruled in 1996 that a family of two shooting victims could proceed with a suit against the gun makers on the theory that manufacturers should take greater steps to stop potential criminals from buying their product. However, another federal judge in New York, Harold Baer (the drug judge we met in Chapter 3), ruled against the victims of Colin Ferguson's murderous rampage on a Long Island commuter train in their attempts to hold the gun maker liable. A panel of the U.S. Second Circuit Court of Appeals upheld Baer's ruling, 2–1, over the dissent of Judge Guido Calabresi, a progressive thinker from Yale who seems enthusiastic about establishing this new tort.

Neither medical battery nor gun-maker liability has gained widespread acceptance in courtrooms—yet. But if they do, the implications for the legal system could be staggering, as an example from the field of employment law makes clear.

Title VII of the 1964 Civil Rights Act prohibits workplace discrimination based on race, sex, and other factors. Courts in the 1970s typically interpreted the law as meaning bosses were forbidden to make put-out-or-get-out demands on female employees. But that didn't satisfy Catharine MacKinnon, the radical feminist theoretician, who suggested, with virtually no foundation, that Title VII also outlawed a "hostile environment," which is to say practically any actions that would offend a "reasonable person's" sensibilities. The Supreme Court adopted this expansive standard in 1986, creating vast new horizons for suits:

- A secretary won $6.9 million (later reduced to $3.8 million) from law megafirm Baker & McKenzie. Among other charges, she accused a partner of dropping some M&Ms into her blouse pocket and asking her, "What's the wildest thing you've ever done?"

- Then there's the $50 million award against Wal-Mart (reduced to $5 million). Among the store's sins was not disciplining a supervisor who referred to women as "goddamn dummies."

- In another hostile environment case, an Atlantic City, New Jersey, female police sergeant won $1.3 million, in part because on one occasion a sanitary napkin marked with sergeant's stripes was hung from the ceiling while she conducted roll call.

Such behavior is clearly boorish, to say the least. But if we want to punish such transgressions with such large fines, elected legislators should pass a law saying so. That's not what happened; these multi-million-dollar payouts are all the judges' and juries' doing.

Politicians, Keep Out

When mere politicians do try to intervene in tort law, judges often tell them to get lost. Since the early 1980s, most state legislatures have passed tort reform statutes, typically to limit punitive damages, joint and several liability (the "deep pockets" rule), or some other aspect of expanding liability. More than sixty state court decisions have been issued since the early 1980s invalidating many of these statutes on the grounds that they somehow violate state constitution guarantees of access to the courts. In 1996, Illinois judges struck down *all* of the tort reforms passed by the legislature the previous year, including caps on noneconomic and punitive damages. One court claimed that the legislature couldn't "usurp the powers of the judicial branch" to regulate torts. (That decision was upheld in 1997 by the Illinois Supreme Court.)

This should come as news to other states, where judges have upheld equally stringent tort reform measures under not very different constitutional provisions. For that matter, if the limitations on legislative power suddenly discovered by the Illinois court had existed decades earlier, it would have been impossible for legislatures to deny injured workers the right to a jury trial in a variety of cases by forcing them into a workers' compensation system governed by administrative boards.

But decisions like the one in Illinois are about as securely grounded in precedent as a dying tree's roots in topsoil. State constitutions give legislatures the authority to pass laws. The state courts are saying, "No, you can't pass laws rolling back our expansions of liability." As in areas such as term limits and abortion, the juristocracy is changing the constitution by ukase.

"Send a Message": The Expansion of Punitive Damages

THE LOEWEN Group, Inc., a Canadian funeral home chain, almost went bankrupt in 1996. It wasn't because the company was badly run or because consumers weren't buying its products. Loewen's misfortune was to come up on the losing side of the punitive damages lottery in America's courts.

A Mississippi jury lit up the company for $100 million in compensatory damages and $400 million in punitive damages, considerably more than its total annual sales. The company's sin? It had crossed the powerful former mayor of Biloxi, who also owned some local funeral homes. The former mayor claimed that Loewen had backed out of an agreement to buy two of his funeral homes and to sell him a small insurance company. "Much of the plaintiff's case was not about contractual matters," said one of Loewen's executives, "but [was] an attempt to paint our company as ruthless predators oppressing the poor people of Mississippi." Indeed, one of the jurors later said she was "really disturbed" that Loewen raises prices at funeral homes it acquires. This, she averred, "makes it too expensive for the poor people to be buried, and I'm one of the poor people."

And where was the judge in all this? State judge James Graves Jr. refused to reduce the jury award, and the Mississippi Supreme Court held that if Loewen wanted to appeal, it would have to post a bond for $625 million within a week. Staring into the bankruptcy abyss, Loewen settled with the plaintiffs, agreeing to pay $175 million over twenty years.

Cases like this demonstrate the devastating effect that punitive damages can have. Compensatory damages are designed to make injured people whole and to force tortfeasors (a.k.a. the bad guys) to internalize the cost of their misconduct. Punitive damages, by contrast, exist to punish unlawful conduct and deter wrongdoing in the future. These are essentially criminal penalties, but with some major differences.

For a start, they're imposed by juries with virtually no guidelines; in the Loewen case, the jurors seemed to pick the $500 million number out of a hat (the properties in question had a value of only $8.5 million). Such fines are often far in excess of comparable criminal penalties—yet judges frequently do nothing to bring these stratospheric awards down to earth.

Also unlike criminal penalties, punitive damages are sought by attorneys who have a big pecuniary stake in the outcome. These plaintiffs' lawyers, who style themselves as private attorneys general, often wind up getting one-third or more of any award—a major incentive to seek the penalty, whether deserved or not. Thus, it's hardly surprising to find that in California, punitive damages are demanded in almost one-third of the suits where they're available. Naturally, lawyers resist like mad any proposal that punitive awards should go to the government or to charity, instead of to them and their clients.

Plaintiffs' lawyers usually urge a jury to "send a message" with their punitive award, a message designed (as a leading trial lawyer put it) to "deter despicable acts by corporate America." But often these awards are made in complex contract case like Loewen's, where the acts in question are far from despicable. And no matter what the conduct, it's usually hard to understand the message the jurors are sending with a punitive award.

Consider one of the most famous tort cases in America. In 1994, Stella Liebeck won $2.7 million (later reduced to "only" $480,000) from McDonald's because she got burned by spilling hot coffee on

herself. The coffee in question was 180 degrees (the same temperature, incidentally, as in most electric home coffeemakers). What is
McDonald's to do? "Will it be insulated from punitive damages by
turning its pots down to 175 degrees, 170, 165?" asks Judge Alex
Kozinski. "There's no telling."

These quasi-criminal penalties are especially unfair when they're
awarded more than once. The Constitution's double-jeopardy clause
protects criminal defendants from being prosecuted twice for the same
crime. But a civil defendant can face multiple punitive damage awards
for essentially the same act, with devastating consequences.

A. H. Robins was driven into bankruptcy by thousands of cases filed
over the Dalkon Shield. In one case, the company was hit for $7.5 mil-
lion in punitive damages; in another, for $6.2 million. Piper Aircraft
Company, a maker of small airplanes, and Johns Manville Corporation,
an asbestos manufacturer, are among the other companies driven onto
the bankruptcy rocks by the scourge of punitive damages. It's almost
impossible, as Judge Henry Friendly once noted, to avoid "overkill" in
awarding punitive damages "in such a multiplicity of actions."

The Disproportionate Impact of Punitive Damages

Unpredictable. Arbitrary. Devastating. Punitive damages are one of
the worst features of the modern litigation system.

In defending punitive damages, lawyers and law professors often
argue that they are rarely given out. True enough. A 1995 Justice
Department study, often cited by defenders of the system like Ralph
Nader, found that punitive damages are awarded in just 6 percent of
cases won by a plaintiff. In the first place, the study is misleading
because it only surveyed major jurisdictions, whereas big punitive
damage awards often occur in places like backwoods Alabama. But
even if punitive awards are rare, that's about as reassuring as saying
that when you play Russian roulette, your chances of splattering your
brains over the dining room rug are only one in six. When the consequences of a misstep are so catastrophic, any prudent individual will
go to considerable lengths to avoid the risk altogether.

In litigation, that means defendants are willing to settle for more
just because the threat of punitive damages always looms on the hori-
zon. Since 98 percent of cases are settled, it's a good bet that punitive

damages have a much larger effect on the civil justice system than the 6 percent figure would suggest.

And thanks to indulgent judges, the effect is getting bigger all the time. Traditionally, punitive damages were reserved for particular types of cases involving intentional wrongs—libel, false imprisonment, malicious prosecution, and the like—but in the last few decades, judges have allowed the expansion of punitive damages into fields such as products liability. "Recently," writes Justice Sandra Day O'Connor, "the frequency and size of such awards have been skyrocketing and it appears that the upward trajectory continues unabated."

- In Texas, the total amount affirmed in punitive damages between 1968 and 1971 was $85,000. Jump ahead two decades to another two-year period: From 1992 to 1994, the courts affirmed *$186 million* in punitive awards.

- In California, the largest punitive damage award between 1872 and 1959 was $10,000. Between 1990 and 1994, by contrast, California juries issued twenty verdicts of *$15 million or greater* (the total amount awarded in punitive damages during this period was $1.7 billion).

Punitive damages have become especially popular in financial cases like Loewen's. A 1997 RAND study found that "punitive damages represent more than half of total damages in financial injury verdicts." The average punitive damage award in these cases more than doubled from 1985 to 1994, to reach a whopping $5.2 million. Mind you, all this money is not awarded for broken limbs or mangled bodies, but for disagreements over how to read a piece of paper.

"*Enough!*"

Judges stood by while this explosion of punitive damages was occurring and did nothing. The Supreme Court finally cried "Enough!" with its landmark 1996 decision in *BMW v. Gore*.

Dr. Ira Gore Jr. of Birmingham, Alabama, bought a BMW 535i in 1990 and drove it for nine months without noticing anything amiss. Then he discovered that the car's paint job had been partially refinished after shipment from Germany. BMW dealers do this routinely with cars that suffer minor damage in transit; it's exactly what most customers would want. But for not disclosing this touch-up job, Dr. Gore took BMW to court.

He hit all the cherries on the tort slot machine: The jury awarded him $4,000 in compensatory damages and a whopping $4 million in punitive damages. (An earlier, virtually identical case in Alabama had brought in just $4,600 in compensatory damages and no punitive damages at all, underlining the capricious nature of the process.) The Alabama Supreme Court decided Gore's award was excessive and reduced the payout to "only" $2 million. Still, not bad: $2 million for a paint job.

The U.S. Supreme Court, by a 5–4 margin, held that even this award violated the Fourteenth Amendment's Due Process Clause. However, the decision was hardly cause for celebration. In the first place, as Justice Scalia and other dissenters pointed out, the Constitution doesn't say anything about punitive damages; the majority in this case thus appears as guilty of activism as the majority that overturned Colorado's anti–gay rights Amendment 2 on that same day. Cutting down punitive damages should be a job for state courts and legislators, not the highest federal court in the land.

The second problem with the *Gore* decision is that it's unclear how much of an impact it will have. Justice John Paul Stevens' majority opinion sets out three "guideposts" for judging whether punitive awards are unconstitutional, but as Justice Ruth Bader Ginsburg noted in her dissent, the court didn't establish any "mathematical formula" or "bright line," so the ruling may not promote greater uniformity and predictability in punitive awards. In Dr. Gore's case, after the U.S. Supreme Court ruling, Alabama's supreme court wound up reducing his punitive award to $50,000; it's hard to see why that represents a "fairer" award for a paint scratch than any other figure.

The punitive damages tidal wave seems likely to keep on washing over American courts for many years to come. Indeed, little more than a year after the *Gore* decision, a jury in New Orleans socked a railroad for $2.5 billion in punitive damages (and a total award of $3.37 billion) for a chemical accident that caused neither serious bodily harm nor major property damage. Such awards will keep on coming until more state judges realize they have a responsibility to assure that outcomes in their courtrooms don't fly in the face of all reason and logic. Individual trial judges should exercise their responsibility by reducing or throwing out sky-high punitive damage awards, but too often they don't.

Compensation Without Causation: The Problem with Mass Litigation

SOMETHING IS seriously amiss in America's courts when judges allow verdicts that violate the most basic principle of common law, which is that in order to collect damages from someone you have to show that the person was responsible for harming you. This age-old rule has gotten tossed overboard in our current enthusiasm for litigation. Watching the development of mass litigation, with questionable experts testifying to just about anything and with the number of suits seemingly more important than their quality, it's easy to conclude that truth is now irrelevant in many courtrooms.

The star witness in support of this alarming proposition is the by-now familiar breast implant saga. Starting in the 1980s, lawsuits began to charge that silicone gel breast implants caused a host of maladies, principally autoimmune diseases. The success of the claims multiplied geometrically. In 1985, a plaintiff won $1.7 million. In 1991, a woman won $7.3 million. In 1994, the award in one Texas case was up to $28 million. That same year, breast implant manufacturers agreed to a whopping $4.2 billion class-action settlement, which proved inadequate when more than 400,000 women—the vast majority of whom didn't even claim to be sick—registered for a handout. But that didn't stop the onslaught of individual suits, so Dow Corning, a multibillion dollar company, was forced into Chapter 11 bankruptcy in May 1995.

Throughout all this litigation, the most salient fact about breast implants, as *Fortune* magazine noted, was this: "*There has yet to be published a single peer-reviewed study that supports the central allegation behind the lawsuits*—that silicone gel implants cause disease." (Italics in original.) In fact, more than twenty peer-reviewed studies have been published by such reputable institutions as the Mayo Clinic and Harvard University, all coming to essentially the same conclusion: "At most, breast implants could be a very weak risk factor for disease," writes Dr. Marcia Angell of the *New England Journal of Medicine*, but "the best evidence now is a relative risk of 1.0, indicating no contribution of

implants to disease." It is undoubtedly true that there are many genuinely sick women with breast implants, which is what you would
expect of any group of more than 1 million people, but as Dr. Angell's
comment indicates, the *percentage* of sick women is no higher than that
among the general population.

The most favorable study for the plaintiffs' cause was published in
the *Journal of the American Medical Association* in 1996. This Harvard
study of 10,830 women reported that those with breast implants had a
slightly higher incidence of connective tissue disease than those in a
control group. But the increase in disease was so small—and based on
self-reporting by women at a time of media hysteria over implants—
that the study's authors themselves didn't think it was very significant.
The lead investigator, Dr. Charles Hennekens of Harvard Medical
School, summed up the results in the *New York Times:* "Our study's
great contribution is to show that the idea that women with implants
had a large hazard of connective tissue disease is not plausible."

It's disheartening to see the consensus of the scientific community,
as summed up by Drs. Angell and Hennekens, diverge so dramatically
from the consensus of the courtrooms. Who is responsible for this
confounding outcome? Plaintiff's lawyers certainly raided the vault,
but it was judges who opened the bank for business.

The judges allowed a traveling road show of "expert" testifiers into
one courtroom after another, where they presented juries with just
enough pseudoscientific mumbo jumbo to justify a verdict in favor of a
sympathetic, sick plaintiff. Such experts included a Houston doctor
who saw 4,700 women with breast implants in two years, all of whom
were referred to him by plaintiffs' lawyers, and diagnosed 93 percent
of them with some illness. And then there's the UCLA pathologist
who marketed a test to detect silicone-induced disease, even though
there's no evidence that such a disease exists. Many of these experts
made hundreds of thousands of dollars a year from their courtroom
activities. None had published a single peer-reviewed study in a reputable scientific journal backing up their claims.

By allowing these experts to testify, countless trial judges violated
their duty to keep junk science out of court. Under the old Frye rule,
judges were bound to keep out of evidence any scientific testimony
that hasn't won "general acceptance." In the 1993 *Daubert v. Merrell
Dow* case, which came in the middle of the breast implant onslaught,

the Supreme Court articulated an arguably stricter standard: Judges are supposed to be "gatekeepers" who must "ensure that any and all scientific testimony or evidence admitted is not only relevant, but reliable." Obviously, the testimony of a handful of professional testifiers—which flew in the face of the consensus in the scientific community—was neither relevant nor reliable. Yet judges allowed these "experts" enough leeway to torpedo the good ship Dow Corning.

In this sea of guilty judges, one deserves extra opprobrium. She is Connie Steinheimer, a state judge in Reno, Nevada. Plaintiffs' lawyers scored a notable victory in her court in 1995—they won a $14.1 million verdict against Dow Chemical, a company that never manufactured implants. Virtually the only connection Dow had with implants was owning 50 percent of Dow Corning; imagine holding an IBM stockholder, even a large one, legally responsible for decisions made by the company's CEO. To avoid such an absurd outcome, judges in New York, Michigan, and California have barred all breast implant claims against Dow. But Judge Steinheimer not only allowed the plaintiffs' lawyers to take their case against Dow to a jury, she later refused to reduce the outrageously high award.

Following Steinheimer's lead, Louisiana state judge Yada Magess allowed a jury to find Dow Chemical liable for breast implant damages in a class-action trial in 1997. By contrast, Texas state judge Michael Schneider, after presiding over a jury trial on the home turf of the plaintiffs' lawyers, showed great bravery in 1995 in throwing out the only other breast implant verdict against Dow Chemical.

In 1996 and 1997, the tide in breast implant cases finally turned against the plaintiffs (though not completely, as the verdict in Judge Magess's court makes clear). Defendants began winning jury verdicts, and judges—at last!—began exercising their *Daubert* responsibility to sift through the science. U.S. district judge Sam Pointer Jr., overseeing the sprawling breast implant class action, appointed a panel of independent scientists to report on whether implants cause disease. So did federal judge Robert Jones, in charge of the Oregon breast implant cases. After his independent experts issued their report, Judge Jones barred the plaintiffs from presenting any more disease claims. Alas, such decisions are coming several years—and several billion dollars—too late.

Blackmail Settlements

The larger problem is that breast implants are far from the only case where the traditional link between causation of harm and collection of damages has been severed. The same thing has happened in all too many other mass torts, where the sheer volume of cases blackmails defendants into settling, and judges fecklessly approve the settlements, no matter the merits.

The case that set the pattern, the archetype, was the Agent Orange litigation, where some 240,000 veterans and their lawyers managed to collect $180 million from Dow and other chemical companies as part of a 1984 settlement essentially forced on the parties by federal judge Jack Weinstein. The judge approved the settlement in order to get the cases out of the court system, an appeals court later wrote, even though "he viewed the plaintiffs' case as so weak as to be virtually baseless."

The trend started by Judge Weinstein reached its natural culmination after a General Chemical Corporation plant released a cloud of sulfuric acid over Richmond, California, in 1993. Ambulance chasers quickly rushed to the scene. Eventually, reports *American Lawyer* magazine, "almost 200 law firms and solo practitioners filed some 150 suits (coordinated into a single state court proceeding) on behalf of roughly 65,000 individuals—who claimed damages for physical injuries, emotional distress, and annoyance." The company, wanting to avoid costly litigation, settled for $150 million. Yet an examination of medical records by *American Lawyer* magazine revealed that fewer than two dozen of these claimants were even hospitalized; there was no evidence that anyone was seriously injured. Federal judge Richard Patsey, living up to his name, rubber-stamped this ridiculous settlement—including $50 million in fees for the lawyers.

Even in the asbestos cases, where there's no doubt that some plaintiffs were genuinely harmed, most of those receiving benefits are no more unhealthy than the lawyers representing them. Experts estimate that just 10 percent of the plaintiffs suffer from cancer and another 10 percent or less suffer from serious asbestosis, a scarring of the lungs. The other 80 percent aren't sick at all; most of them have nothing more than "pleural plaques," or darkenings on their chest X rays, which, according to the scientific literature, don't interfere with lung functions or predispose them to early death.

Yet the legal system allows the uninjured to cash in. And how. Over the past several decades, more than 250,000 asbestos cases have been filed, with the total cost for handling them estimated at $15 billion to $20 billion. Defendants have won most of the trials, but few cases are adjudicated on their merits. Instead, hundreds and even thousands of cases are bunched together, forcing defendants to settle rather than face a "bet the company" trial. As part of these aggregations, judges have set up a tort assembly line where plaintiffs can automatically get money according to complex formulas. The only "proof" required to collect is to claim that you were exposed to asbestos, usually on the job, and that you now suffer some lung impairment. Neither courts nor defendants ever check the validity of most claims. In this kind of environment, it's hardly surprising that defendant Owens Corning found that some 40,000 plaintiffs falsified their medical records.

But falsified or not, the fact remains that you don't have to prove a link between asbestos and disease in order to collect money. In fact, some plaintiffs have actually won jury verdicts simply because they *feared* they might one day develop cancer. So much for the hallowed principle of causation. Judges don't have time for such niceties any more. They've decided it's more important to push mass tort cases through the system, whether the issue is breast implants, asbestos, or Agent Orange, rather than quibble about whether each—or any—of the plaintiffs was actually injured.

In their own defense, judges say they have no choice, given the overwhelming number of cases clogging up their dockets. But is this vast increase in litigiousness really due to the inherent dangers of society? That's what defenders of the legal system argue. But think back to the early years of the twentieth century, to the days of Upton Sinclair's *The Jungle*, when tainted food products and injured workers were far more commonplace, yet there was far less litigation. In the years since, America has become a much safer place by any indication—yet the number of suits has skyrocketed. It's hard not to conclude that litigation is increasing not in response to actual harms but simply because it's so easy to file suit. And who's responsible for opening the courthouse doors? Hint: They wear black robes. Judges have nobody to blame but themselves if they now find their dockets so swamped that they can't sort out good cases from bad.

The Class Struggle:
How Judges Abet Class-Action Scams

WHEN ASKED why he robbed banks, Willie Sutton famously replied, "That's where the money is." Today, Willie would no doubt be a class-action lawyer. Judges have made class actions a lucrative hunting ground for trial lawyers—and a costly one for consumers.

Modern class actions were born in 1966 from the loins of the judicial, not the legislative, branch. That was the year the Judicial Conference of the United States adopted a new Rule 23 of the Federal Rules of Civil Procedure. The new rule, crafted by a committee of lawyers and judges handpicked by Chief Justice Earl Warren, and fired up by what one of its members later called a "fairly simplistic good guy–bad guy outlook on the world," radically expanded the class-action device to do battle with the evils of segregation.

The biggest change was the nature of the opt-out device. Previously, plaintiffs had to actively "opt into" a class action to be represented. From that time on, however, a class action was assumed to represent all the potential plaintiffs who didn't actively "opt out." Since most class members aren't even aware of suits filed on their behalf, few opt out, so this has created an opportunity for plaintiffs' lawyers to bring cases on behalf of thousands of clients—without actually signing them up.

In Joseph Conrad's *The Secret Agent*, a terrorist stalks though London, carrying in his pocket a bomb that he threatens to detonate at any minute, should the police close in on him. The effect of Rule 23—though it wasn't intended by its idealistic drafters—was to place in the hands of plaintiffs' lawyers a bomb of their own that they could use to extort settlements from countless companies. When a judge certifies a class action, the effect is much like that of punitive damages, tremendously enhancing the potential destructive power of a lawsuit, as the Agent Orange and breast implant cases made clear. Most defendants shirk from the danger and gladly produce their wallet to stop the bomb from detonating.

From the perspective of plaintiffs' lawyers, the class-action device has one other major advantage: The actual clients have no say over the outcome, so they're unlikely to object to deals that benefit primarily the lawyers. "While in theory the class action lawyers must be responsive to their clients," notes former senator William Cohen, who once introduced (unsuccessful) legislation to reform class actions, "in practice the lawyers control all aspects of the litigation."

The only protection for plaintiffs—a.k.a. consumers—is afforded by judges. A trial judge has broad discretion, bound only by vague and general rules promulgated by higher courts, about whether to certify a class action. And once certified, the judge has a great deal of leeway to reject a settlement or to demand changes before accepting it. But most judges find it easier to just go along with the settlement rather than undertake the difficult and time-consuming work of scrutinizing the details. As a result, class actions have turned into the scam-of-the-month club.

Nothing better exemplifies this trend than a Texas case settled in 1996. This class-action suit, filed by Dallas lawyer John R. W. Cracken, alleged that Allstate and Farmers Insurance ripped off Texas drivers through an obscure practice known as "double rounding."

When calculating premiums, the insurers rounded once to calculate the yearly rate and then rounded a second time to calculate each six-month payment. If the annual premium was $1,000.50, the insurers would round it up to $1,001. Then they would round up the semiannual premium again—from $500.50 to $501. So in this example, the driver would pay $1,002 per year, or an extra $1.50.

Obviously, this wasn't a very costly practice. The plaintiffs' lawyers themselves calculated that in a typical scenario, a driver may have been overcharged $35 over ten years. Yet the plaintiffs demanded $109 million on behalf of all Texas drivers.

In response, the insurers solicited affidavits (unpaid, they say) from the bureaucrats at the Texas Department of Insurance who actually oversaw auto policies, and they all said that double rounding was not only legal but required by the state. Texas insurance commissioner Elton Bomer confirmed that as recently as 1991, his department informed insurance companies (erroneously, he says) that double rounding was the law. So here was the spectacle of insurance companies being sued for doing what the state told them to.

And where did the lawyers choose to file their blockbuster suit? Not, heaven forbid, in any of Texas's major cities, where most of the drivers live. Instead, they filed in Zavala County, a plaintiff-friendly, dirt-poor jurisdiction located near the Mexican border. Among the "lead" plaintiffs whom Attorney Cracken represented down there was José Barajas, who admits that he's illiterate in both English *and* Spanish. This handicap has disqualified him from jury duty in the past—but apparently not from "representing" the interests of millions of Texas drivers in a high-stakes class action. Speaking through an interpreter during a deposition, he acknowledged that he is "totally dependent" on the plaintiffs' lawyers: "Because since I don't know English very well, when the lawyers start talking, I'm not going to understand."

To help cinch the home-court advantage, Cracken hired a local lawyer who, conveniently enough, went to high school with the judge hearing the case. State judge Amado Abascal III duly certified a class action. Allstate and Farmers, knowing they couldn't get a fair hearing in this notoriously pro-plaintiff jurisdiction, quickly capitulated.

Here's what they agreed to: Each Texas driver insured by the two companies will be eligible for $5.50 in compensation—enough to buy a celebratory meal at McDonald's. The plaintiffs' counsel, meanwhile, got $10.3 million, or 28.9 percent of the $35.7 million total settlement. Insurance Commissioner Bomer was livid. "Class action lawsuits rarely help the consumer, but they always help the lawyer," he told me.

The commissioner added that he "can't blame the companies, because they didn't ask to be sued." Nor does it make sense to blame an entrepreneurial lawyer like John Cracken, who simply played by the rules. Blame should be affixed on judges like Amado Abascal who endorse such extortionate tactics.

Millions for the Lawyers, Pennies for the Clients

Lest you think the Texas case an aberration, I would urge you to grab a magnifying glass and carefully examine your mail or the "tombstone" ads in the back of the *Wall Street Journal*. This is where you can usually find announcements—written in tiny type and impenetrable legalese—of the latest class-action settlements.

If you can figure out the fine print, you'll invariably discover that the court-approved settlements provide millions to the lawyers and pennies to the class members. Sometimes literally. One class member sent me a check for 86 cents that he had received from a settlement with a mortgage company. Some other notable examples:

- In 1995, nine major airlines negotiated a settlement of a class-action suit charging them with fixing prices from 1988 to 1992. The lawyers got $14.4 million. The class members—4.2 million airline passengers—got coupons that would give them a small discount on future travel. The passengers couldn't even pool their certificates, so the biggest discount a traveler could get on a $204 ticket from Washington to Miami would be $10, or 5 percent. U.S. district judge Marvin Shoob in Atlanta approved this settlement, which one Naderite critic accurately described as a "glorified promotional fare offer."

- Also in 1995, General Mills settled a class-action suit accusing the company of selling millions of boxes of cereal made from oats treated with a pesticide not approved for such use. There was no public health danger; the pesticide in question was approved for use in other foods. Under the settlement approved by Cook County circuit judge Lester Foreman, the plaintiffs' lawyers got $1.75 million. Consumers received coupons in their Sunday newspapers good for a free box of cereal if presented along with proof of purchase of another General Mills product. The company was happy; it got to sell more cereal. The lawyers were happy; they got rich. And what did consumers get? Indigestion.

- The best (or worst) example is undoubtedly the Bank of Boston settlement. The bank deposited up to $8.76 in each class member's account, but to pay $8.5 million in lawyers' fees, the bank then withdrew up to $90 from some accounts. In other words, the settlement wound up *costing* some plaintiffs money. This Alice-in-Wonderland deal was approved by Alabama judge Braxton L. Kittrell Jr. Some of the outraged class members tried suing their putative attorneys, but the cases were tossed out of state and federal court.

A few judges have declared war—call it class warfare—on such unfair suits. Led by Judge Richard Posner of the Seventh U.S. Circuit Court of Appeals, some federal courts have begun to carefully scrutinize attempts to bring class actions in product liability cases. Realizing that merely certifying the class coerces most defendants into settling regardless of the merits, they have actually begun to deny some requests. In 1996, for instance, the Fifth Circuit decertified the Mother of All Class Actions, the *Castano* case filed against the cigarette makers on behalf of every smoker of the last several decades. The courts have decided that in such suits, the plaintiffs are so differently situated—some seriously ill, others not—that it doesn't make sense to pool their claims.

Some judges are also giving more careful scrutiny to coupon settlements that deliver few benefits for plaintiffs. Federal judge John Nagle reduced from $33 million to $10 million the fees for plaintiffs' lawyers in a class settlement over a purportedly defective heart valve made by Pfizer. The U.S. Court of Appeals for the Third Circuit tore up a settlement that would have provided coupons worth $1,000 to the owners of GM pickup trucks with side-mounted fuel tanks while giving the lawyers $9.5 million. And federal judge Morey Sear tossed out a class action over the Ford Bronco II that offered the plaintiffs $200 for parts and repairs, the lawyers $4 million in cash.

But these overturned settlements are still very much the exception, not the rule. And even though federal judges are getting tougher, lawyers can always find pliable state judges to approve settlements—as in the Bank of Boston and General Mills examples—that bind class members across the nation. More fundamental reforms seem unlikely. The Judicial Conference is tinkering with Rule 23, but attorney John Frank, one of the original drafters of the rule in 1966, says, "I do not believe this rule [change] will end any of the abuses of class actions." He's got a point: Substantial reform of class actions—which would require changing Rule 23 to eliminate opt-out class actions—seems a long way off. And in the meantime, attorneys will continue to use consumer class actions—just as they use the public policy class actions that we examined in Chapter 5—to impose their will on millions of Americans who have no say in the matter.

Conclusion: More Activism, Please

WHAT'S THE solution to the problem of runaway liability? The legislative approach would be to cap punitive damages, impose the English Rule (loser pays), abolish opt-out class actions, limit junk science, and so on. Those are all good ideas. But there's an even simpler solution—oddly enough, judicial activism.

I know, I know. I've spent most of the rest of the book decrying activist judges. But as I keep emphasizing, the problem isn't judicial activism per se, it's activism in areas where the courts don't belong, such as setting social policy. The proper outlet for judicial energy is disposing of frivolous cases that are clogging up the courts and wasting money. If judges got serious about doing their duty, they could effectively cure the problem of excessive litigation, instead of merely addressing its symptoms (for example, punitive damages or "junk science"), as legislative proposals attempt to do.

A good precedent has been set in this regard by Stanley Mosk, the liberal lion of the California Supreme Court, appointed in the 1960s by Governor Pat Brown. Judge Mosk and his colleagues ruled in 1996 in a landmark case involving electromagnetic fields. The electromagnetic field (EMF) scare was launched by Paul Brodeur, a *New Yorker* writer who had previously drummed up hysteria about microwaves, asbestos, and ozone. In 1989, he moved on to claiming that high-voltage power lines cause leukemia and brain cancer. The understated titles of his works give you the flavor: A *New Yorker* article called "Calamity on Meadow Street" and two books, *Currents of Death* and *The Great Power-Line Cover-Up.*

Talk about a high-voltage scare! By one estimate, half of all American homes are located close enough to power lines to be affected. That's enough potential litigants to dwarf the 400,000 who signed up for the breast implant settlement. Never mind that the scientific evidence supporting Mr. Brodeur's conclusions was, to be charitable, shaky. Lack of causation has never been a bar to mass torts; as we've seen, plaintiffs' lawyers simply pile up enough cases to zap defendants into submission.

Indeed, by the early 1990s, a perceptive observer could see the EMF litigation powering up like the Death Star in *Star Wars.* Plaintiffs' lawyers organized themselves into a consortium called the Electromagnetic Radiation Case Evaluation Team and filed more than two dozen cases—some with as many as thirty-three plaintiffs—against utilities nationwide. The lawyers marshaled "expert" witnesses, and hordes of "victims" organized support groups. The plaintiffs even came up with a novel theory to get around the inconvenient lack of causation evidence: demanding money not because power lines are objectively dangerous but because the *perception* of their danger could drive down home values. If that's the case, perhaps they should be suing Paul Brodeur, who's more responsible for that perception than the utility companies.

A leading EMF suit was filed by the Covalt family, alleging all sorts of horrors after San Diego Gas and Electric increased the number of power lines near their backyard. The trial judge wanted to let a jury hear the case, but the state court of appeals stepped in to say that power lines are the domain of the California Public Utilities Commission, which hasn't found EMF to be a threat. The Covalts appealed. In response, the state supreme court not only affirmed the appeals court decision but issued such a sweeping ruling that similar suits might be laughed out of court in the future.

The unanimous opinion, written by Justice Mosk, is peppered with such phrases as "misses the mark," "unsound," "lacks merit," and "untenable." In judgespeak, that's like saying, "Gimme a break!" The ruling included a thorough review of the science on EMF. This was not an inquiry that could have had a happy outcome for the scaremongers, since fourteen leading scientists, including six Nobel laureates, filed a brief concluding "that the evidence does not justify the fears that are claimed by the plaintiffs." Indeed, Justice Mosk dismissed the one alarmist study cited by the plaintiffs, noting that the American Medical Association, the Oak Ridge National Laboratory, and the American Physical Society have all debunked the EMF bogeyman. "The bottom line is that this decision kills the mass tort marketing effort for EMF in California," said a lawyer for San Diego Gas and Electric.

The best part of this ruling is the way Justice Mosk deferred to the legislative and executive branches. He wrote that the Public Utilities Commission is welcome do something about EMFs, but the courts won't intervene: "An award of damages . . . would interfere with the policy of the commission on power-line electric and magnetic fields."

The EMF case is a welcome recognition that there are some complex policy questions that the courts, ruling on a case-by-case basis, aren't very good at sorting out. Lawmakers and regulators are far from perfect, but how many would tell utilities to spend billions of dollars—which means adding thousands of dollars to each customer's bill—to deal with speculative power-line problems? How many would voluntarily remove swing sets from playgrounds just because a child occasionally gets injured? Or stop the introduction of new and improved IUDs because of the Dalkon Shield mess? That kind of lunacy can only occur if judges allow juries to haphazardly issue half-baked verdicts.

The moral of the EMF story: It's not hard to stop meritless litigation. We don't even need any new laws. All we need is for more judges to show the humility of Stanley Mosk in recognizing that courts shouldn't provide relief to everybody with a toxic grievance.

CHAPTER 7

Justice for Rent

JUDGES WHO

ARE ETHICALLY

CHALLENGED

I don't want to know what the law is, I want to know who the judge is.
ROY COHN, *The New York Times*

IT WILL NOT have escaped the attentive reader's notice that many of the tort atrocities mentioned in the last chapter were concentrated in a few places, such as Texas and California. Many others occur in Alabama, Mississippi, and a handful of other states. This is no coincidence. These are all areas where juries are fired up by populist resentments to sock it to big defendants, and judges all too often look the other way—sometimes after taking campaign donations from one of the parties appearing before them.

The results can be pretty rotten. For evidence, look no further than the flyspeck town of Decatur in North Texas, seat of Wise County (population 34,679). In 1995, a jury there awarded a whopping $204 million to eight local families. The cause of action? Smelly water.

Seems that the water in the neighboring town of Boyd has a foul odor, reminiscent of rotten eggs. The locals knew of the water's poor quality when they first moved into the area; it had smelled for years.

But the residents suddenly decided that the cause of their problems was Mitchell Energy and Development Corporation of faraway Houston, which owned some local natural gas wells. A group of Boyd residents took Mitchell to court, blaming their smelly water on hydrogen sulfide from Mitchell's wells.

To establish Mitchell's liability, the plaintiffs brought in two "expert" witnesses. Neither one could point to credible scientific evidence that Mitchell's wells were the cause of the problem. Indeed, an appeals court would later rule that there was not a "scintilla of evidence that hydrogen sulfide was present in Mitchell's gas wells." Nevertheless, one of the expert witnesses uttered a magic incantation—he was sure to "a reasonable degree of scientific certainty," he testified, that Mitchell was at fault. That was excuse enough for the jury to light up the out-of-town company like a Las Vegas slot machine.

The staggering damages awarded by the jurors were out of all proportion to any harm suffered by the plaintiffs. Even the plaintiffs' attorney, W. T. Womble, acknowledged to me that the evidence of physical harm "was not overwhelming." In fact, it amounted to a few headaches, lethargy, and the like. Yet the jury awarded $412,500 for physical pain and another $3.3 million for "mental anguish, discomfort, annoyance and inconvenience." The other harm suffered by the plaintiffs was the cost of buying bottled water. The jury awarded economic damages of $340,000, which buys a lot of Perrier.

The award got truly staggering because the jury decided to sock the out-of-town company with punitive damages of $200 million, four times its net earnings the previous year. Mr. Womble says the jurors were "aggravated" by evidence he presented that Mitchell allegedly hid its pollution from Texas regulators. But if the company was genuinely cheating on pollution laws, that should be a job for law enforcement. It shouldn't be an excuse for a handful of plaintiffs and their lawyers to become richer than the Beverly Hillbillies.

Up until this point, the Mitchell verdict appears to be nothing more than another punitive damage atrocity, of the kind chronicled in the previous chapter. But it's worse than that. Now, as Paul Harvey says, the rest of the story.

Turns out that local judge John Fostel, who oversaw this staggering jury verdict (and who subsequently refused to overturn the jury's decision), may not exactly have been impartial. Before winning a state district court seat in the November 1994 election, John Fostel was a name partner in the local law firm Woodruff, Fostel, Wren, & Simpson. Just thirty-three days after he assumed his seat, his former law firm filed the smelly-water suit. This case was assigned to Judge Fostel along with several others that had been filed in 1987, and he subsequently presided over the whopping jury award to the plaintiffs. His former law firm, of course, would share in the $60 to $80 million in contingency fees. Talk about backwoods justice.

But Mitchell Energy alleges that the judge had an even more direct conflict of interest. The company says that when Mr. Fostel joined the bench, he signed a buyout agreement with his law partners. That agreement promised that until January 1, 1997, Judge Fostel would continue to collect 20 percent of the contingency fees in sixty-four cases (mainly involving breast implants) that his firm was working on when he left. In short, while hearing the smelly-water case, *Judge Fostel was actually receiving compensation from the plaintiffs' lawyers.*

Mitchell alleges that the judge had another stake in the litigation as well. In 1978, the company says, Mr. Fostel bought an 80-acre property in Wise County that draws water from the Trinity Aquifer, the very aquifer that the plaintiffs allege was polluted by Mitchell's wells. Although Judge Fostel turned over the land in 1994 to his ex-wife, the company argues that Mr. Fostel or his family could file a claim against Mitchell, too. Thus, the company suggests, he "is in a position to directly benefit from his own rulings in this case."

For whatever reason, Judge Fostel refused to throw out or reduce the outrageous verdict against Mitchell. A three-judge appeals court panel, based in Fort Worth, had to do the job instead. In 1997, two years after the original verdict, the appellate judges reversed the jury award against Mitchell on the grounds that the plaintiffs should have been barred from bringing their claims by the statute of limitations and that the plaintiffs had failed to prove that Mitchell was the cause of their "injuries." The unanimous appeals court ruling is a stunning rebuke of Judge Fostel's handling of the case.

In the first place, the appeals court noted, Fostel allowed the jury to hear the testimony of two "expert" witnesses who did not have scientific evidence to back up their claims. Such unreliable evidence is inadmissible in Texas courts, and it's up to trial judges to exclude it. But Fostel didn't.

The judge did even worse on the statute of limitations question. The appeals court noted that in Texas, plaintiffs have to bring suit within two years of becoming aware of their injuries. In this case, many of the plaintiffs had lived in Boyd—and had been aware of the smelly water—for a decade before filing suit. The defense attorneys had petitioned Fostel to throw out the jury verdict on precisely that ground. But he refused to do so. By not acting, the judge subjected both sides to needless delay, worry, and expense.

These were judgment calls, of course, and there's no evidence that the judge made his decisions in bad faith. But the stench of impropriety continues to linger over his handling of the smelly-water case.

The most amazing aspect of this case is that Fostel didn't bother to inform defense lawyers about his lucrative agreement with the plaintiffs' lawyers. "It was not related or relevant in this case," Fostel told me. Mitchell Energy only discovered the relationship after the huge verdict by reading the judge's divorce decree, which promised half of the money to his former wife. At that point, Fostel, who had already ratified the jury's decision and denied defense motions for a retrial, agreed to recuse himself from the case.

But Fostel refused to retroactively disqualify himself from the already concluded trial, which would have meant vacating the $204 million verdict. A visiting judge who heard the matter backed up his colleague on the grounds that the original trial wasn't tainted, offering this curious explanation: "I see no reason why [judges] just have to give up every dime they've earned simply because they are going to move from Main Street to the courthouse."

Mitchell next filed a motion to get the judge thrown off a copycat smelly water suit brought by another group of Wise County residents represented by the judge's old law firm. Two former Texas Supreme Court justices testified on behalf of Mitchell that Fostel had a clear conflict in presiding over the litigation. The judge, while saying he "disagree[d]" with the defendants over the merits of the motion, agreed to recuse himself from the pending case. "Because of the magnitude and the size of the case . . ." the judge said, "if there is anyone that does not want me sitting on this case, I am not going to do it." Fostel, however, changed his mind when a third smelly-water case came along. This one, he wanted to hear; another judge had to recuse him at the defendant's request.

And what happened in the copycat case that Fostel recused himself from? The trial took place in 1997 with a visiting judge from Fort Worth presiding. This jurist excluded one of the plaintiffs' "expert" witnesses who wanted to testify about the supposed health effects of the smelly water; defense lawyers say that Judge Fostel, by contrast, denied all their motions to exclude dubious testifiers. The result? The jury in the second case ruled unanimously in favor of Mitchell on all counts.

Different judge, different result. A coincidence? Perhaps. But cases like this one make clear that there's something rotten in our civil justice system. Maybe it's something in the water.

Injudicious Politics:
Campaign Donations and the Juristocracy

A LOT OF goo-goos (old-fashioned slang for good-government advocates) get overly alarmed when they see money flooding into House and Senate races. In and of itself, however, there's nothing particularly wrong with congressional candidates accepting campaign cash from donors with an interest in legislation. Nobody but the most pursed-lips Common Cause type could possibly expect politicians to be disinterested arbiters of the policy process. Lawmakers are openly, admittedly, gloriously partisan, and if they happen to represent the interest groups that donated to them, then so be it; other politicians presumably speak for competing causes, and the clashing interests are somehow reconciled in the legislative cauldron.

But judges aren't politicians, at least in theory. They're not supposed to represent any interest other than the law. Yet while Lady Justice may be blind, it's hard to escape the impression that in many places her scales are tilted in favor of whichever lawyer has given the most money to the local juristocracy. Sometimes, as we'll see, those contributions take the traditional form of bags of cash slipped under the table; sometimes the money comes in the form of contingency fees, of the kind Judge Fostel received. But more often these days, the contributions are perfectly legal—they're called "campaign donations." No matter what you call it, though, it creates a conflict of interest for judges to take money from current or future litigants.

The problem is especially acute in states like Texas, where judges are selected in partisan elections. Like any other political candidates, judges have to raise money for their campaigns. And who contributes to these (usually) obscure candidates? Who else but lawyers—and often lawyers who will have business pending before the very judicial candidates they're supporting.

The litigation explosion of recent years has vastly increased the amount of money sloshing around judicial campaigns. Both plaintiffs' lawyers and business defendants realize that judges can hold the key to their livelihood in years ahead, so they're both determined to make their impact felt in judicial races. In Ohio, business interests, plaintiffs lawyers, unions, and various other special interests poured more than $600,000 into political action committees that ran advertising campaigns backing state supreme court candidates in 1996. The four court candidates themselves spent $1.2 million. In Texas, candidates for three state supreme court seats spent $10.7 million in 1994, after the legislature passed a tort reform bill that was widely expected to be challenged in court.

Trying to figure out the relationship between inputs (campaign donations) and outputs (court decisions) poses a chicken-and-egg problem. Do various interests give more to judicial candidates because the legal system is suddenly more lucrative, or is the legal system more lucrative because various interests are giving more to judicial candidates? Ultimately, it doesn't matter; what counts is that such heavy spending raises the specter of ethical problems dogging the bench.

"If You Build a Brothel . . . ": One Judge's Campaign

In such a competitive, high-stakes environment, it should hardly be surprising that some judges are willing to use fund-raising tactics normally associated with Clinton campaign aides trolling Buddhist temples. Indeed, Larry Starcher could probably have enjoyed a fine career as a Democratic National Committee fund-raiser if he wasn't already a judge.

In 1996, Starcher, a circuit court judge in Morgantown, West Virginia, decided to seek a vacant seat on the state supreme court. Since West Virginia remains a state of yellow-dog Democrats (they'd sooner vote for a yellow dog than a Republican), Starcher was a shoo-in for the post, if he won the Democratic primary. But to win that race, he had to overcome a tough opponent—and to do that he had to raise a lot of money.

The tactics that Judge Starcher used to raise that money were revealed in a motion filed by defendants seeking to disqualify him from a mass asbestos trial. The motion pointed out that the judge's campaign had been largely financed by plaintiffs' lawyers with asbestos claims before his court. According to the defendants, asbestos plaintiffs' lawyers contributed more than $60,000 to Judge Starcher's campaign. A local tort reform group says the judge got $143,700 in all from plaintiffs' lawyers. A number of leading asbestos plaintiffs' lawyers were also active in Judge Starcher's election committee; an economist who frequently appears as an expert witness for the plaintiffs even served as his campaign treasurer.

In his own defense, Judge Starcher told me that it's not considered unethical in West Virginia for judges to accept campaign contributions from lawyers who appear before them. That, of course, is a telling commentary on judicial ethics in that state. But even by local standards, Judge Starcher may have gone too far.

Richard Yurko, a lawyer with an asbestos-defense firm in Clarksburg, West Virginia, filed a sworn affidavit in which he says that after he appeared before Judge Starcher on March 5, 1996, the judge "stated that he was not getting any significant contributions from defense counsel. . . . He informed me that while he would not do anything illegal with respect to any decisions he would make while on the bench, he would remember who had supported him and who did not support him." Not too subtle, that message.

A few days later, Judge Starcher wrote to a local labor union (many of whose members are asbestos plaintiffs) appealing for support. In his letter, the judge called his opponent, who had defended asbestos companies, "a lawyer who has made his living on the backs of labor." By contrast, the judge bragged, "I have steadfastly moved nearly 20,000 of these cases through court in order that injured workers can receive compensation." And he promised, "Neither *you* nor labor will be disappointed with a justice such as me on the high court." All of this, the defendants' motion suggests, "raises the spectre of a judge who has prejudged such cases."

Judge Starcher told me he couldn't comment on the specifics because the recusal motion concerned pending litigation. He did say that he's "friends with asbestos defense lawyers," and he's even had them over to his house for cookouts. But he's run the asbestos litigation in a manner that favors the plaintiffs, many of whom (as we saw in Chapter 6) have spurious cases. At one point, Judge Starcher had scheduled a mass trial with 7,000 asbestos plaintiffs and 120 defendants. Such consolidated litigation is an awful idea because it puts inexorable pressure on defendants to settle even really weak claims or face crippling damages. Now here was Starcher soliciting campaign donations from union officials associated with the plaintiffs. What's wrong with this picture?

From Larry Starcher's standpoint the answer has to be: nothing. The hard sell paid off—Judge Starcher is now Justice Starcher of the Supreme Court of West Virginia. But at what cost to the already tattered reputation of the bench in that state?

I don't mean to pick on Judge Starcher. Well, not too much, anyway. Neither his handling of the asbestos cases nor his heavy-handed appeals for political support are any worse than the conduct of lots of other state judges. That is precisely the point.

Richard Neely, a former member of the West Virginia Supreme Court (and a supporter of Judge Starcher's), points out that this is what happens when judges must compete for votes. "If you build a brothel," he says, "you shouldn't be surprised when you come back and find it's inhabited by whores."

"Home-Court" Advantage: Does Cash Corrupt?

PERHAPS Neely's view will strike some as unusually cynical. Surely, idealists will argue, it's possible for a judge to remove his politician's hat once he dons the black robes and decides cases impartially. Perhaps that's true in some cases; maybe even in many cases. But a good deal of justice depends on the appearance of justice being done. Indeed the American Bar Association's Model Code of Judicial Conduct states that a judge must "act at all times in a manner that promotes public confidence in the integrity and impartiality of the judiciary." That confidence is badly tarnished when judges solicit or even accept contributions from actual or potential litigants, whether plaintiffs or defendants. "Many people think we can't separate the money from our decisions," acknowledges Chief Justice Thomas Moyer of Ohio, who's pushed bills to limit contributions to judges.

This isn't just a perception problem, as Justice Moyer's comment may imply. It's hard to get around the fact that there is a link between lawyers' contributions to judges and the outcomes of cases that those lawyers are involved in. In 1995, *Forbes* magazine surveyed the richest lawyers in America. Five out of the seven came from Houston or nearby Beaumont, Texas, both places where judges receive copious contributions from leading lawyers. No doubt the lawyers in question—the likes of Joe Jamail and John O'Quinn—are men of extraordinary ability. But would they be doing as well if they didn't have "home-court" advantage?

A partial answer to this question is provided by the lengths to which some lawyers are willing to go to make sure that their cases are heard by a favorably disposed judge. Harris County, Texas, like most other jurisdictions around the country, is supposed to have random assignment of cases, but, the *Houston Chronicle* reports, a clerk in the Harris County courthouse was allegedly taking bribes to steer certain cases to certain judges. The clerk was quietly fired and the case never received much publicity, but this provides a clear indication that lawyers—not just the cynical public—believe that it really does matter who hears which case.

The Victim

It's hard to sympathize when the victim of these machinations is a faceless corporation like General Motors or Dow Corning. But what happens when the victim is herself a vulnerable would-be plaintiff?

Mary Klager is a housewife who received breast implants in 1979. Like many other women, she was scared stiff by all the adverse publicity about breast implants—"ticking time bombs," the lawyers called them—so in January 1992 she went to O'Quinn, Kerensky, McAninch, & Laminack. Run by the legendary John O'Quinn, who according to *Forbes* made $40 million in 1994 (a number he denies), the law firm was amassing some 2,000 breast implant plaintiffs. One of Mr. O'Quinn's partners, Richard Laminack, quickly put Ms. Klager on the medical assembly line set up to process plaintiffs.

The O'Quinn law firm directed Ms. Klager to L. Fabian Worthing III, a plaintiffs' expert witness, a plastic surgeon who had removed implants from at least 1,000 women. Dr. Worthing performed the operation on Ms. Klager in March 1992. The implants and biopsy samples wound up at the O'Quinn law firm, where they were stored in a refrigerated "Tupperware-type container" along with hundreds of others—a ghoulish display of evidence for pending cases.

O'Quinn's law firm sent Ms. Klager's tissue samples for testing to a couple of plaintiffs' "experts," one of whom reported back with an alarming finding: the tissue contained "intraductal carcinoma." *Breast cancer.* In December 1992, Dr. Worthing called Ms. Klager in and told her she'd have to consider a double mastectomy. Although a mammogram was negative, Ms. Klager did have a surgeon remove both breasts. But when the pathology report came back, it turned out Ms. Klager didn't have breast cancer. It now appears that the tissue that tested positive for carcinoma may not have been Ms. Klager's—one DNA test found the tissue wasn't hers, while another was inconclusive.

In short, due to a horrifying mix-up either at the O'Quinn law firm or at one of the doctors' offices, Ms. Klager had needlessly undergone a double mastectomy. And due to the way the scar tissue has formed, she won't be able to have breast reconstruction. If Ms. Klager's tissue samples *were* switched, it means that another woman actually had breast cancer but didn't realize it. Nobody knows who she is, or whether she's still alive.

Mr. O'Quinn insists that "we've done nothing wrong." He says the mix-up occurred "in a lab somewhere," but adds, "If I were Mary Klager, I'd be mad as hell, too." In fact, she was so mad that she did what Mr. O'Quinn likes to do: She sued everyone in sight, which in this case meant the O'Quinn law firm as well as the doctors. Normally, Ms. Klager might have expected her case—no matter the merits—to get a sympathetic hearing from a judge in the plaintiff's paradise of Harris County. But as she quickly discovered, a plaintiff's odds of prevailing change dramatically when the defendant is not an out-of-state corporation but rather a famous local trial attorney.

The complaint against Mr. O'Quinn never even made it to a jury. On July 6, 1994, Judge Carolyn Marks Johnson issued summary judgment in favor of the O'Quinn law firm, a decision not based on any published finding of fact. The judgment, which Judge Johnson refuses to publicly explain, is defensible on the merits, but it should raise a few eyebrows when considered in light of her history. It turns out that the judge, as much as anyone, has been responsible for helping the local plaintiffs' attorneys make a fortune from their weak breast implant claims.

Who is Judge Johnson? The wife of a local personal injury attorney, she was appointed to a vacancy on the bench in 1993 by then governor Ann Richards, who had received $155,000 in contributions from John

O'Quinn over the years. During the 1994 campaign (all judges in Texas are elected), Ms. Johnson's Republican opponent charged that Mr. O'Quinn's influence was responsible for putting her on the bench. Both Mr. O'Quinn and Ms. Johnson deny the accusation.

It is undeniable that since her appointment, Judge Johnson has acquired a reputation among local lawyers as a plaintiff's judge, not a fair judge. In a 1995 Houston Bar Association survey, she received the second-highest "poor" rating among the nineteen state civil district court judges in Houston.

During a Republican landslide in 1994, Ms. Johnson was the only Democratic judge to win a race in Harris County. Her narrow victory—she prevailed by less than half a percentage point—can be attributed in part to her prodigious fund-raising. According to her campaign disclosure forms, she received $402,768.73, mainly from plaintiffs' lawyers.

Her largest single donation—$6,250—came from Mr. O'Quinn on November 8, 1993. Four months later, Judge Johnson presided over a whopping $27.9 million jury verdict against breast implant manufacturers 3M, McGhan Medical Company, and Inamed. The plaintiffs' attorney? John O'Quinn. "The verdict helped set the market price for breast implant cases," says Jon Opelt of Citizens Against Lawsuit Abuse in Houston. Thanks to the verdict in Judge Johnson's court, it was a very generous price for Mr. O'Quinn, who typically takes 40 percent of his clients' winnings.

Judge Johnson has a long history with breast implant litigation. In 1994, she presided over two other implant cases brought against Baxter Healthcare. By Friday, December 2, 1994, the jury had been out for ten days, and consternation was growing among the plaintiffs' attorneys, who had expected a quick verdict in their favor. Suddenly, Judge Johnson granted their motion for a mistrial, claiming that the jury had been unable to reach a verdict. The jurors were so outraged that eleven of them together issued a rare public statement protesting the judge's decision. In their statement, the jurors said they were "making substantial progress"—they had already decided in favor of the implant manufacturers in one case and were within a day or two of a verdict in the other case. "We are appalled," the jury added, "at not being asked if we were making progress during the latter days of the deliberations."

Judge Johnson later told the *Houston Chronicle* that the jurors "did not fully understand the court process." But they thought they did: As one juror told the *Houston Post*, "I think when the plaintiffs saw it wasn't going in their favor, they decided to pull out." By granting a mistrial, Judge Johnson stopped the jury from issuing Harris County's first-ever verdict in favor of breast implant manufacturers. (At a retrial in 1995, Baxter won the case anyway—in a different courtroom.)

Here is the irony of Judge Johnson's jurisprudence: In the breast implant litigation, where multiple studies have shown there is not a shred of scientific evidence that the plaintiffs suffered any harm caused by the manufacturers, she has allowed the charges to go to a jury. Yet in Mary Klager's case—where the harm suffered was undeniable, though the culprit was unclear—Judge Johnson tossed out the case early on.

The Texas Court of Appeals decided in August 1996 that Judge Johnson had erred. The four-judge panel did agree with her dismissal of Ms. Klager's suit against the surgeon who removed her implants. However, when it came to Mr. O'Quinn's law firm, the higher court held: "We recognize that OKM&L [O'Quinn, Kerensky, McAninch, & Laminack] had no duty to have Klager's tissue samples tested for cancer, but OKM&L, as custodian of the implants and tissue samples for evidentiary purposes, has an obligation to ensure that the samples being tested correspond to the individuals to whom test results are given."

But Ms. Klager still faced a David versus Goliath battle. Her odds of prevailing appear especially slim because her case, still continuing as of this writing, was referred back to Judge Johnson's courtroom. Anybody who challenges the trial lawyer establishment in a place like Texas, it seems, can expect no favors from the bench.

One State's Descent into Tort Hell: A Study in the Impact of Campaign Cash

THE WORST-CASE scenario of what happens when money and politics get inextricably intertwined with justice may be found in Alabama. In recent years, this state has gotten a reputation as (in the words of *Time* magazine) "tort hell." Presiding over this particular nether region, of course, is the local juristocracy. The situation is particularly bad in a handful of rural Alabama counties where a single judge hears all the cases and local plaintiffs' lawyers routinely haul national companies into court for a judicial mugging.

How absurd is the Alabama judicial system? "These days the situation seems to be that if I take my jacket to the cleaners and it is damaged, I don't just want a new jacket, I want $25 million," a local business professor told Scripps Howard News Service. "It used to be that a million-dollar verdict distinguished a plaintiff's lawyer," Yale law professor George Priest told me. "Now down here in Alabama that's considered a defense victory."

One of the worst offenders is Lowndes County, scene of the $150 GM verdict described in Chapter 1; the judge allowed a local plaintiff named Alex Hardy to hit all the cherries in the tort slot machine, despite strong evidence that the defendant hadn't done anything wrong.

Another offender is Barbour County. For years, the only judge in this county was William H. Robertson, and the leading trial lawyer was Jere Beasley, who also counts the GM case among his many triumphs. He's a former quarterback of the local high school and, more important, a former law partner of Judge Robertson. Beasley has won so many multimillion-dollar verdicts in jury trials presided over by Judge Robertson that it's hard to keep track. Suffice it to say that, by one count, Barbour County juries under Judge Robertson's supervision awarded a staggering $150 million in punitive damages between 1989 and 1996. (Juries in the whole state awarded more than $767 million in punitive damages during that period.)

Robertson told me, in his own defense, that a leading local defense attorney is one of his former partners, too. How comforting.

Most of these cases, unlike *Hardy v. GM*, did not involve serious bodily harm. Most were "paper" injury suits, where the plaintiff claims to have been defrauded by a financial services company. Usually, the evidence of fraud isn't found in a written contract but rather in oral misrepresentations allegedly made by a local salesman for an insurance company. So the case amounts to the plaintiff's word versus the defendant's, and when the plaintiff is a local and the defendant is a big out-of-state company, it's not hard to predict how the case will come out.

One of the biggest such verdicts occurred in 1994. Mr. Beasley won $50 million from Illinois-based Mercury Finance Company, which he claimed had inflated the cost of an auto loan for his client by $1,000. The evidence of wrongdoing was tenuous, at best, but that's not the point. How could a dispute so minor possibly result in such a big payout? True, Judge Robertson eventually reduced the award to "only" $2.5 million and the parties settled out of court, but that doesn't change the fact that in his courtroom, minor wrongs can suddenly result in major paydays.

Robertson insisted to me "that any jury anywhere would have done the same thing based on the same set of circumstances." He further claimed that Mercury's later troubles—three years after the trial in Barbour County, the firm's former controller was accused of artificially inflating profits—justified the verdict; but there was in fact no proof of the firm bilking consumers. For some strange reason, national companies like Mercury manage to evade the attention of big-city district attorneys with large fraud squads at their disposal; they only get "caught" by juries in small rural counties in Alabama, where trials are presided over by the likes of William Robertson.

Judge Robertson's reign in Barbour County ended abruptly in the fall of 1996, when the judge announced his retirement before his term was over. Perhaps not so coincidentally, his retirement came shortly after the state Office of the Examiners of Public Accounts found that the judge had misused $4,167.85 in public money, "borrowing" some of it to pay his own personal expenses. The judge insisted it was all a "sincere mistake" that had been immediately rectified; but isn't that what the big out-of-state defendants also said in his courtroom, just before they were socked for multimillion-dollar damages? The state still found Robertson guilty of violating the canons of judicial ethics, and he finally stepped down.

While William Robertson is off the bench, plenty of other Alabama jurists continue to issue verdicts that make a lot of plaintiffs' lawyers very happy. In most courts across the country, certifying a class action—which usually blackmails a defendant into settling—is a laborious process involving lengthy arguments from both sides. Not in Alabama. In rural Coosa County, plaintiffs' lawyer Kenneth Ingram Jr.—son of an Alabama Supreme Court justice—sued Exxon, Shell, Texaco, and every other major oil company, claiming to represent everyone in the nation living near a leaking underground oil tank. The first the companies heard about it was when they received notice in the mail that a class action had *already* been certified by Judge John Rochester. Such one-sided decisions are common in the land of the Crimson Tide. No wonder class-action lawyers are flying in from as far away as San Francisco and Boston to file suit in Alabama.

Presiding over this mess is the Alabama Supreme Court, which has been pulling the plaintiffs' gravy train for years. Between 1989 and 1996, the justices affirmed $80.3 million in punitive damages, mainly against out-of-state defendants, more than four times the total in the neighboring states of Georgia, Tennessee, and Mississippi *combined*. That's according to a study conducted by Yale's George Priest. The starting date of that study—1989—is significant because that's the year Ernest "Sonny" Hornsby took his seat as chief justice of the state supreme court. Many businesspeople blame Hornsby, a plaintiffs' lawyer who had been president of the Alabama Trial Lawyers Association, for contributing substantially to Alabama's current reputation as the world capital of litigation.

One of the Hornsby court's most significant actions was to overturn a package of tort reforms—including a $250,000 cap on punitive damages—passed by the state legislature in 1987, on the grounds that the laws limited the "right to jury trial." Hornsby had actually lobbied against the bills before joining the court, and although he recused himself from the deliberations, the rest of the justices effectively enacted the trial lawyers' agenda.

With the justices playing such an outsize role in the future of the tort system, it was inevitable that the state supreme court elections would become excessively politicized. In 1994, business interests ran a Republican challenger against Democrat Hornsby. The challenger was leading by fewer than 300 votes out of 1.1 million cast, when the Democrats tried to count more than 2,000 absentee ballots that had been improperly cast in traditionally Democratic areas. The all-Democratic state Supreme Court voted 4–1 that the ballots "substantially complied" with Alabama election laws, thus apparently giving the election to their colleague Hornsby. (Three of the four justices in the majority had personally contributed to the Hornsby campaign.) It took federal court intervention to throw the disputed ballots out and remove Hornsby from his seat on the court.

The next state supreme court election, in 1996, was almost as nasty. Business interests supported law professor Harold See in a challenge to pro-plaintiff Justice Kenneth Ingram. Plaintiffs' lawyers rallied to Ingram's defense, contributing at least $2.38 million through a variety of front organizations. One of the trial lawyers' groups, called deceptively enough the Coalition for Family Values, ran ads accusing See of deserting his family in Chicago, committing adultery with his secretary, and dating one of his law students. Another memorable trial-lawyer ad showed a skunk walking down the road as an announcer intoned, "This is Harold See." See ultimately won, however, after spending at least $2.59 million, much of it raised from business interests.

His election, along with the U.S. Supreme Court's decision in *BMW v. Gore* and several other cases reversing Alabama punitive damage awards, may signal a "See-change" for Alabama's courts. But no matter what the future holds, it's distressing to see how politicized the state's judiciary has become. Whether it's Sonny Hornsby and William Robertson being accused of carrying water for the plaintiffs' lawyers or Harold See purportedly running on behalf of business interests, judges are no longer seen as impartial. Many now view them, fairly or not, as representatives of special interests. As a leading plaintiffs' lawyer told the *American Lawyer*: "I think every justice on that [supreme] court will admit—well, they won't admit it to you—that when they sit down to resolve a case, one of the first considerations is the . . . political issue. . . . Which is really awful. Justice is supposed to be that lady who's got that blindfold on."

Awful it may be, but the situation in Alabama is only marginally worse than conditions in many other states, ranging from Texas to West Virginia. Many have protested what they view as the spectacle of justice for sale. But it might be more accurate to say that justice is for rent, with the bill coming due every election.

Graft Galore: Beyond Conflicts of Interest

So FAR, we've focused only on conflicts of interest and other ethical imbroglios in which judges have become embroiled. But that is not to suggest that this is the extent of the problems dogging the nation's courts. Indeed, outright illegality appears to run rampant; the only trouble is finding proof. It's usually impossible for mere reporters to show that judges have taken bribes, as opposed to simply engaging in questionable conduct. But once law enforcement gets involved, with its wiretaps and subpoenas and stings, it's possible to show that many courts have become corrupted to a greater degree than the public generally suspects.

Exhibit A for this proposition may be found in San Diego. Not a city that's known as a den of inequity, San Diego was the site of a massive judicial corruption scandal in 1996 that revealed how easily friendly relations between judges and lawyers can cross the line into illegality. Two judges and Patrick Frega, a well-known local personal injury attorney with a long list of multimillion-dollar verdicts, were convicted of racketeering, conspiracy, and mail fraud. Another judge pled guilty to bribery. The evidence uncovered by the FBI showed that Frega had established cozy relations with the three judges, who handled many of his cases.

Superior court judge G. Dennis Adams awarded Jim Williams, a client of Frega's, $5 million in a bench trial of a suit he'd filed against a local bank. Judge Adams later showed up at the car dealership owned by Williams, where attorney Frega kept a special account to pay for purchases by judges. Frega paid for car repairs for Adams and his family and helped buy vehicles for his father and teenager daughter; the attorney even hired a ghostwriter to pen a novel for the judge. Frega wound up spending some $65,000 altogether through the special car account.

Another judge helpful to Frega was Michael Greer. As presiding judge of the superior court, Greer was responsible for assigning cases; he personally handled many of Frega's cases and, at Frega's request, assigned other cases to judges who he knew would be favorably disposed toward the plaintiffs' lawyer. Prosecutors presented evidence that Greer himself made many favorable rulings for Frega's clients, in cases that resulted in multimillion-dollar verdicts.

The third superior court judge in the scandal, James Malkus, received not only free car repairs from Frega but also such favors as a health club membership and a job for his son. In return, prosecutors showed, the judge met secretly with Frega to discuss his cases.

Prosecutors may have cracked this case, but they're not fooling themselves into thinking they've managed to clean up all the improper behavior in the San Diego courts. "I think we put an end to the corruption with a big C," the lead federal prosecutor in the case said. "But there is still stuff that didn't rise to the level of federal criminal conduct: the winks and the nods and the hometownism that has gone on for years." It's not easy to deter such misconduct when even jurists caught with their hand in the cookie jar are dealt with leniently. A federal judge allowed Adams and Malkus to stay out of jail pending appeal of their conviction; Judge Greer received nothing but probation. And, on top of that, Greer gets to keep collecting his $55,000-a-year pension.

The problem of judicial corruption, needless to say, is hardly confined to San Diego. Indeed, the template for the San Diego probe was cut in Chicago, where the FBI uncovered an even more pervasive pattern of corruption in the 1980s. Eighteen Cook County judges and more than 60 others, including lawyers, clerks, and police officers, were convicted as part of Operation Graylord, a sting operation designed to clean up the courts. FBI agents posing as prosecutors, defense attorneys, crime victims, and criminals staged more than 100 phony cases and caught on tape the spectacle of judges taking bribes. And not just to fix parking tickets, either.

Judge Thomas J. Maloney was convicted of fixing three murder cases in exchange for bribes. In one case, he took a share of some $100,000 in payoffs for acquitting three New York gang members for the murder of a rival in Chicago. In another case, Maloney took $4,000 to $5,000 to allow an accused murderer to plead guilty to a reduced charge of manslaughter. A murder defendant convicted in Judge Maloney's court later appealed on the grounds that the judge was biased against him because he hadn't paid a bribe!

Chicago's corruption was more blatant than San Diego's—it was more along the lines of cash in brown bags, not free car repairs—but my bet is that if federal authorities were so inclined, they could make similar cases in virtually every major court system in the country. In Miami, for instance, Operation Court Broom, a sting operation, snared four judges who took $250,000 in bribes from FBI agents. In Nashville, Tennessee, a probate judge committed suicide after he learned he was being investigated by a federal grand jury for soliciting bribes, including free rental vehicles.

Starting to see a pattern here? The only reason more of these scandals don't come to light isn't because there's a scarcity of them out there; it's because prosecutors are naturally wary of going after judges, who, after all, hold the fate of their cases in their hands.

Corruption on the Federal Bench

Thus far, we've concentrated exclusively on the peccadilloes of state judges. This is by no means to suggest that the Olympian occupants of the federal bench are immune to pecuniary temptations. Indeed, since the 1980s a record number of federal judges have been either convicted or impeached, or both. The rogues' list:

- U.S. district judge Robert Collins of New Orleans became the first black federal judge in the modern-day Deep South when he was appointed by President Carter. In 1991, he was found guilty of scheming to split a $100,000 bribe from a marijuana smuggler. He was caught with $16,500 in FBI-marked money, after the drug smuggler turned informant. He continued to collect his $133,600 annual salary while in prison for two years before he finally resigned under threat of Senate impeachment.

- U.S. district judge Robert Aguilar, appointed to a vacancy in San Jose, California, by President Carter, was convicted in 1990 of leaking a wiretap to a mobster and lying to the FBI. He became the target of an FBI probe after an organized crime investigation uncovered evidence that Judge Aguilar was helping a former teamsters' official overturn an embezzlement conviction. Eventually, Aguilar's conviction was overturned on appeal, but he made a deal with the government to resign his seat in exchange for prosecutors' not refiling criminal charges.

- In 1989, the Senate voted to impeach U.S. district judge Alcee L. Hastings of Miami, another Carter appointee. The case revolved around charges that Hastings had conspired with a prominent Washington, D.C., lawyer to shake down two embezzlers for $150,000 in exchange for reducing their prison sentences and restoring their seized assets. A jury acquitted Hastings of those charges, but the Senate held that the judge had lied to the jurors. Kicked off the federal bench, Hastings found a more congenial home: the House of Representatives.

- Just two weeks after impeaching Hastings, the Senate removed from the bench U.S. district judge Walter Nixon of Mississippi. Nixon had earlier been convicted of perjury for denying that he'd intervened in the marijuana smuggling case of a wealthy local man. The marijuana smuggler's father later helped Nixon obtain a lucrative oil and gas investment.

- In 1986, Harry Claiborne of Reno, Nevada, became the first federal judge since the 1930s to be impeached. Claiborne, yet another Carter appointee, had been indicted on charges of bribery and tax evasion after an FBI investigation. The bribery count resulted in a hung jury, but he was convicted of failing to report $106,000 in income.

Surprised to see some of the most powerful judges in America behaving like Chicago aldermen? You shouldn't be. After all, as we've seen in previous chapters, no public officials are as unaccountable as federal judges, and as a result, no members of the judiciary suffers from gavelitis more than federal judges.

Simply consider the difference in supervision between federal judges and executive or legislative officials. The latter are policed by a constant array of special counsels, in matters ranging from Whitewater to Dan Rostenkowski's shady financial dealings. But whoever heard of a Lawrence Walsh or Kenneth Starr for the third branch of government? To recap what was pointed out in Chapter 1: The only checks on the federal judiciary are fellow judges sitting in judicial councils (which are relatively toothless) and the Senate, which, despite the examples cited earlier, is usually loath to activate the cumbersome impeachment machinery.

Given those circumstances, it's to be expected that some members of this exclusive circle would be tempted to abuse their position not just for ideological ends—as with Judge Thelton Henderson's overturning the California Civil Rights Initiative or Judge Leonard Sand's telling Yonkers officials how to vote on public housing—but also for purely pecuniary advantage. Indeed, having a few federal judges on the take may be less harmful to the country as a whole than having these judges routinely act as Platonic Guardians, usurping the democratic process whenever it pleases them. Of course, we now have the worst of both worlds—judges transgressing the law for both financial and ideological reasons.

Conclusion: Time for a Bench-Clearing Brawl

IN THIS chapter, we've seen a wide array of unsavory conduct, ranging in seriousness from judges who rule on cases involving campaign contributors (for instance, Judge Johnson presiding over the suit against John O'Quinn) to judges who take outright payoffs to influence their decisions (for instance, the San Diego case). What are we to make of all this? It's not very helpful to observe that there are a lot of crooks hiding behind black robes; there are undoubtedly crooks in every walk of life. But we can reach some specific conclusions about the causes of, and cures for, judicial misconduct.

First, let's look at the "root causes" of judicial corruption. Not all the corruption surveyed in this chapter was tied to giant liability awards to plaintiffs. There was also corruption involving criminal cases, and in particular drugs—as with federal judges Robert Collins and Walter Nixon, who helped marijuana smugglers. There's no question that the war on drugs, along with the rising litigation tide, has been one of the main sources of corrupting cash for the court system. The obvious answer would be to legalize drugs, hence ending the war on drugs and its inducements to corruption. But clearly, such a major policy change should not be based entirely on a desire to cut down on corruption, especially since plenty of other factors—for example, concerns about increases in addiction—suggest that many narcotics should remain illegal.

When it comes to the corruption associated with liability awards, however, we've already seen in Chapter 6 that there is no good policy reason to keep the current system as is, but there are plenty of reasons—such as reducing the "tort tax"—to rein in litigation anyway. The corruption and conflicts of interest detailed in this chapter provide further cause for cutting back plaintiffs' ability to strike it rich with dubious claims: By reducing the amount of money available in the civil justice system, we could also reduce the stench of impropriety that lingers around litigation such as the smelly-water case in Decatur, Texas, or the $50 million Mercury Finance verdict in Barbour County, Alabama.

The second general conclusion about corruption concerns state systems of selecting judges. It's no coincidence that virtually all the examples of misconduct in this chapter involve states that pick their judges through partisan elections. This method of judicial selection, whether in Alabama, Texas, or Illinois, puts judges in the unenviable position of West Virginia Supreme Court justice Larry Starcher: having to accept campaign funds from current or future litigants. Even the most pure-hearted judges find it hard to preserve their reputation for probity in such a system.

Of course, selecting judges through nonpartisan retention elections (where voters simply turn thumbs up or down on a sitting judge) is no guarantee of integrity. Witness the corruption in San Diego, which, like the rest of California, selects its judges in this manner. But while no system can produce perfect rectitude as long as fallible humans, instead of Platonic Guardians, are appointed to the bench, some systems are more prone to conflicts of interest than others, and it's clear that nonpartisan retention elections are preferable to the partisan variety if we're to preserve the good name of the bench.

This brings us to the third and final conclusion: No matter how judges are selected, the key deterrent to corruption is having a tough system in place for policing the juristocracy's ethics. It is precisely the lack of such a system for most judges that, I believe, breeds much of the wrongdoing surveyed in this chapter. As we saw in Chapter 1, the judiciary has less oversight than any other branch of government, so it's only natural to expect that its members would be prone to abuse their positions.

The key to reducing judicial corruption, it seems to me, is getting more supervision by those outside the judicial process, that is, not lawyers or judges. One way to do this would be through a strengthened, formal judicial discipline process. Judicial conduct commissions already exist at the state level; their powers should be strengthened, and more outsiders should be brought in to oversee their operations.

Make no mistake: Not even a battalion—nay, an entire army—of judicial overseers will ever totally clean up judicial corruption. That's a mission impossible. But with greater oversight, tort reform, and nonpartisan elections, we have a chance to greatly reduce the opportunities for unethical behavior inherent in the current system. That will go a long way toward restoring confidence that our courts are deciding cases on the merits, not based on which party greased the judge's hands.

CHAPTER 8

Dethroning the Juristocracy

HOW TO DEAL WITH

JUDGES WHO ARE

TOO ACTIVIST—

AND WITH THOSE

NOT ACTIVIST ENOUGH

There is no happiness, there is no liberty, there is no enjoyment of life, unless a man can say when he rises in the morning, I shall be subject to the decisions of no unjust judge today.

DANIEL WEBSTER, SPEECH, NEW YORK, 1831

THE ECONOMIST and author Thomas Sowell once came to a *Wall Street Journal* editorial board meeting and was asked to comment on some proposed piece of legislation that concerned the issue he had recently written a book about. "I don't offer solutions," he replied, in all seriousness. "I just analyze problems. That's more than enough to keep me occupied for the rest of my life."

Nearing the end of this book, I've developed a lot of sympathy for

Sowell's outlook. The problems of junk judges are so deep-seated, so ingrained, so intractable that there simply isn't a three-point (or four-point, or five-point) plan that will magically transmogrify the judiciary into a model of rectitude, responsibility, and responsiveness. It's a sure bet that most of the problems chronicled in this book—lazy judges, stupid judges, arrogant judges, incompetent judges—will be with us as long as we have a judicial system. The best that we can hope to accomplish in this imperfect world is to ameliorate some of the destructive consequences of these problems.

To begin formulating solutions, we must be clear about what problems bedevil the bench. Judges are most commonly assailed for an excess of activism. This is no doubt a major problem. As we've seen in Chapters 2, 3, 4, and 5, judges have been wantonly overturning state laws that range from term limits to abortion regulations; imposing pro-defendant laws on the states in matters ranging from the exclusionary rule to the death penalty; and personally running institutions ranging from schools to prisons, even raising taxes in the process.

And as we've seen in Chapters 1 and 7, the arrogance, the gavelitis, that leads judges to issue these rulings often leads them into ethically dubious conduct in both their personal and public lives; think of Sol Wachtler terrorizing his former girlfriend or the San Diego judges taking payoffs from a local personal injury lawyer.

But, as we've also seen in Chapters 2 and 6, the judiciary just as frequently errs by not being activist enough—by not throwing the book at criminals and by not pulling the plug on absurd jury verdicts in civil cases. The offenders here range from New York's Lorin Duckman, who released onto the streets a thug who subsequently killed his girlfriend, to Mississippi's James Graves Jr., who refused to reduce a $500 million verdict against a Canadian funeral home chain. This problem also manifests itself in judges who are simply unable to control their courtrooms, from Lance Ito to A. Ted Bozeman (he of the $150 million verdict against General Motors).

What's the unifying thread between the failures of the judiciary in these disparate fields? Why are judges sometimes too activist—and at other times not activist enough?

The common problem, it seems to me, is that much of the judiciary is pursuing a fairly radical conception of justice. The courts are trying to provide a remedy for every conceivable "victim," and in the process, they hold no one accountable for his own conduct. In the world according to many of today's judges, plaintiffs deserve big payoffs because their injuries must have been somebody else's fault; criminals deserve understanding, not punishment, because their transgressions must be rooted in society's ills; and various "minorities"—whether a smelly panhandler kicked out of a public library or politicians kicked out of office by term limits—deserve protection from the vicissitudes of fortune.

This worldview serves not only the ideology of the bar but also, conveniently enough, its bottom line. After all, creating endless avenues of legal redress—as the courts have done in criminal, civil, and constitutional law—also creates plenty of work for the juristocracy. Writes law professor John O. McGinnis:

> The lawyers' ideal is a government sufficiently powerful enough to entangle every area of human activity with intricate rules combined with due-process rights sufficiently boundless to allow every citizen to contest their application. Endless regulatory wrangles result in ever higher income for lawyers.

Alas, what's ideal for lawyers is hell for everybody else. Yet that's where we are today: in an America dominated by laws, but one where neither the criminal nor the civil courts seem to do a very good job, and where judges routinely involve themselves in matters that in earlier times were considered none of their business.

To improve the performance of the courts, then, we must limit judges' opportunities for ill-advised activism, while providing incentives for them to practice the kind of activism that ought to keep them busy—the kind designed to minimize the crime rate and the tort tax. And if, along the way, we can somehow improve the caliber of judges in general and cut down on their ethical problems, that's a nice bonus.

In previous chapters, some specific solutions to the problems discussed have been suggested: increase mandatory sentences for criminals, eliminate the exclusionary rule and Miranda, stop judges from overturning state policies, end judicial management of public institutions, roll back outrageous civil verdicts, and reduce corruption on the bench. All these reforms are designed to decrease judges' discretion and improve the quality and consistency of the justice they mete out. In this chapter we'll review some broader, structural solutions aimed at judicial activism, then move on to more general approaches that work within the existing laws and address both major failings of the juristocracy—excessive activism *and* insufficient activism.

Structural Solutions: How to Curb Activism—and How Not To

UNFORTUNATELY, many of the prescriptions bandied about by opponents of judicial activism are worse than the problem. Possibly the worst idea is impeaching federal judges for merely issuing bad decisions, a plan advanced by House Majority Whip Tom DeLay of Texas. His throw-the-bums-out approach may be emotionally satisfying, but it doesn't stand up to much scrutiny.

This becomes obvious when we examine one of the targets of DeLay's ire, U.S. district judge Fred Biery of San Antonio. His sin? Judge Biery had the temerity to issue an injunction preventing two Republicans from taking office as sheriff and county commissioner, pending resolution of a suit claiming that their winning margin had been provided by 800 soldiers who had voted illegally by absentee ballot (Democratic lawyers uncovered evidence that none of the 800 voters actually lived in the district). This is judicial activism? Perhaps, but if so, then an Alabama federal judge was equally guilty when he ruled that a bunch of absentee ballots had been illegally cast for Democratic chief justice Sonny Hornsby, a decision that threw the election to his GOP challenger. Why isn't DeLay calling for the head of the Alabama judge? Or why isn't he calling for the impeachment of federal judge John E. Sprizzo, who refused to enforce the law keeping abortion clinics clear of demonstrators because the defendants claimed to be acting from religious motives?

This double standard reveals the DeLay impeachment talk as mere partisan grandstanding, not a serious proposal to reform the judiciary. It is reminiscent, in some ways, of the attempt in 1805 by President Thomas Jefferson's Democratic partisans to remove the Federalist Samuel Chase from the Supreme Court because they didn't like his politics. Chase survived the impeachment vote by the slimmest of margins, and since then, the tradition has been that it takes more than par-

tisan differences to impeach a federal judge. As Professor Ronald
Rotunda of the University of Illinois College of Law puts it, "The
impeachment clause requires high crimes and misdemeanors to remove
any federal official. There's not a lesser standard for judges, and wrong
decisions are not high crimes and misdemeanors. What legislators
ought to be doing is carefully considering the candidates who are nominated. That's their only real role under the Constitution."

The Bork Revolution

Some other, even more radical solutions to the problem of judicial
activism have been bandied about by former judge Robert H. Bork, the
author of this book's foreword. He writes in a conservative magazine:

> If, as some suggest, a constitutional amendment doing away with
> judicial review altogether were adopted, we would then govern our-
> selves in the same fashion as the United Kingdom and continental
> democracies have for centuries. That would surely be better than
> the present situation, unless you think, as many liberals do, that the
> people of the United States are irredeemably fascist at heart.

Bork's other answer:

> I have suggested a constitutional amendment making any court
> decision, state or federal, past or present, subject to legislative revi-
> sion by a majority vote. In the case of state court decisions, the revi-
> sion would be by the state legislature; Congress would be able to
> revise federal court decisions.

Bork is trenchant in his analysis of the judiciary's problems (indeed
his book, *The Tempting of America*, offers the single best description of
where judges have gone wrong in constitutional law), and he's
undoubtedly right that his ideas would not usher in the dark night of
despotism. But his proposals raise more questions than they answer.

Why would it be preferable to have Congress rather than the
Supreme Court in effect rewriting the Constitution? Why virtually
sweep away judicial review of *federal* laws, a power that is seldom exercised but one that is often essential to protect liberty? What happens if
Congress is unhappy with a Supreme Court ruling (say, allowing flag
burning) and overrides it, but then doesn't specifically invalidate the

line of cases that led to that decision? How will courts rule on future disputes that aren't quite identical to the case overridden by lawmakers? And why get rid of an essential check on the majoritarian impulse? Weren't the Founders worried about the abuse of minorities by untrammeled democracy?

These objections, however, are almost beside the point. Bork's plan is reminiscent of proposals, happily debated in late-night bull sessions by countless college professors and students over the years, to impose British-style parliamentary democracy in the United States. Bork, too, would graft a major feature of the British system—little or no judicial review of legislators' decisions—onto our government, with unpredictable consequences. This makes for a fun debate, comparing the advantages and disadvantages of the two systems. But while intellectually stimulating, it's also wholly unrealistic.

Not just because it will never happen—that's no reason to avoid talking about something—but because it *should* never happen, for a reason that Edmund Burke pointed out: It's simply not a good idea to sweep away centuries of tradition and impose a new system of government, no matter how appealing its theoretical virtues. For a government to be secure, it must evolve naturally over the course of centuries. "[V]ery plausible schemes, with very pleasing commencements, have often shameful and lamentable conclusions," Burke warned. "[I]t is with infinite caution that any man ought to venture upon pulling down an edifice which has answered in any tolerable degree for ages the common purposes of society, or in building it up again without having models and patterns of approved utility before his eyes."

Burke was arguing against the French Revolution, but his argument applies equally well against the Bork revolution. The British and American systems of government grew up organically in different political soils, and important features of each system simply shouldn't be transplanted from one to the other. Conservatives, of all people, should recognize the power of this argument for tradition.

There is another, more practical problem with the Bork solution: As Bork concedes in the foreword, it hasn't worked elsewhere. Since 1982, Canada has allowed its federal parliament, acting in conjunction with one of the provincial parliaments, to overrule any decision of the Canadian Supreme Court. But this has never happened in practice, because it would cause such a brouhaha—just imagine the headlines about obstructing the rule of law if the politicians ever overrode the judges. What really preserves judicial power, it turns out, is not formal devices but simply the towering respect and esteem in which the judiciary is held by the public and politicians. Alas, the Bork plan would do little to change that.

Judicial Term Limits

Another radical idea gaining support these days is limiting the terms of judges. California attorney general Dan Lungren, fuming over all the court decisions blocking California ballot initiatives, has announced his support for ending lifetime tenure for federal judges, which of course would require amending the Constitution. What would be the alternative? One idea would be to force federal judges to submit to periodic reconfirmations by the Senate. Another idea, introduced as a constitutional amendment by Senator Bob Smith of New Hampshire, would be to impose a ten-year term limit on all federal judges, including Supreme Court justices.

This idea is seductive; if we're going to limit the terms of many legislators, why not also those of judges? But this is ultimately not a convincing solution—for two reasons. First, term limits would deny the public the services of such eminent and long-serving jurists as Richard Posner and Antonin Scalia. Many of the leading judges in American history—the likes of Cardozo and Story, Holmes and Hand—spent decades on the bench. It would be a shame to force their successors into retirement because of an arbitrary time limit. This, in and of itself, is not dispositive, however. There's no denying, as I've argued throughout the book, that many judges are not of high caliber, so it would be no great loss if they were forced off the bench. And certainly I would have shed no tears if term limits had limited the near-record tenure of William Brennan Jr.

But there's a second, more powerful reason to resist the lure of judicial term limits: There's no guarantee that they will produce the result reformers want, namely, a more timid, less activist judiciary. The result could easily be the opposite: Knowing that they'll only be on the bench a short while, judges might be more determined to make a splash right away by issuing groundbreaking activist decisions that will earn them a place in legal history. Remember, after all, one of the principal arguments advanced by George Will et al. for legislative term limits: that free of the pressures of reelection, lawmakers would be more willing to make tough, unpopular decisions. The problem with the judiciary hasn't been its unwillingness to make unpopular decisions; in fact, just the opposite. So term limits might well backfire in this instance.

A More Cautious Approach: The Hyde Plan

A more timid—and more realistic—solution is being advanced by chairman Henry Hyde of the House Judiciary Committee. His bill combines a host of limited and sensible measures: It would require that only a three-judge panel, not a single judge like Thelton Henderson, could issue an injunction to stop the implementation of a state voter initiative; and that panel's decision could be appealed straight to the U.S. Supreme Court. It would give each side in a federal civil case one peremptory challenge to reassign a judge. It would send complaints filed against a federal judge to a circuit other than the one where the judge sits. It would allow for fast-track appeals of class-action certifications. And it would impose a series of six conditions—for example, no loss of property values—before judges can impose a tax hike as part of a remedial measure.

The most controversial of these ideas is the three-judge requirement for striking down voter initiatives, but in fact—unlike the Bork or the term-limits proposals—it's solidly rooted in American history. Congress actually mandated in 1910 that all challenges to state laws would be heard by three-judge courts at the trial level, with appeal directly to the Supreme Court. This law was a response to the judicial activism of an earlier era, specifically to *Ex Parte Young*, the 1908 case in which the Supreme Court upheld the authority of federal courts to enjoin the enforcement of a state statute that was challenged as a violation of the U.S. Constitution. Progressive legislators feared, with good reason, that conservative activists on the courts would use this authority to block state regulation of business activity, so they tried to limit a single judge's discretion.

The three-judge requirement wasn't dropped by Congress until 1976. By then, all the pooh-bahs of the legal establishment, led by Chief Justice Warren Burger, had lined up against the law, ostensibly because it created too great a burden on the judiciary, though I suspect the real reason was because they didn't like any limits on the power of federal judges. But even in repealing the law, Congress reserved the three-judge requirement for two categories of cases: those involving challenges to congressional or statewide legislative districts (which the politicians naturally decided were more important than other disputes) and those asserting a violation of the Voting Rights Act. Since then, thanks to the Prison Litigation Reform Act of 1995, the three-judge requirement has been extended to some prisoner suits.

So, it would hardly be a radical step to extend the three-judge requirement, as Congressman Hyde proposes, to cases involving voter initiatives. Yet the legal establishment, predictably, has lined up solidly against the Hyde plan, with the U.S. Judicial Conference and various civil rights groups testifying against the three-judge requirement. Chief Judge Harry Edwards of the D.C. Circuit U.S. Court of Appeals complains that this would be "a terribly burdensome process." Precisely. That's the point. It *should* be burdensome for unelected and unaccountable judges to overturn the will of state voters.

If there's a problem with the Hyde plan, it's that it may not be burdensome *enough*. Between 1986 and 1997, only ten cases would have fallen under the requirements of the new law. Yet many more state laws were invalidated during that period; however, many of those overturned laws, such as those governing abortion or panhandling, were not imposed by voter initiative, so they wouldn't be affected by the Hyde plan. Why should only state laws passed by voter initiative receive protection from judicial usurpation?

A Better Way: The Two-Thirds Option

My own preference is for a structural solution that's a little more wide-ranging than Hyde's but not as radical as Bork's. I like the idea put forward by Don Stenberg, the Harvard-educated attorney general of Nebraska. He wants to remove all constitutional challenges to state and federal laws from the purview of the lower federal courts. Under the Stenberg plan, only the Supreme Court could deem a statute unconstitutional—and then only by a two-thirds vote.

I would tinker with this plan a bit. There's no need to extend the two-thirds requirement to federal statutes, since there's no problem with the courts' cavalierly overriding acts of Congress; and there's no reason not to allow two-thirds of an appeals circuit to override a law, too, for the sake of judicial efficiency. But basically the two-thirds plan is sound, because it avoids the blunderbuss approach of the term limits or Bork plans and focuses like a laser on the key problem of judicial activism—federal courts unfairly striking down state laws.

In our federalist system, a federal judge should only overrule state laws when it's absolutely clear that they violate the Constitution. Yet many of the most important Supreme Court decisions overruling state statutes are reached by a 5–4 vote. If four justices of the Supreme Court think a law is constitutional, that's prima facie evidence that it's not *clearly* unconstitutional. We should not be allowing a swing vote on the Supreme Court to decide many of the most controversial policies of our society, governing life and death. But as things stand now, it's a lot easier for the government to decide how to handle abortion—all this takes is a bare Supreme Court majority—than some obscure sugar subsidy, which to be enacted requires approval of a majority of both houses of Congress, plus presidential approval. On the really major questions—for example, an impeachment or treaty approval—a two-thirds vote of the Senate is required. It should be at least as difficult for the juristocracy to overturn a state law passed by millions of people as it is for the Senate to impeach a single member of the federal judiciary.

The two-thirds requirement has another great advantage over the Bork or term limits plans: It's at least arguable that it wouldn't require a constitutional amendment to enact it. Article 3, after all, gives Congress the right to regulate federal appellate jurisdiction and to determine the size of the Supreme Court. Presumably, Congress could impose a two-thirds requirement for all cases simply by reducing the size of the Supreme Court to three members. If Congress can impose such a de facto requirement, why not a de jure one? The reason, of course, is that absent a constitutional amendment, the Supreme Court may be unlikely to allow such an abridgment of its own power. But it's at least worth a shot.

If the two-thirds requirement were enacted, incidentally, it wouldn't necessarily be an instrument that would always help the conservative political cause. Many on the right would be disappointed with the Stenberg plan because many recent conservative victories in the

Supreme Court—especially in the federalism and reverse discrimination cases—have involved overturning state or federal laws on 5–4 votes. So the short-term impact of the two-thirds plan might well be "liberal." But the long-term consequences would be neither liberal nor conservative; they would be democratic. The two-thirds plan would return power to voters and take it away from unelected judges. That can only be good for the health of the republic.

Working Within the Law:
How to Improve the Judiciary Right Away

ANY OF THE structural solutions just discussed face substantial obstacles before they can become law. But we don't need to change the law, at least not in a major way, in order to improve the judiciary. There are plenty of things that can be done more or less within the existing system. And many of these improvements address not only the problem of judges who do too much but also that of judges who do too little—that is, judges who are incompetent or ethically challenged.

Picking State Judges

Chapter 7 explained why, in my view, the best system for minimizing judicial corruption is the Missouri plan: The governor picks judges based on the nominations of a selection committee; his appointees are then subject to an up or down vote after a trial period (pardon the pun) on the bench. This is also the best system for choosing competent judges—provided that the governor and his advisers choose wisely. At the very least, judicial candidates should be forced to pass a written test, perhaps similar to the Bar Exam, displaying a basic familiarity with the law.

Unfortunately, too many governors don't pay enough attention to judicial selection and thus wind up with judges who traduce many of their most treasured principles. The example of two Republican governors makes the point.

In New York, Governor George Pataki touts his law-and-order record and his opposition to liberal activist judges. So who did Governor Pataki reappoint to the key appeals court in Manhattan?

None other than Justice Joseph Sullivan. (Under New York's peculiar system, appellate judges serve a set term, then go back to the trial bench unless reappointed by the governor.) You may remember Justice Sullivan from Chapter 3: He's the author of the infamous opinion holding that the exclusionary rule protects a high-school student caught carrying a loaded handgun; and he joined his appellate colleagues in excluding as evidence the body found by state troopers in a car stopped for speeding. Governor Pataki criticized both decisions, yet in 1997 wound up reappointing Sullivan, on the lame grounds that the judge was only "following precedent," an excuse later exploded by the state's high court, which reversed Sullivan in both cases. The truth appears to be that Pataki was afraid of the howls of the legal establishment if he dumped Sullivan, so he quietly chose the path of least resistance.

Similar pusillanimity was shown by California's Pete Wilson, another governor who often decries judicial activism but whose words aren't matched by deeds. In 1991, Wilson appointed Ronald George to the California Supreme Court, and in 1996, the governor elevated him to chief justice. The foolishness of this choice soon became apparent in a case involving a law that required a parent's or judge's consent before a minor can have an abortion. Similar laws have been upheld by the U.S. Supreme Court, and, indeed, in California minors are prohibited from getting most medical procedures, including even routine X rays, without a parent's permission.

Yet when abortion rights activists challenged the new law as an invasion of teens' privacy, George decided that the law was unconstitutional. He lost the first vote on the case: The court, by 4–3, upheld the constitutionality of the statute. The majority opinion was written by no less than Justice Stanley Mosk, a long-serving liberal appointed to the court by Governor Pat Brown. Thus, George wound up espousing a "right" to privacy that not even a liberal justice recognized.

And George eventually got his way. Just six weeks after the court upheld the law, two new Wilson appointees came aboard and, with George, voted to rehear the case. In 1997, the court voted 4–3 to reverse the law—the exact opposite of the outcome in 1996, with the two new appointees providing the margin of victory. Leave aside the merits of the case; it's hard to dispute that this was activism pure and simple, since the result was so clearly dependent on the composition of the court.

"Californians regularly endure the rulings of federal judges who disregard the will of the electorate and their democratically elected representatives," complained State Attorney General Dan Lungren, whose office defended the constitutionality of the parental consent law. "Unfortunately today's majority decision provides an astonishingly similar example of disregard for legislative authority within our state courts." Lungren has nobody to blame but his fellow Republican, Pete Wilson.

If governors like Wilson and Pataki—both ostensibly and loudly committed to judicial restraint—only chose judges more wisely, they'd have a lot less reason to complain about the judiciary during the course of their campaigns. Perhaps, however, that's precisely why they *don't* act on their rhetoric. A cynical thinker might suggest that these professional politicos don't want to lose a surefire crowd-pleasing issue.

Picking Federal Judges

The annals of the federal judiciary are filled with similar failures. The very presidents who most often decry judicial activism are the ones who appoint the biggest activists to the courts. Indeed, some of the most liberal Supreme Court justices of the last half century were GOP appointees—Earl Warren and William Brennan (Eisenhower); Harry Blackmun (Nixon); John Paul Stevens (Ford); and David Souter (Bush). By contrast, two leading advocates of judicial restraint—Justices Felix Frankfurter and Byron White—were appointed by Democrats Franklin Roosevelt and John F. Kennedy, respectively.

Of course, there's a long tradition of judges who disappoint their political patrons once they get on the bench: President James Madison, for instance, nominated fellow Democrat Joseph Story to the Supreme Court and then was horrified to see his appointee join forces with the Federalist chief justice John Marshall. But though such betrayals have happened often enough, there is some evidence that careful screening by a president bent on judicial restraint can produce like-minded nominees. It's worth noting, for example, that none of Reagan's Supreme Court nominees (Scalia, O'Connor, Kennedy, and Rehnquist as chief justice) has turned into another Blackmun or Warren. Naturally, if a president is trying to put activists on the bench, he can achieve that, too; witness Bill Clinton's selection of Ruth Bader

Ginsburg and Stephen Breyer or Lyndon Johnson's appointment of Thurgood Marshall.

It may be impossible to keep all activists off the bench, but presidents, especially Republican presidents, can certainly try harder. And so can the chamber charged with "advice and consent." Naturally, the Senate should give a president a great deal of leeway to choose whom he likes for the courts; that's one of the prerogatives of winning an election. But the Senate also has a duty to determine, to the best of its admittedly limited ability, whether judicial nominees will follow the law or make up their own.

Unfortunately, the upper body—even when it's in the hands of Republicans who claim to be alarmed about judicial activism—has done a shoddy job of inspecting judicial nominees. During President Clinton's first term, for instance, the Senate, despite all the hot air about judicial activism, approved all two hundred judges he nominated. Not a single one was rejected. Even more shameful, roll call votes were held on only four judges, two of them Supreme Court nominees; the others were approved by unanimous consent, which means that few members even bothered to study the pros and cons of the nominees very closely.

No wonder James Ware won a lifetime appointment to the federal district court in 1990 and was almost confirmed to the Ninth U.S. Circuit Court of Appeals in 1997, despite having fabricated his life history. (The judge claimed to be the brother of a black teenager shot to death by racists in Alabama in 1963 during the civil rights struggle, a canard eventually exposed by another federal judge, not the Senate's crack investigators.)

Instead of taking on questionable judicial nominees, Senate Republicans, in a misdirected offensive against racial quotas and preferences, focused their fire on two nominees for assistant attorney general for civil rights, Lani Guinier and Bill Lann Lee. What's the point? Whoever the president appoints to the Justice Department will carry out the administration's policy—and rightly so. Indeed, one of the nominees the Senate did approve for the civil rights post, Deval Patrick, was every bit as pro-affirmative action as Guinier or Lee. But judges are supposed to be held to a higher standard; they're supposed to administer the law impartially, not advance a president's agenda. So why aren't senators challenging judicial, rather than Justice Department, nominations?

Perhaps, you say, the explanation is that all of Clinton's nominees were uniformly wonderful, and none was guilty of activism. But a study of the record of Clinton judges by libertarian lawyer Clint Bolick reveals that although not as activist as Carter appointees, they're much more activist than Reagan or Bush judges in a host of areas. Yet even the most activist judges were approved with Republican votes, the two most striking examples being H. Lee Sarokin and Rosemary Barkett.

In 1994, Rosemary Barkett was confirmed by the Senate, 61–37, for a seat on the U.S. Court of Appeals for the Eleventh Circuit in Florida. In her first two years on the court, she wrote opinions in seven criminal cases, siding with the defendants each time. She also wrote an opinion holding that a fifth grader pestered by another fifth grader could sue the school district for sexual harassment under Title IX of the 1972 Education Amendments. The dissenting judge castigated her opinion for its "unprecedented expansion" of the law.

None of this should have been a surprise to anyone. When she was still on the Florida Supreme Court, Barkett voted to strike down the state's antiobscenity law on the grounds that such laws are inherently unconstitutional; she voted to create a right to abortion under the Florida Constitution; and she wrote an opinion striking down Tampa's antiprostitution ordinance as unconstitutionally vague. Yet none of this stopped the Senate from confirming her, with some prominent Republicans going along.

Then there's H. Lee Sarokin, confirmed by a vote of 63–35 to a seat on the U.S. Court of Appeals for the Third Circuit in New Jersey (he's since retired). Prior to his confirmation in 1994, Sarokin was for fifteen years one of the most controversial U.S. district judges in the country. As we saw in Chapter 4, he gained nationwide fame with his opinion holding that a smelly vagrant had a right to frequent the Morristown library. And that was only the tip of the iceberg. The *New Jersey Law Journal* reported that Sarokin "may be the most reversed federal judge in New Jersey when it comes to major cases." Among these cases was the landmark *Cippolone* suit against tobacco manufacturers. In 1992, the Third Circuit—the very court he was later to join—removed Sarokin from the case because the judge had become too cozy with the plaintiffs and their lawyers.

There'd be no need for talk of impeachment or constitutional amendments to rein in activist judges if the Senate simply carried out its advise and consent duty a little more diligently and kept nominees like Sarokin and Barkett off the courts. A small step in that direction was taken by Senate Judiciary Committee chairman Orrin Hatch when he announced in 1997 that the American Bar Association would no longer enjoy a privileged position in rating the qualifications of judicial nominees. The ABA, which has taken stands on everything from gay rights to a nuclear freeze, has let politics intrude on its ratings process; it's even given mixed ratings to such clearly qualified candidates as Robert Bork (a former judge on the U.S. Court of Appeals for the D.C. Circuit, Yale law professor, and solicitor general) and Ralph Winter (a former Yale law professor, now chief judge of the Second Circuit Court of Appeals). But while getting the ABA out of the judicial selection process is an important symbolic step, it's hardly enough to win the battle against activist nominees.

GOP senators will have to show the courage to do something about bad nominees—which they have not yet done. In 1997, for instance, the Senate GOP caucus rejected a proposal by Phil Gramm that would have forced the Judiciary Committee to kill a nomination if it was objected to by a majority of the Republican senators within that judicial circuit. So far, it seems, senators have shown as little willingness as some governors to ensure a higher quality of judge.

Rating Judges

Oversight of judges shouldn't end once they get on the bench. The real key to improving the quality of the judiciary is to encourage greater public oversight of the juristocracy. Only by opening up the judicial process to more public inspection can we curb the tendencies of judges to do too much or too little, to act incompetently and arrogantly.

A promising approach for increasing public scrutiny is to rate the performance of judges. This is already starting to happen in many places, though judges aren't happy about it. In New York, for example, lawyers contribute anonymous comments to *New York Judge Reviews*, a thick book rating state judges. Many of the comments are less than flattering: One judge is described as "hotheaded," another as "cantankerous," a third as "very high-strung." Citizens for Judicial Review, a group based in Tulsa, Oklahoma, has been compiling similar reviews for other states, ranging from Alabama to Texas. The problem with such information is that the audience is usually limited to lawyers, who use the ratings to gain a competitive advantage in the courtroom. The public, however, doesn't derive much benefit. The New York book, for example, at 537 pages and a cost of $125 per copy, is not likely to become a best-seller.

That's just the way judges like it, of course. They usually lobby to keep local lawyers' reviews secret if at all possible. To improve the performance of the judiciary, we need to publicize these ratings, to inform the public before election day of how judges have performed in office. Local bar associations, political parties, and other groups interested in the judicial process should post the reviews on the Internet and mail them to voters in some easy-to-read form.

It is important that judicial reviews not be simply an academic exercise—they should be the basis for firing and promoting judges, either by ballot or by other methods. In New York, Chief Administrative Judge Jonathan Lippman has instituted an innovative system to annually rate the performance of all 104 acting state Supreme Court justices (meaning trial judges). These judges are assessed according to temperament, work ethic, scholarship, competence, and comprehensibility of written opinions. As a result of these evaluations, four judges were actually demoted in 1997.

These are good methods that should be more widely replicated across the country. Above all, voters shouldn't be afraid to express their displeasure at the ballot box. While impeachment must be reserved for high crimes and misdemeanors, there's no requirement—as some judges and lawyers would have you believe—that every judge who's not a crook is entitled to reelection. It is perfectly proper for voters to vote out judges—for example, California chief justice Rose Bird or Tennessee chief justice Penny White—whose decisions they don't like.

"Judges perform a constitutional, as opposed to a majoritarian function," notes Richard Lee Price, a New York judge and former president of the American Judges Association, "and it is constitutional for the public to vote out a judge who does not enforce the laws passed by the majority."

Cameras in Court

Reviews of judges are all well and good; we certainly need more of them. But in this TV-centered society, unless something appears on the air, it has scant chance of penetrating the public consciousness. This leads to the unavoidable conclusion that to increase the judiciary's accountability we need to increase its visibility on the tube.

TV in court has gotten a bad reputation because of the O.J. Simpson and Oklahoma City bombing trials—the former showing the destructive potential of TV, the latter showing how smoothly a trial can run in its absence. There have been a number of studies that show that cameras are, by and large, a positive influence in the courtroom, forcing all the parties to be on their best behavior. But most judges, it seems, have become convinced by the Simpson case that televising trials isn't a good idea. And it's undeniable that in some cases, TV *can* bias the outcome.

But no matter what your view of cameras in jury trials, cameras in appellate courts are another matter. These proceedings take place before judges alone, so there's no need to worry about biasing the jury. And these hearings are the ones that are really important to publicize. Trial courts don't make law. Appellate courts, and especially the U.S. Supreme Court, do. This is where the decisions usurping legislative powers take place—out of the public sight. As John Leo points out, "perhaps the most galling aspect of the revolution in the courts is that it remains invisible to most Americans. In part, this is because we get most of our news about the courts from reporters who share the principles of the cultural left and are thus part of the problem."

Letting cameras into court would change that. Viewers could bypass those of us in the print media and find out for themselves what is going on by turning on Court TV or C-Span. In addition, providing footage of appellate arguments would create an incentive for network news shows to cover these proceedings.

At the moment, many state courts are open to TV, but most federal judges remain unalterably opposed to TV in court (as good an argument as any for opening up their proceedings, in my view). The U.S. Judicial Conference has banned district judges from allowing TV into their courts. In 1996, the conference did allow appellate arguments to be televised with the judges' permission, but so far, only two of the thirteen federal circuits have taken up the invitation.

Congress has the ability to change that overnight. Lawmakers should pass legislation that gives federal trial judges the *option* of having cameras in the court but makes it virtually *mandatory* for appeals courts, and especially the U.S. Supreme Court, to throw open their doors. It's clear that if given its druthers, the Supreme Court, as currently composed, would never televise oral arguments. The justices have said in the past that they don't want to lose their treasured anonymity. But while anonymity is fine for obscure bureaucrats in the Bureau of Labor Statistics, it's not acceptable for arguably the most powerful public officials in the land. If the justices insist on wielding as much power as they do, they should at least do so in the public eye.

We don't need to have the judges' say-so to throw open the doors on their activities. They work for the taxpayers, and the presumption should be that whatever they do should be exposed to the voters' scrutiny.

Conclusion: Repeal the Doctrine of Judicial Infallibility

REVIEWING judges' performance and televising their proceedings are ultimately only means to an end, the end being greater judicial accountability. The surest way to achieve that goal is to publicly criticize judges who misbehave or issue wrongheaded decisions. This can pay off as much as any structural reform. Witness the way the U.S. Supreme Court, in the face of overwhelming public opposition, backed off its 1970s decisions mandating forced busing and an end to capital punishment. And then there's Judge Harold Baer's much publicized volte-face after he was hung out to dry for his exclusionary ruling.

Judges—even Supreme Court justices (perhaps *especially* Supreme Court justices)—do follow the election returns, and they know the dangers of staying on a path that brings them into conflict with the people and their elected representatives. Even when judges seem to be flying in the face of public opinion—for example, in *Brown v. Board of Education* or the assisted-suicide cases—on closer examination it can usually be determined that the courts are following, not leading, elite opinion.

So when the voters—and especially journalists—become upset with judicial decisions, they shouldn't be shy about letting the judges know.

It's even a good idea to publicly debate schemes such as impeaching judges, although it's not a good idea to actually impeach them. Just talking about it can have the desired effect of forcing the judiciary to tread more carefully.

You would think this advice would be unobjectionable. After all, I'm not suggesting that judges be flogged or even impeached for bad decisions; only that they be held up for public opprobrium. But even that is too much for the fainthearted judiciary. After I'd written some columns denouncing specific judges, a leading member of the American Bar Association wrote in their journal, "The corrosive effect of these attacks upon the judicial system and the society it serves cannot be overstated." Similar criticism is leveled at anyone who dares to criticize the gavelers.

After Judge Baer was attacked for excluding from evidence 80 pounds of drugs, for instance, four members of the U.S. Court of Appeals for the Second Circuit issued a letter claiming, "These attacks do a great disservice to the principle of an independent judiciary" and "threaten to weaken the constitutional structure of this nation." The ABA even convened a Commission on Separation of Powers and Judicial Independence, whose essential mission was to stifle all attacks on the judiciary. ABA president Jerome Shestak went so far in 1997 as to call attacks on judges "un-American."

Judicial infallibity seems to be one of the tenets of the Gospel According to the ABA. If we assume, however, that judges make mistakes like everyone else, it's hard to see why they alone should be exempt from criticism. Certainly no one suggests that our system of government is being undermined when critics publicly castigate the president of the United States; indeed, this is widely touted as being the essence of democracy. Why should it be any different when the subject of criticism isn't the leader of the whole nation but a mere federal judge?

The suggestion is sometimes made that judges don't rule based on their own preferences; they rule based on the law. Therefore, defenders of the judiciary argue, it's not proper to criticize judges for merely applying the rules made by others. Balderdash. If this book has shown nothing else, it has demonstrated that judges all too often make decisions based on their own personal whims—in contravention of the intentions of the law's drafters. If they're going to make such high-handed rulings, if they're going to act in essence like politicians, then judges shouldn't be surprised to be treated like politicians.

A little public scrutiny seems essential to temper the juristocracy's natural inclination to abuse its vast powers. As Chief Justice Warren Burger once observed: "A court which is final and unreviewable needs more careful scrutiny than any other. Unreviewable power is the most likely to indulge itself and the least likely to engage in dispassionate self analysis. . . . In a country like ours, no public institution, or the people who operate it, can be above public debate."

Burger's comments notwithstanding, a lot of judges are sure to be upset by the idea that they should be subjected to withering criticism whenever they issue decisions not clearly grounded in the law. But there's a simple way the judiciary can avoid public opprobrium: by becoming once again what Alexander Hamilton thought it would be— "the least dangerous branch." If judges confine their activism to cutting the tort tax and the crime rate instead of meddling in essentially political matters, they will reclaim the esteem that is their due as the defenders of the rule of law.

Until then, judges will get, and deserve, less public approbation. While we should always retain a high level of respect for the judiciary in principle, we shouldn't be afraid to treat individual occupants of the office with the contempt and scorn they deserve when they issue bad rulings.

H. L. Mencken summed up the situation perfectly:

> My own favorite object of mirth is one of the most austere and venerable figures in our society, to wit, the judge. If I frequent courtrooms little, it is only because I have a high theoretical respect for his office, and so do not want to be tempted to laugh at him. That temptation, in his presence, is almost irresistible. There he sits for hour after hour, listening to brawling shysters, murkily dozing his way through obvious perjury, contemplating a roomful of smelly loafers, and sadly scratching himself as he wonders what his wife is going to have for dinner, all the while longing horribly for a drink. If he is not a comic figure, then there is none in the world.

Only when judges give us less cause to laugh at their follies will the judicial profession be restored to the place of honor it deserves.

Notes

For brevity's sake, authors' names and titles of newspaper news articles have been omitted. They are provided only for newspaper op-eds and for magazine articles. No page numbers are listed for either newspapers or magazines, on the assumption that they are not necessary for on-line researchers.

Chapter 1: The Injudicious Judiciary

5 Brazoria County case: *National Law Journal*, March 24, 1997.

5 Racial bias prohibited in jury selection: *Edmonson v. Leesville Concrete Co. Inc.*, 500 U.S. 614 (1991) (civil cases); *Batson v. Kentucky*, 476 U.S. 79 (1986) (prosecutors in criminal cases); *McCollum v. Georgia*, 112 S.Ct. 2348 (1992) (defense attorneys in criminal cases).

5 Jury pool: *Detroit News*, June 21, 1996.

5 Alleged juror misconduct: Defendant's Memorandum of Law in Support of Motion for Judgment Notwithstanding the Verdict, *Hardy v. General Motors Corp.*, No. CV-93-56 (Ala. Circ. Ct. Lowndes Cnty. September 1996); Plaintiff's Brief in Opposition to Motion for Judgment Notwithstanding the Verdict, *Hardy v. General Motors Corp.*, No. CV-93-56 (Ala. Circ. Ct. Lowndes Cnty. September 1996).

7 Bozeman's alleged conflict of interest: Defendant's Petition for Writ of Mandamus, *Hardy v. General Motors Corp.*, No. 1951247 (Ala. May 13, 1996); advisory opinion, Alabama Judicial Inquiry Commission, May 23, 1996.

7 Bozeman's background: Martindale-Hubbell; Montgomery Advertiser, December 18, 1997.

8 *Hardy v. GM*: Max Boot, "In the Land of Lawsuits," *Wall Street Journal*, October 30, 1996. Judge Bozeman did not return calls seeking comment on his handling of the case.

9 "The judge is under a duty": Benjamin N. Cardozo, *The Nature of the Judicial Process* (New Haven: Yale University Press, 1921), 133–134.

10 "Most judges": Charles W. Collier, "The Use and Abuse of Humanistic Theory in Law: Reexamining the Assumptions of Interdisciplinary Legal Scholarship," *Duke Law Journal* 41 (1991), 191, 221.

12   Judicial selection: Department of Justice, *State Court Organization 1993* (Washington, D.C., January 1995); Daniel R. Deja, "How Judges Are Selected: A Survey of the Judicial Selection Process in the United States," *Michigan Bar Journal* (September 1996), 904–909. Note that in many states, different selection methods are used for various levels of judges.

12   Politically active judges: Sheldon Goldman, *Picking Federal Judges: Lower Court Selection from Roosevelt Through Reagan* (New Haven: Yale University Press, 1997), 352, 357.

13   Charles "Bud" Stack: *Washington Times*, March 1, 1996; *Adarand Constructors, Inc. v. Peña*, 515 U.S. 200 (1995).

13   Judicial selection in Europe: See, for example, Mary L. Volcansek and Jacqueline Lucienne Lafon, *Judicial Selection: The Cross-Evolution of French and American Practices* (Westport, Conn.: Greenwood Press, 1988), 129–134.

13   Gallagher's drug bust: *USA Today*, December 27, 1995; *Plain Dealer*, August 13, 1995.

14   "Terribly addicted": Author's interview with Mark Marein, attorney for Michael Gallagher, November 10, 1997.

14   "Candidates with the name": *Plain Dealer*, August 13, 1995.

16   "I blame Ito": Vincent Bugliosi, *Outrage: The Five Reasons Why O. J. Simpson Got Away With Murder* (New York: Island Books, 1996), 74. Judge Ito refused to comment to me on his handling of the Simpson trial.

16   Larry King story: Jeffrey Toobin, *The Run of His Life: The People v. O. J. Simpson* (New York: Random House, 1996), 231–232.

16   "Cameras": Christopher Darden, with Jess Walter, *In Contempt* (New York: HarperCollins/Regan Books, 1996), 260.

16   "Size small": Toobin, *Run of His Life*, 324.

16   None were true: Associated Press, May 6, 1997.

17   Nullification: Jack Weinstein, "Considering Jury 'Nullification': When May and Should a Jury Reject the Law and Do Justice?" *American Criminal Law Review* 30 (1993), 239.

17   "A jury has": *U.S. v. Washington*, 705 F.2d 489, 494 (D.C. Cir., 1983). The panel that issued this opinion included Ruth Bader Ginsburg, before her elevation to the Supreme Court.

18   Keating case: *Charles H. Keating Jr. v. Robert Hood and Daniel Lundgren*, 922 F.Supp. 1482 (C.D.Cal. 1996).

19   Only 1 percent removed: Susan J. Carbon, "Retention elections in the United States," *Judicature* 64 (1980), 213.

20   Baby Richard: *Peoria Star Journal*, September 18, 1994; Associated Press, July 13, 1994; *Chicago Tribune*, May 2, 1995, July 17 and 13, 1994.

21   "The trouble he's in": *Chicago Tribune*, April 2, 1997.

21   "Appearance of impropriety": *Chicago Tribune*, March 28, 1997.

21   Remained on the court: Associated Press, May 2, 1997.

21   "The judicial disciplinary process": *Wall Street Journal*, March 3, 1997. Justice Heiple did not return a call seeking comment on his conduct.

22 "A federal judge can be": Richard Posner, *Overcoming Law* (Cambridge, Mass.: Harvard University Press, 1995).

22 "Not even a scarecrow": Merrill D. Peterson, ed., *The Portable Thomas Jefferson* (New York: Penguin Books, 1977), 562.

22 The clerk incident: Author's interview with Judge Duff, October 30, 1997; *Chicago Tribune*, October 11, 1996.

23 "Irascibility" and "Barnett": Interview with Duff; *Chicago Tribune*, October 11, 1996.

23 "Observers in his courtroom": *Chicago Sun-Times*, October 11, 1996.

24 "New orifice": Associated Press, October 12, 1996.

25 The mental health class action: *In the Matter of James R. Edgar v. K.L., et al.*, No. 96–2641 (7th Cir., July 18, 1996).

25 Reversal rate: Associated Press, October 12, 1996.

25 "If there was a sealed complaint": Interview with Duff.

27 Wachtler memoir: Sol Wachtler, *After the Madness: A Judge's Own Prison Memoir* (New York: Random House, 1997).

27 "I had been given": Ibid., 63.

27 "We should continue" and "There are many people here": Ibid., 267, 93.

27 "The governor sought to treat": Ibid., 332.

28 "How could my judgment" and "When I went into a place": Ibid., 314, 338.

30 Judge Matsch: *Wall Street Journal*, June 3, 1997; *Washington Post*, May 12, 1997; Timothy Sullivan, "Can One Judge Save the System?" *American Lawyer* (March 1997), 95.

Chapter 2: "Perverse Failures"

32 "I look for the good in people": Letter to author from Judge McDonald, November 4, 1997.

32 Roberson case: *San Antonio Express-News*, March 29 and 26, April 23, 1995.

32 In his own defense: Letter to author from McDonald.

33 Other cases: *Ex parte Roberts*, 468 S.W.2d 410 (Tex.Crim.App. 1971) ("affirmed bail of $75,000 in robbery case"); *Ex parte Goosby*, 685 S.W.2d 440 (Tex.App.-Houston [1st Dist] 1985) ("reduced $250,000 bail to $100,000 in each capital murder case").

33 Safety of relatives: "[A] close relative of a deceased victim is entitled to . . . the right to have the magistrate take the safety of the victim or his family into consideration as an element in fixing the amount of bail for the accused." Tex. Code Crim. Proc.Ann.art.56.02(a)(2).

33 "This guy": *San Antonio Light*, November 6, 1992.

33 "The circumstances": Letter to author from McDonald.

33 Resendez case: *San Antonio Light*, September 7, 1991.

34 "I offered five years": Letter to author from McDonald. The judge added: "That District Attorney has endorsed me in every judicial election." See also *San Antonio Light*, February 12, 1990.

34 Reelected: *San Antonio Express News*, November 16, 1994.

34 "Bad boy": *San Antonio Express-News*, October 23, 1996.

34 "My son was not convicted": Letter to author from McDonald.

34 Life sentence: *San Antonio Express-News*, July 2, 1996.

35 Crime rate per 100,000: U.S. Bureau of the Census, *Statistical Abstract of the United States: 1995* (Washington, D.C., 1995), 199; U.S. Bureau of the Census, *Historical Statistics of the United States, Colonial Times to 1970, Part 1* (Washington, D.C., 1975), 413.

35 "Crime is down": *USA Today*, April 14, 1997.

35 "Crime bomb": John J. DiIulio Jr., "Why Violent Crime Rates Have Dropped," *Wall Street Journal*, September 6, 1995.

35 "I now know": Wachtler, *After the Madness*, 266.

36 Murder during the Great Depression: David Rubinstein, "Don't Blame Crime on Joblessness," *Wall Street Journal*, November 13, 1992.

36 Little impact: *New York Times*, April 16, 1997.

36 Favorite solutions: Former Judge Wachtler urges: "Continue to explore punishment alternatives to imprisonment." See *After the Madness*, 267.

36 Increased incarceration: John J. DiIulio, Jr., "Tougher Law Enforcement Is Driving Down Urban Crime," *Policy Review* (Fall 1995), 12–16.

37 "It strains credulity": U.S. Department of Justice, "The Case for More Incarceration," in Robert James Bidinotto, ed., *Criminal Justice? The Legal System vs. Individual Responsibility*, 2d ed. (Irvington-on-Hudson, N.Y.: Foundation for Economic Education, 1995), 212.

37 "A thug in prison": Quoted in William J. Bennett, John J. DiIulio Jr., and John P. Walters, *Body Count: Moral Poverty . . . And How to Win America's War Against Crime and Drugs* (New York: Simon and Schuster, 1996), 112.

37 Imprisonment: "The Bureau of Justice Statistics estimated that arrest-based imprisonment rates for robbery were 49 percent in the United States, 52 percent in Canada, and 48 percent in England." Department of Justice, in Bidinotto, *Criminal Justice?* 222.

37 Costs of committing crimes: James Wootton, "Truth in Sentencing: Why States Should Make Violent Criminals Do Their Time," in Bidinotto, *Criminal Justice?* 243, 244.

38 "Come apart at the seams": Associated Press, April 24, 1996. Roberts was objecting to a plan to lengthen jail sentences for first-time violent offenders.

38 103 percent of capacity: Department of Justice, Bureau of Justice Statistics, *Correctional Populations in the United States, 1995* (Washington, D.C., June 1997).

38 3.8 cents: Department of Justice, Bureau of Justice Statistics, *Expenditures and Employment Statistics* (Washington, D.C., 1997).

38 Comparative cost of prisons: John J. DiIulio, Jr. and Ann Morrison Piehl, "Does Prison Pay?" *The Brookings Review* (Fall 1991), 28–35; Ann Morrison Piehl and John J. DiIulio, Jr., "Does Prison Pay? Revisited," *The Brookings Review* (Winter 1995), 21–25.

38 Prison costs: Construction costs per bed vary from $11,000 to almost $100,000. Operating costs in fiscal year 1990 averaged $15,513 per inmate. Department of Justice, in Bidinotto, *Criminal Justice?* 223.

39 Benefits of incarceration: DiIulio and Piehl, "Does Prison Pay?"; Piehl and DiIulio, "Does Prison Pay? Revisited."

39 Costs and benefits: The National Institute of Justice estimated that the *total* costs (including annualized construction costs, an inmate's lost legitimate income, and so forth) of incarcerating a criminal for one year range from $34,000 to $38,000, while the benefits of incarcerating that one inmate range between $172,000 and $2,364,000. That evaluation of the benefits of incarceration doesn't even include homicide (except when committed during another felony), rape, or drug crimes. See Department of Justice, in Bidinotto, *Criminal Justice?* 226.

39 85 percent say courts don't deal "harshly enough": U.S. Department of Justice, Bureau of Justice Statistics, *Sourcebook of Criminal Justice Statistics* (Washington, D.C., 1997), 172, 173.

40 Freed an assault suspect: The judge was Bradford Timbers, who has since been removed from the bench. *In re Bradford Clark Timbers*, 674 A.2d 1217 (Pa.Ct. Jud. Disc. 1996). Timbers attributed his actions to alcoholism.

40 "Perverse failures": John J. DiIulio Jr., "A Philadelphia Crime Story," *Wall Street Journal*, October 26, 1994.

41 Benito Oliver case: *New York Times*, March 14, 1996; *Washington Post*, March 14, 1996.

41 Maximo Peña case: Associated Press, February 18, 1996.

41 "Persons accused": Kurt X. Metzmeier, "Preventive Detention: A Comparison of Bail Refusal Practices in the United States, England, Canada and Other Common Law Countries," *Pace International Law Review* 8 (1996), 399.

42 History of bail: Esmond Harmsworth, "Bail and Detention: An Assessment and Critique of the Federal and Massachusetts Systems," *New England Journal on Criminal and Civil Confinement* 22 (1996), 213; Peggy Tobolowsky and James F. Quinn, "Pretrial Release in the 1990s: Texas Takes Another Look at Nonfinancial Release Conditions," *New England Journal on Criminal and Civil Confinement* 19 (1993), 267.

43 "Memorize *Hamlet*": *Bangor Daily News*, May 29, 1996.

43 $10,000 bail and personal recognizance: Department of Justice, Bureau of Justice Statistics, *Felony Defendants in Large Urban Counties, 1992* (Washington, D.C., July 1995).

43 Pretrial release: Ibid.

43 Released again and personal recognizance: Ibid.

43 Statistics on pretrial release: Ibid. Most misconduct consisted of missing a court appearance, but 14 percent of released defendants were rearrested for a new offense, usually a felony.

45 Judge Duckman: Max Boot, "Rule of Law: What Does It Take to Fire a Judge?" *Wall Street Journal*, September 17, 1997.

45 Up to one thousand cases: *Salt Lake Tribune*, February 7, 1993.

46 "Probation was an alternative": Lawrence M. Friedman, *A History of American Law*, 2d ed. (New York: Simon and Schuster, 1985), 596. See also Sharon M. Bunzel, "The Probation Officer and the Federal Sentencing Guidelines: Strange Philosophical Bedfellows," *Yale Law Journal* 104 (1995), 933, and Mihal Nahari, "Due Process and Probation Revocation: The Written Statement Requirement," *Fordham Law Review* 56 (1988), 759.

46 No time behind bars: Department of Justice, *Felony Defendants in Large Urban Counties, 1992*.

46 3.1 million on probation: Department of Justice, Bureau of Justice Statistics, *Correctional Populations in the United States, 1995*, (Washington, D.C., June 1997).

47 Lorenzia Wright case: Author's interview with Judge Lopossa, October 31, 1997; *Indianapolis Star*, June 14, 1996.

47 Stewart case: Interview with Lopossa.

47 "Look forward": *Indianapolis Star*, November 24, 1991.

47 Rearrested: Department of Justice, in Bidinotto, *Criminal Justice?* 215.

47 Simpson's probation: *Daily News* (Los Angeles), August 23, 1994.

48 Juvenile crime: *U.S. News and World Report*, March 25, 1996. The number of juveniles arrested for weapons-law violations increased 103 percent during that period.

48 Juvenile cases: Department of Justice, Office of Juvenile Justice and Delinquency Prevention, *Offenders in Juvenile Court, 1994* (Washington, D.C., October 1996).

48 "The judge isn't taking a chance": Author's interview with Peter Reinharz, June 17, 1997.

48 "His involvement at best": Author's interview with Judge Ramirez, November 4, 1997.

48 "Wrong profession": *Rocky Mountain News*, April 21, 1996.

49 Judge Ramirez: *Rocky Mountain News*, November 11 and 5, 1996, April 21 and 4, 1996.

50 Probation programs: John J. DiIulio Jr., "Reinventing Probation and Parole," *Brookings Review* (Spring 1997), 42.

50 Sentences: Department of Justice, Bureau of Justice Statistics, *Felony Sentences in State Courts, 1994* (Washington, D.C., January 1997); Department of Justice, *Felony Defendants in Large Urban Counties, 1992*.

50 Far more criminals on probation than parole: As of 1995, there were 700,000 parolees in the country and nearly 3.1 million probationers. Department of Justice, Bureau of Justice Statistics, *Correctional Populations in the United States, 1995* (Washington, D.C., June 1997).

50 Parole and indeterminate sentences: Friedman, *History of American Law*, 597.

51 More than 60 percent rearrested: Department of Justice, *Recidivism of Prisoners Released in 1983* (Washington, D.C., April 1989). In addition, 46.8 percent of prisoners released are reconvicted of a crime within three years.

51 Arrest records: Department of Justice, *Felony Defendants in Large Urban Counties*, 1992.

51 RAND estimate: Department of Justice, in Bidinotto, *Criminal Justice?* 217.

52 "At almost every step": *Record* (northern New Jersey), May 16, 1993. Conrad Jeffrey case: *Record*, December 17, 1995, May 17 and 16, 1993; *Star Ledger* (Newark), June 23, 1996.

52 Amanda Wengert: *Star Ledger* (Newark), March 13, 1994.

53 Judges don't like guidelines: Former congressman Don Edwards surveyed federal judges on the guidelines, and of 265 who responded, 244 said they opposed fixed terms. See Gannett News Service, November 1, 1993.

53 Sentencing guidelines: Department of Justice, Bureau of Justice Statistics, *Federal Prison Terms Increasing Under Sentencing Guidelines* (Washington, D.C., June 21, 1992).

53 Morin case: *U.S. v. Andrew Scott Morin*, No. 95–5300 (4th Cir., April 5, 1996).

53 "The district court was obligated": *U.S. v. Daniel Perkins*, No. 95–5750 (4th Cir., March 10, 1997).

55 Overturning the death penalty: *Furman v. Georgia*, 408 U.S. 238 (1972).

55 Death row parolees: *Sacramento Bee*, November 12, 1995.

56 Death penalty upheld: *Gregg v. Georgia*, 428 U.S. 153 (1976).

56 "Individual justice": Alex Kozinski, "Tinkering with Death," *New Yorker*, February 10, 1997, 52.

56 Second thwack at the piñata: I'm grateful to Judge Frank Easterbrook for this metaphor, which he used in an entirely different context.

56 Executions carried out: Department of Justice, Bureau of Justice Statistics, *Capital Punishment, 1994* (Washington, D.C., February 1996); U.S. Bureau of the Census, *Statistical Abstract of the United States: 1995* (Washington, D.C.), 220.

56 Most polls: See, for example, *Sourcebook of Criminal Justice Statistics 1995*, 183: In a 1995 Gallup survey, 77 percent said they favored the death penalty for those convicted of murder; only 13 percent said they were opposed.

57 Robert Alton Harris: *Los Angeles Times*, April 23, 1992; *San Diego Union-Tribune*, April 26, 1992;

57 $1.7 million: Associated Press, May 25, 1992.

59 Judge John Nixon: *Nashville Banner*, April 4 and February 11, 1997; *Commercial Appeal* (Memphis), December 7, 1996, August 2 and February 14, 1995; *Boston Globe*, June 14, 1995; *Tennessean*, February 26, 1997, July 29, 1995; *Nashville Banner*, February 20, 1997, August 1, 1995; *Knoxville News-Sentinel*, February 13, 1997, July 30, 1996.

59 Objections to death penalty: "The death penalty is not a deterrent. It is extremely costly; it clogs the courts; it doesn't reduce prison populations." Wachtler, *After the Madness*, 161.

60 Thompson case: *Washington Post*, August 6, 1997.

61 Wisconsin judges: *Milwaukee Sentinel-Journal*, June 1, 1997.

61 Outside the public eye: Joseph M. Bessette, "In Pursuit of Criminal Justice," *Public Interest* (Fall 1997), 8.

61 Small claims court: *Indianapolis News*, December 20, 1996.

61 Duckman's removal: *New York Times*, October 25, 1997.

61 "In the court of law": Ralph Waldo Emerson, "The Sovereignty of Ethics," in *Collected Works of Ralph Waldo Emerson* (1904), 187.

Chapter 3: Criminal Exoneration

62 Most dangerous school in New York: *Newsday*, July 17, 1995, November 23, 1993.

63 "The outline of the gun": *Juan C. v. Cortines*, 223 A.D.2d 126, 133 (N.Y. App. Div. 1ˢᵗ Dept. 1996).

63 Civil proceedings exempted: See, for example, *INS v. Lopez-Mendoza*, 468 U.S. 1032 (1984) (exclusionary rule does not apply in civil deportation hearings).

63 Liquor license: *Matter of Finn's Liquor Shop v. State Liquor Authority*, 24 N.Y. 2d 647 (1969).

63 Police disciplinary matter: *Jon C. Boyd v. Constantine*, 81 N.Y. 2d 189 (1993).

64 "If security aides": *In the Matter of Juan C. v. Cortines*.

64 "We should not lose sight": *Juan C. v. Cortines*, N.Y. Lexis 322 (April 1, 1997).

66 "Far from looking at the warrant as a protection": Cited in *U.S. v. Leon*, 468 U.S. 897, 972 (1984) (Stevens, J., concurring and dissenting).

66 Preexclusionary rule history: Akhil Amar, *The Constitution and Criminal Procedure: First Principles* (New Haven: Yale University Press, 1997), 11.

67 "[T]he evidence is admissible": *United States v. LaJeune Eugenie*, 26 F.Cas. 832, 844 (C.C.D. Mass. 1822), cited in Amar, *Constitution and Criminal Procedure*, 21.

67 Creation of exclusionary rule: *Boyd v. U.S.*, 116 U.S. 616 (1886).

67 Federal criminal law: *Weeks v. U.S.*, 232 U.S. 383 (1914) (letters taken from the accused's house constituted a denial of constitutional rights).

67 "The criminal is to go free": *People v. Defore*, 242 N.Y. 13, 718 (1926).

67 Exclusionary rule opinion: *Mapp v. Ohio*, 367 U.S. 643 (1961).

68 Exclusionary rule does not apply: *Wolf v. Colorado*, 338 U.S. 25 (1949). The rump caucus is described in Bernard Schwartz, *A Book of Legal Lists* (New York: Oxford University Press, 1997), 132.

68 Black went along: *Mapp*, 367 U.S. 661–662 (Black, J., concurring). ("The Fourth Amendment does not itself contain any provision expressly precluding the use of such evidence, and I am extremely doubtful that such a provision could properly be inferred from nothing more than the bare command against unreasonable searches and seizures.")

68 "Judicially created remedy": *U.S. v. Calandra*, 414 U.S. 338, 348 (1974).

68 "To compel respect": *Elkins v. U.S.*, 364 U.S. 206, 217 (1960).

68 "Curb police misconduct": *Plain Dealer* (Cleveland), October 25, 1995.

69 DEA agents: Nat Hentoff, "Lethally Lawless Federal Police," *Village Voice*, March 7, 1995.

69 Clearance rates: Testimony of Paul J. Larkin Jr., House Judiciary Committee, January 20, 1995. 1995 WL 20738 (F.D.C.H.).

70 Vannatter: Alan M. Dershowitz, *Reasonable Doubts: The Criminal Justice System and O. J. Simpson* (New York: Touchstone/Simon and Schuster, 1997), 46–48.

70 "They are lying": *Boston Globe*, November 15, 1995.

70 "Considerable cost": *Malley v. Briggs*, 475 U.S. 335, 344 (1986).

71 ABA report: American Bar Association, Criminal Justice Section, "Criminal Justice in Crisis" (Washington, D.C., November 1988).

71 "Many of these": *U.S. v. Leon*, 468 U.S. 897, 908 (1984).

71 Arrest figures: Department of Justice, Bureau of Justice Statistics, *Sourcebook of Criminal Justice Statistics* (Washington, D.C., 1997), 394. The FBI's Uniform Crime Reports define violent crimes as murder, non-negligent manslaughter, forcible rape, robbery, and aggravated assault. Police made 778,730 arrests for these offenses in 1994.

72 "Because of search and seizure issues": ABA, "Criminal Justice in Crisis," 18.

74 Coffey's dissent: *U.S. v. Lenin Jerez and Carlos M. Solis*, 108 F.3d 684 (7th Cir. 1997).

75 Inadmissible evidence: *People v. Leonardo Turriago*, 644 N.Y.S.2d 178 (N.Y. App. Div. 1996).

75 Turriago indictment: *Times Herald Record*, November 8, 1996.

75 Might be admitted: *People v. Leonardo Turriago*, 1997 WL 253205 (N.Y., May 13, 1997).

77 "The ultimate test": *Culombe v. Connecticut*, 367 U.S. 568, 602 (1961), cited in Joseph D. Grano, *Confessions, Truth, and the Law* (Ann Arbor: University of Michigan Press, 1993), 59–60. The following history of pre-*Miranda* law draws heavily on Grano.

78 Mississippi case: *Brown v. Mississippi*, 297 U.S. 278, 287 (1936).

78 Upheld confessions: *Crooker v. California*, 357 U.S. 433 (1958); *Cicenia v. La Gay*, 357 U.S. 504 (1958).

78 Right to have counsel: *Escobedo v. Illinois*, 378 U.S. 478 (1964).

78 "The Constitution does not provide": *State v. Murphy*, 87 N.J.L. 515, 530 (1915), cited in Grano, *Confessions*, 157.

79 Overturned decades of precedence: *Miranda v. Arizona*, 384 U.S. 436 (1966).

80 Upshot of *Miranda*: *Miranda v. Arizona*, 384 U.S. 436, 542 (1966) (White, J., dissenting).

81 Cassell study: Paul G. Cassell, "*Miranda*'s Social Cost: An Empirical Assessment," *Northwestern University Law Review* 90 (1996), 387; Cassell, "*Miranda*'s 'Negligible' Effect on Law Enforcement: Some Skeptical Observations," *Harvard Journal of Law and Public Policy* 20 (1997), 327. For a critique, see Stephen J. Schulhofer, "*Miranda*'s Practical Effect: Substantial Benefit and Vanishingly Small Social Costs," *Northwestern University Law Review* 90 (1996), 552.

81 Natural-born killers: *Boston Globe*, March 15, 1997; Associated Press, March 14, 1997.

82 Thomas Damiano case: *Providence Journal-Bulletin*, May 15, 1996.

82 Miranda's death: *Arizona Republic*, July 15, 1996.

83 Affirmed *Miranda*: See, for example, *Thompson v. Keohane*, 116 S.Ct. 457, 133 (1995) (federal courts must review the facts in state court Miranda rulings de novo).

83 Public safety exception: *New York v. Quarles*, 467 U.S. 649 (1984).

83 "Fruit" allowed: See *United States v. Gonzalez-Sandoval*, 894 F.2d 1043 (9th Cir. 1990).

83 Threw out the confession: *People v. Steven Oquendo*, *New York Law Journal*, April 8, 1997.

84 Grand jury: *United States v. Calandra*, 414 U.S. 338 (1974).

84 Deportation hearings: *INS v. Lopez-Mendoza*, 468 U.S. 1032 (1984).

84 "Inevitable discovery": *Nix v. Williams*, 467 U.S. 431 (1984).

84 Dog sniff: *United States v. Place*, 462 U.S. 696 (1983).

84 "Open fields": *United States v. Dunn*, 480 U.S. 294 (1987).

84 "Good faith" exception: *U.S. v. Leon*, 468 U.S. 897 (1984) (evidence not excluded if officers relied on mistakenly issued warrants); *Illinois v. Krull*, 480 U.S. 340 (1987) (evidence not excluded if officers relied on statute authorizing warrantless search).

84 No good faith exception in New York: Peter Reinharz, "The Court Criminals Love," *City Journal* (Winter 1996). "Is the state Constitution so different from the federal one that such differences are inevitable? Hardly: the Fourth Amendment and the parallel state provision read exactly the same. The difference lies entirely in the eye of the judicial beholder."

84 Metal detectors: *National Treasury Employees Union v. Von Raab*, 489 U.S. 656 (1989).

84 Sobriety checkpoints: *Michigan Department of State Police v. Sitz*, 496 U.S. 444 (1990).

84 Federal workers: *Stigile v. Clinton*, 110 F.3d 801 (D.C. Cir., 1997).

84 "No-knock" searches: *Wilson v. Arkansas*, 514 U.S. 927 (1995) (officers knocking and announcing presence and authority before entering dwelling is factor to be considered in determining reasonableness of search); *Richards v. Wisconsin*, 117 S.Ct. 1416 (1997) (Fourth Amendment does not permit a blanket exception to knock-and-announce requirement for felony drug investigations).

85 "Mess" and "embarrassment": Amar, *Constitution and Criminal Procedure*, 1, 147.

85 Inordinate amount of time: "The rule obligates defense counsel to move for suppression in every case, regardless of the merit of the defendant's claim, if for no other reason than to avoid the charge of providing ineffective assistance of counsel." Former Justice Department lawyer Paul Larkin Jr., in testimony before the House Judiciary Committee, January 20, 1995. 1995 WL 20738 (F.D.C.H.).

86 New York decisions: *People v. Edwin Gomez and John Alburquerque*, 628 N.Y.S.2d 927 (1995) (random stops of every taxicab in high crime area were

reasonable); *People v. Christopher Carty*, 624 N.Y.S.2d 771 (1995) (police officers' stop of taxi for purposes of handing out safety pamphlets was reasonable
and doesn't violate the Fourth Amendment); *People v. Isaac Leary*, see *New
York Law Journal*, March 21, 1997.

86 Baer's ruling: *United States v. Carol Bayless*, 913 F.Supp. 232 (S.D.N.Y. 1996).

87 Reversal: *United States v. Carol Bayless*, 921 F.Supp. 211 (S.D.N.Y. 1996).

87 "Largely ignored": Grano, *Confessions*, 202.

87 Can override: See, for example, Larkin, House Judiciary Committee, January
20, 1995: "Congress enjoys the power to revise or abolish the exclusionary
rule for cases tried in the federal courts."

88 Growing police power: Amar, *Constitution and Criminal Procedure*, 41.

88 "Demoralizing message": Cited in ibid., 119.

88 "Search for truth": *Nix v. Whiteside*, 475 U.S. 157, 166 (1986).

Chapter 4: Juristocracy

90 Forum shopping: *San Francisco Chronicle*, March 2, 1997; *San Diego Union-
Tribune*, January 19, 1997.

91 Henderson's conflicts: "Statement of Facts Supporting WLF's Judicial Misconduct Complaint," *Washington Legal Foundation*, July 8, 1992; "Judge
Wrongly Suspends CCRI," *Center for Equal Opportunity*, December 10, 1996.

91 "Substantial burden": *Coalition for Economic Equity v. Wilson*, 946 F. Supp.
1480 (N.D. Cal. 1996).

91 Ninth Circuit decision: *Coalition for Economic Equity v. Wilson*, No. 97–15030
(9th Cir. April 8, 1997).

92 Under fire: "Prof. Erwin Chemerinsky, who teaches constitutional law at the
University of Southern California Law Center, said he fears that the April 9
ruling 'opens the door to a real manipulation of the system by lawyers and
judges.'" *National Law Journal*, April 21, 1997.

92 "Legal limbo": Testimony of Representative Richard Mountjoy before the
Senate Subcommittee on Courts and Intellectual Property, May 14, 1997.

92 "Every conservatively based initiative": Remarks of Governor Pete Wilson
before the *Wall Street Journal* editorial board, May 1, 1997.

92 Henderson's past rulings: Matthew Reese, "The Judge Who Hates CCRI,"
Weekly Standard, December 16, 1996.

93 "Judicial power": *Coalition for Economic Equity v. Wilson*, No. 97-15030 (9th
Cir. April 8, 1997).

93 Oregon initiative: Judge Hogan's injunction was vacated by the Ninth Circuit. Associated Press, February 27, 1997.

94 Abortion protesters: *New York Times*, April 23, 1997.

94 "A preexisting rule was there": Benjamin N. Cardozo, *The Nature of the Judicial Process* (New Haven: Yale University Press, 1921), 124.

94 "Only between the gaps" and "The law is so clear": Ibid., 113, 129.

95 Scalia argument: Antonin Scalia, "Common Law Courts in a Civil Law Sys-

tem," in *A Matter of Interpretation: Federal Courts and the Law*, ed. Amy Gutmann (Princeton: Princeton University Press, 1997). "The brilliance of one's own mind": 7. "What it *ought* to mean" and "If it is good": 39.

95 "Serve as a laboratory": *New State Ice Co. v. Liebmann*, 285 U.S. 262, 311 (1932) (Brandeis, J., dissenting).

96 The advantages of federalism: For an invaluable discussion, see Steven G. Calabresi, "'A Government of Limited and Enumerated Powers': In Defense of *United States v. Lopez*," *Michigan Law Review* 94 (1995), 752.

96 "Any truly new thing": Richard S. Kay, "Adherence to the Original Intentions in Constitutional Adjudication: Three Objections and Responses," *Northwestern University Law Review* 82 (1988), 226, 254.

96 After *Marbury*: Lawrence M. Friedman, *A History of American Law*, 2d ed. (New York: Simon and Schuster, 1984), 122.

97 Approving New Deal legislation: *NLRB v. Jones & Laughlin Steel Corp.*, 301 U.S. 1 (1937) (upholding National Labor Relations Act); *U.S. v. Darby*, 312 U.S. 100 (1941) (upholding federal minimum wage and maximum hours laws); *Wickard v. Filburn*, 317 U.S. 111 (1942) (upholding wheat quotas even if wheat isn't intended for interstate commerce).

97 Exceeded enumerated authority: *U.S. v. Lopez*, 115 S.Ct. 1624 (1995).

97 Brady Act: *Printz v. United States*, No. 95-1478 (S.Ct., June 27, 1997).

97 Religious Freedom Restoration Act: *City of Boerne v. Flores*, No. 95-2074 (S.Ct., June 25, 1997).

97 Property rights: See, for example, *Nollan v. California Coastal Commission*, 483 U.S. 825 (1987); *Lucas v. South Carolina Coastal Council*, 505 U.S. 1003 (1992); *Dolan v. City of Tigard*, 512 U.S. 374 (1994).

98 Political speech: *Buckley v. Valeo*, 424 U.S. 1 (1976).

98 Communications Decency Act: *Reno v. American Civil Liberties Union*, No. 95-511 (June 26, 1997).

99 Power of Congress: *Powell v. McCormack*, 395 U.S. 486 (1969).

100 Term limits decision: *U.S. Term Limits, Inc. v. Thornton*, 115 S. Ct. 1842 (1995).

100 Contraceptives: *Griswold v. Connecticut*, 381 U.S. 479 (1965); *Eisenstadt v. Baird*, 405 U.S. 438 (1972).

100 Abortion: *Roe v. Wade*, 410 U.S. 113 (1973).

100 Prayer in public schools: *Engel v. Vitale*, 370 U.S. 421 (1962).

100 Invocation of God: *Lee v. Weisman*, 505 U.S. 577 (1992).

100 Pornography: *Miller v. California*, 413 U.S. 15 (1973) (establishing "obscenity" standard); *Brockett v. Spokane Arcades, Inc.*, 472 U.S. 491 (1985) ("obscenity" does not include material that excites "normal, healthy sexual desires").

100 Antisodomy law: *Bowers v. Hardwick*, 478 U.S. 186 (1986).

100 Overturning Colorado law: *Romer v. Evans*, 116 S.Ct. 1620 (1996).

102 Begging decision: *Loper v. New York City Police Department*, 999 F.2d 699 (2d Cir. 1993).

102 "It seems fair to say": *Young v. New York City Transit Authority*, 903 F.2d 146 (2d Cir. 1990).

102 Begging rights: See, for example, *Mark Chad v. City of Fort Lauderdale, Florida*, 861 F.Supp. 1057 (1994) (declining to enjoin antibegging law on public beaches, but holding that panhandling is a First Amendment activity). For a critique, see Peter Nichols, "The Panhandler's First Amendment Right: A Critique of *Loper v. New York City Police Department* and Related Academic Commentary," *South Carolina Law Review* 48 (1997), 267.

102 "Poor people, nonconformists": *Papachristou v. City of Jacksonville*, 405 U.S. 156 (1972).

103 Third Circuit: *Kreimer v. Bureau of Police for the Town of Morristown*, 958 F.2d 1242 (3d. Cir. 1992).

103 Pennsylvania Station: *Streetwatch v. National Railroad Passenger Corp.*, 875 F.Supp. 1055 (S.D.N.Y. 1995).

103 "The virtue of a democratic system": *U.S. v. Virginia*, 116 S.Ct. 2264 (1996) (Scalia, J., dissenting).

104 Separate but equal: *Plessy v. Ferguson*, 163 U.S. 537 (1896).

104 Second-greatest of all time: Bernard Schwartz, *A Book of Legal Lists* (New York: Oxford University Press, 1997), 52.

104 "Inconclusive": *Brown v. Board of Education of Topeka*, 347 U.S. 483 (1954).

104 "In the fractured discipline": Michael W. McConnell, "Originalism and the Desegregation Decisions," *Virginia Law Review* 81 (1995), 947, 952.

104 Varying degrees of success: For perhaps the best conservative defense of *Brown*, see McConnell, "Originalism." McConnell argues that even if education was not a "civil right" in 1868, it had clearly become one by the 1950s, with the spread in taxpayer-supported schools and mandatory schooling laws. Therefore, he suggests, the Warren Court was right to demand equality in public education.

For criticism, see Michael J. Klarman, "Brown, Originalism and the Constitutional Theory: A Response to Professor McConnell," *Virginia Law Review* 81 (1995), 1881, 1918. Klarman points out that McConnell's argument, if taken seriously, can easily be used to justify just about any aspect of modern judicial activism. "Thus, for example," he writes, "the same argument that would authorize expanding civil rights to include public education would justify expanding protected groups to include women, aliens, gays, etc." Presumably, this is not the result McConnell, or other champions of restraint, would want to achieve.

105 Rational basis: See, for example, *Goesaert v. Cleary*, 335 U.S. 464 (1948); *Hoyt v. Florida*, 368 U.S. 57 (1961).

106 Idaho law: *Reed v. Reed*, 404 U.S. 71 (1971).

106 Military rule: *Frontiero v. Richardson*, 411 U.S. 677 (1973).

106 Oklahoma law: *Craig v. Boren*, 429 U.S. 190 (1976).

106 Virginia Military Institute case: *U.S. v. Virginia*, 116 S.Ct. 264 (1996). For the background of the VMI case, see Anita K. Blair, "How We Got the ERA," *Women's Quarterly* (Spring 1997).

107 All-female nursing college: *Mississippi University for Women v. Hogan*, 458 U.S. 718 (1982).

108 "No practical difference": *Richmond Times-Dispatch*, March 8, 1997.

108 Nineteenth Amendment: See Antonin Scalia, "A Theory of Constitutional Interpretation," remarks at the Catholic University of America, October 18, 1996.

109 "Anyone who has seriously thought": Judy Mann, "Boys and Girls Apart," *Washington Post*, October 20, 1996.

110 Supreme Court went along: *Romer v. Evans* (1996).

112 Gay marriage: "*Romer v. Evans* would in fact call into question the authority of a state in refusing to honor gay marriages." Hadley Arkes, "A Culture Corrupted," *First Things* (November 1996), 30. See also Melanie Kirkpatrick, "Gay Marriage: Who Decides," *Wall Street Journal*, March 13, 1996; David Orgon Coolidge, "At Last, Hawaiians Have Their Say on Gay Marriage," *Wall Street Journal*, April 23, 1997.

112 Supreme Court justices: Thomas, Scalia, Rehnquist, Kennedy, and O'Connor.

112 "Remedying the effects": *Metro Broadcasting, Inc. v. FCC*, 497 U.S. 547 (1990) (O'Connor, J., dissenting).

112 Set-asides: *City of Richmond v. J. A. Croson Co.*, 488 U.S. 469 (1989); *Adarand Constructors, Inc. v. Pena*, 115 S.Ct. 2097 (1995).

112 Congressional districts: *Shaw v. Reno*, 509 U.S. 630 (1993).

112 Race at the University of Texas: *Cheryl Hopwood v. Texas*, 84 F.3d. 720 (5th Cir. 1996).

112 Conservative activism: Jeffrey Rosen, "The Color-Blind Court," *American University Law Review* 45 (1996), 791; Rosen, "Originalist Sin," *New Republic*, May 5, 1997.

113 "To remedy disadvantages": *Regents of University of California v. Bakke*, 438 U.S. 265 (1978).

113 "To do away with": *Palmore v. Sidoti*, 466 U.S. 429 (1984). I'm grateful to law professors Stephen Calabresi of Northwestern and Eugene Volokh of UCLA for this interpretation of the court's race doctrine.

114 "Long gone": Professor Herman Schwartz of American University Law School, quoted in *New York Times*, May 18, 1997.

114 Not fully endorsed by Tribe: See Laurence H. Tribe, "Comment," in Gutman, *A Matter of Interpretation*, 83.

114 Substantive due process: *Dred Scott v. Sandford*, 60 U.S. 393 (1857).

115 "Interfere with the liberty": *Lochner v. New York*, 198 U.S. 45 (1905) (Holmes, J., dissenting).

115 *Lochner* line ended: *West Coast Hotel Co. v. Parrish*, 300 U.S. 379 (1937).

115 *Griswold v. Connecticut*: 381 U.S. 479 (1965).

115 *Roe v. Wade*: 410 U.S. 113 (1973).

115 *Doe v. Bolton*: 410 U.S. 179 (1973).

116 Research at the Mayo Clinic: See Bob Woodward and Scott Armstrong, *The Brethren: Inside the Supreme Court* (New York: Simon and Schuster, 1979), 272. See also, at 276: "The clerks in most chambers were surprised to see the Justices, particularly Blackmun, so openly brokering their decisions like a group of legislators."

116 Liberal critics of Roe: Stuart Taylor Jr., *"Meese v. Brennan,"* *New Republic*, January 6 & 13, 1986.

116 *Casey* decision: *Planned Parenthood of Southeastern Pennsylvania v. Casey*, 505 U.S. 833 (1992).

117 Ninth Circuit: *Compassion in Dying v. Washington*, 79 F.3d, 790, 798 (9th Cir. 1996).

117 Second Circuit: *Vacco v. Quill*, 80 F.3d 716 (2nd Cir. 1996).

117 Unanimously repudiated: *Washington v. Glucksberg*, No. 96-110 (S.Ct., June 26, 1997); *Vacco v. Quill*, No. 95-1858 (S.Ct., June 26, 1997).

118 *Cruzan v. Director, Missouri Department of Health:* 497 U.S. 261 (1990).

121 Greatest good for the greatest number: "Assume that there are only two states, with equal populations of 100 each. Assume further that 70 percent of State A, and only 40 percent of State B, wish to outlaw smoking in public buildings. The others are opposed. If the decision is made on a national basis by a majority rule, 110 people will be pleased, and 90 displeased. If a separate decision is made by majorities in each state, 130 will be pleased, and only 70 displeased. The level of satisfaction will be still greater if some smokers in State A decide to move to State B, and some anti-smokers in State B decide to move to State A." Michael McConnell, "Federalism: Evaluating the Founders' Design," *University of Chicago Law Review* 54 (1987), 1484.

Chapter 5: Juristocracy II

124 Philadelphia consent decree: Based mostly on Sarah B. Vandenbraak, "Bail, Humbug! Why Criminals Would Rather Be in Philadelphia," *Policy Review* (Summer 1995), 73–76. Detective Boyle's quotes come from his testimony before the House Judiciary Committee, January 19, 1995. For the consent decree "experiment," see *Pittsburgh Post-Gazette*, March 9, 1997.

125 IBM decree: *Infoperspectives*, August 1, 1996.

125 Denver bilingual education: *Denver Post*, June 23, 1996.

125 Judge Giddings: *Grand Rapids Press*, May 13, 1997.

126 State economic regulations: *Ex parte Young*, 209 U.S. 123 (1908).

126 Block protests: *In re Debs*, 158 U.S. 564 (1895).

126 "May enjoin": *Osborn v. Bank of the United States*, 24 U.S. (9 Wheat.) 738 (1824).

126 History of injunctions: John C. Yoo, "Who Measures the Chancellor's Foot? The Inherent Remedial Authority of the Federal Courts," *California Law Review* 84 (1996), 1128–1130.

127 *Brown v. Board of Education II:* 349 U.S. 294 (1955).

128 1964 Civil Rights Act: "Nothing herein shall empower any official or court of the United States to issue any order seeking to achieve a racial balance in any school by requiring the transportation of pupils or students from one school to another or one school district to another in order to achieve such racial balance, or otherwise enlarge the existing powers of the court to insure compliance with constitutional standard" (Section 2000c-6).

128 Approved the plan: *Swann v. Charlotte-Mecklenburg Board of Education*, 402 U.S. 1 (1971).

128 "Under this theory": *Missouri v. Jenkins III*, 515 U.S. 70 (1995).

128 Boston school busing: J. Anthony Lukas, *Common Ground: A Turbulent Decade in the Lives of Three American Families* (New York: Alfred A. Knopf, 1985).

130 "High schools" and "patch and repair": *Missouri v. Jenkins II*, 495 U.S. 33 (1990) (Kennedy, J., dissenting).

131 "The power of taxation": Ibid.

131 "The District Court": *Missouri v. Jenkins II* (1990).

131 "Pedagogical sociology": Quoted from Eighth Circuit Court of Appeals dissent in *Missouri v. Jenkins III* (1995).

132 "Large expenses": *Washington Times*, April 18, 1997.

132 Another judge: *Kansas City Star*, August 22 and April 18, 1997.

132 End court decrees: *McDowell v. Board of Education of Oklahoma City*, 498 U.S. 237 (1991) (laying out criteria for judging when a school district has achieved "unitary" status); *Freeman v. Pitts*, 503 U.S. 467 (1992) (trial courts should "return schools to the control of local authorities at the earliest practicable date"); *Missouri v. Jenkins III* (1995).

132 "Many school boards": Testimony of Charles J. Cooper before the House Judiciary Committee, April 16, 1996.

133 Quotes approving consent decrees: Owen M. Fiss, "The Supreme Court, 1978 Term—Foreword: The Forms of Justice," *Harvard Law Review* 93 (1979), 1, cited in Yoo, "Who Measures the Chancellor's Foot."

134 "The pattern": *Wall Street Journal*, September 15, 1988.

135 *Spallone v. U.S.*: 493 U.S. 265 (1990).

135 Build six hundred units: *New York Times*, May 4, 1997.

135 "Using a word processor to cook dinner": Lillian R. BeVier, "Judicial Restraint: An Argument from Institutional Design," *Harvard Journal of Law and Public Policy* 17 (1994), 7.

136 Providence COLAs: *Providence Journal-Bulletin*, September 23 and March 28, 1996, December 13 and October 10, 1995.

137 D.C. decrees: *Washington Post*, April 7, 1997.

137 "For protection": *Munn v. Illinois*, 94 U.S. 113, 134 (1877).

137 Prisons under court order: Department of Justice, *Correctional Populations in the United States, 1995* (Washington, D.C., June 1997).

137 Prison law library: *Bounds v. Smith*, 430 U.S. 817 (1977).

137 Not share a cell with a smoker: *Helling v. McKinney*, 113 S.Ct. 2475 (1993).

139 New York consent decree: Testimony of Laura A. Chamberlain, assistant corporation counsel, before the Senate Judiciary Committee, September 25, 1996. See also *New York Times*, May 31, 1996; *Wall Street Journal*, April 8, 1996.

139 Second Circuit reinstated: David Schoenbrod and Ross Sandler, "Rule of Law: In New York City, the Jails Still Belong to the Judges," *Wall Street Journal*, September 10, 1997.

140 Contempt of court: *Arizona Republic*, June 8, 1994.

140 "A mockery": *Arizona Daily Star,* December 16, 1995.

140 Overrode Muecke: *Evan Arthur Hook v. Arizona,* 98.F.3d 1177 (9th Cir. 1996).

140 "The order": *Lewis v. Fletcher Casey Jr.,* 116 S.Ct. 2174 (1996) (Thomas, J., concurring).

140 Supreme Court overrode: *Lewis v. Fletcher Casey Jr.,* No. 94-1511 (S.Ct., June 24, 1996).

140 Impeachment: *Arizona Republic,* June 8, 1994.

141 228 state prisons: Department of Justice, *Correctional Populations in the United States, 1995* (Washington, D.C., June 1997).

141 Prison overcrowding: Jeff Bleich, "The Politics of Prison Crowding," *California Law Review* 77 (1989), 1125.

143 *Lynce v. Mathis:* 117 S.Ct. 891 (1997).

143 Armstrong case: *Orlando Sentinel,* Dec. 10 and 13, 1997.

143 Florida consent decree: "Judges' Jail Break" (editorial), *Wall Street Journal,* March 17, 1997.

145 "The Court": Yoo, "Who Measures the Chancellor's Foot," 1133.

145 Prison Litigation Reform Act: Ibid., 1175.

145 "At some point": *Missouri v. Jenkins III* (1995).

Chapter 6: The Civil Injustice System

147 Wrenicide: *Washington Post,* December 1, 1995, *Richmond Times-Dispatch,* June 28, 1996.

147 Woman bites landlord: *Trial,* October 1, 1996.

147 Electrocution: *Jae Boon Lee v. Chicago Transit Authority,* 205 Ill.App.3d 163 (1990); *Urban Transport News,* May 27, 1993.

148 Judicial mugging: Gannett News Service, December 2, 1993; *Newsday,* April 6, 1993, March 11, 1990.

148 "No litigation explosion": Ralph Nader and Wesley J. Smith, *No Contest: Corporate Lawyers and the Perversion of Justice in America* (New York: Random House, 1996), 263.

149 "Expanding theories of liability": Jon Newberry, "Protect Assets Before Lawsuit Arises," *American Bar Association Journal* (January 1996), 89.

149 "Tendentious macro-anecdotes: Marc S. Galanter, "News from Nowhere: The Debased Debate on Civil Justice," *Denver Law Review* 71 (1993), 100.

149 Their own anecdotes: See the section on "The Tort System Benefits All of Us," in Nader and Smith, *No Contest,* 314–319.

149 "What we think we know": Michael J. Saks, "Do We Really Know Anything About the Behavior of the Tort Litigation System—and Why Not?" *University of Pennsylvania Law Review* 140 (1992), 1147, 1149.

150 Tort filings increased: State Justice Institute, *Examining the Work of State Courts, 1994: A National Perspective from the Court Statistics Project.*

150 Federal tort cases: Statistics Division, Administrative Office of the United

States Courts, *Judicial Business of the U.S. Courts, 1995 Report to the Director* (Washington, D.C., 1995; 1997 update), 139. The ABA argues, at 2, that "with the exception of asbestos cases, product liability filings in federal courts declined dramatically during the 1980s." That's sort of like saying "with the exception of Ted Bundy and Jeffrey Dahmer, the number of serial killers in America has declined."

150 Employment cases: *Washington Post*, May 12, 1997.

150 "One of the most remarkable features": Saks, "Do We Really Know Anything," 1188.

151 "[I]n the vast majority of cases": Samuel Jean Brakel, "Using What We Know About Our Civil Litigation System: A Critique of 'Rate-Based' Analysis and Other Apologist Diversions," *Georgia Law Review* 31 (1996), 104. I am indebted to Brakel's article for his general analysis of the "there is no litigation explosion" arguments.

151 Justifications: Nader and Smith argue in *No Contest*, at 266: "If there has been any kind of litigation explosion, it has not been fueled by personal injury victims, investors, or other individual citizens. Rather it has been in businesses suing businesses." So what? What critic of the system argues that only suits filed by individuals are objectionable? Who defends frivolous suits filed by corporations?

Nader and Smith also cite, at 276, findings of Jury Verdict Research: "In product liability cases, plaintiffs' verdicts dropped from 59 percent in 1989 to 41 percent in 1993." This, the authors claim, "belie[s] the claim that jurors are pro-plaintiff and antibusiness." Just as plausibly, these numbers indicate that 59 percent of all product liability cases—the ones that plaintiffs lose—are meritless.

151 Dog food: Nader and Smith, *No Contest*, 278–279.

151 Fire and police protection: U.S. Bureau of the Census, *Statistical Abstract of the United States: 1995* (Washington, D.C., 1995), 300. The combined figure is $55.6 billion.

151 $900 per household: Paul H. Rubin, "The High Cost of Lawsuits," *Investor's Business Daily*, March 4, 1996.

151 Tort tax for individual products: Bob Eaton, "No Joking Matter," *Newsweek*, September 23, 1996; "A Citizen's Guide to Lawsuit Abuse," *Citizens for a Sound Economy*, April 1995; *USA Today*, January 23, 1996.

151 Health costs: Daniel Kessler and Mark McClellan, "Do Doctors Practice Defensive Medicine?" *Quarterly Journal of Economics* 111 (May 1996), 387.

152 Playgrounds: *San Francisco Chronicle*, January 21, 1997.

152 IUDs: *Washington Post*, August 6, 1996.

153 Volunteers: *New York Times*, May 19, 1996.

153 Cookies: "Revenge of the Reptiles" (editorial), *Wall Street Journal*, March 7, 1995.

153 RAND finding: "The Lawyers' Veto" (editorial), *Wall Street Journal*, May 3, 1996.

153 $5,000 per hour: Testimony of Lester Brickman before the Senate Judiciary Committee, November 7, 1995.

153 Growth in lawyers: Marc Galanter, "Law Abounding: Legalization Around the North Atlantic," *Modern Law Review* 55 (1992), 1, 2.

153 "The fundamental problem": Paul Burka, "The Tort Tax," *Texas Monthly* (June 1996), 7–8.

154 "There is a duty": William L. Prosser, "Palsgraf Revisited," *Michigan Law Review* 52 (1953), 15.

154 "How can society best allocate": Peter W. Huber, *Liability: The Legal Revolution and Its Consequences* (New York: Basic Books, 1990), 7.

154 European-style health insurance: This preference is explicit in the writings of federal Judge Jack Weinstein, one of the leading modern tort theorists. See Jack B. Weinstein, *Individual Justice in Mass Tort Litigation: The Effect of Class Actions, Consolidations, and Other Multiparty Devices* (Evanston, Ill.: Northwestern University Press, 1985), 4–5, 120 (suggesting that the United States needs national health care and federal disability benefits for everyone).

154 "A rule from time immemorial": *Pennsylvania R.R. Co. v. Aspell*, 23 Pa. 147 (1854).

155 "We used to have immunities": Interview with Thomas F. Lambert Jr. (columnist for the *Law Reporter*), in *Trial* (July 1996), 33.

155 Lawyer advertising: *Bates v. State Bar of Arizona*, 433 U.S. 350 (1977).

156 "Long and arduous process": *National Law Journal*, May 19, 1997.

156 Medical battery: Ibid.

156 Guns: *New York Times*, May 3, 1996.

157 Hostile environment: *Meritor Savings Bank v. Vinson*, 477 U.S. 57 (1986).

157 Female police sergeant: Max Boot, "Rule of Law: What If Paula Jones Had Sued a CEO?" *Wall Street Journal*, January 15, 1997.

157 More than sixty state court decisions: Victor Schwartz, Mark Behrens, and Mark Taylor, *Who Should Make America's Tort Law: Courts or Legislatures?* (Wshington, D.C.: Washington Legal Foundation, 1997), 2.

158 "Usurp the powers": *Best v. Taylor Machine Works*, No. 96-L-167 (Ill. Cir. Ct. Madison City, August 20, 1996). See also *National Law Journal*, December 9, 1996.

158 Judges taking over the job of legislators: See Schwartz, Behrens, and Taylor, *Who Should Make America's Tort Law*, 21–27.

159 Loewen case: Walter Olson, "A Small Canadian Firm Meets the American Tort Monster," *Wall Street Journal*, February 14, 1996; *Wall Street Journal*, January 25, 1996; *Forbes*, June 17, 1996; *Profit*, February 1, 1996.

159 Demanded in one-third of California suits: A study of all 1,024 lawsuits filed in San Francisco County Superior Court during a one-month period in 1991 found that where punitive damages were available, plaintiffs asked for them in 27 percent of the cases. See Steven Hayward, *The Role of Punitive Damages in Civil Litigation: New Evidence from Lawsuit Filings* (San Francisco: Pacific Research Institute, February 1996). A study by the Association for California Tort Reform of civil filings in four major counties confirms that "nearly a third of all contract and tort cases involved demands for punitive damages."

See John H. Sullivan, "New State Data Confirms Runaway Abuse of Punitive Damages," *Washington Legal Foundation* 12 (February 7, 1997), 2.

160 "Deter despicable acts" and "Will it be insulated?": Alex Kozinski, "The Case of Punitive Damages v. Democracy," *Wall Street Journal*, January 19, 1995.

160 Dalkon Shield: Don Dempsey, "Punitive Damages: The PowerBall Game of the Litigation Lottery," *Citizens for a Sound Economy*, April 26, 1995.

160 "Overkill": *Roginsky v. Richardson-Merrell, Inc.*, 378 F.2d 832, 839 (2d Cir. 1967).

160 6 percent of cases: Department of Justice, Bureau of Justice Statistics, *Civil Justice Survey of State Courts, 1992* (Washington, D.C., July 1995). What the Naderites don't mention is that the study also found that punitive damages accounted for about 10 percent of the total money awarded to plaintiffs and that while the median award was $50,000, 12 percent of the punitive damage awards were over $1 million.

161 "The frequency and size of such awards": *TXO Production Corp. v. Alliance Resources Corp.*, 113 S.Ct. 2711, 2742 (1993) (O'Connor, J., dissenting).

161 Texas and California punitive damages: Brief of Amici Curiae, Life Insurance Co. of Georgia, et al., in *BMW v. Ira Gore Jr.* (U.S., October term, 1994).

161 RAND findings: *Punitive Damages in Financial Injury Jury Verdicts* (Santa Monica, Calif.: RAND Institute for Civil Justice, 1997).

162 "Guideposts": Courts must judge punitive awards based on "the degree of reprehensibility of the defendant's conduct," the ratio between punitive and compensatory damages, and the "civil or criminal penalties that could be imposed for comparative misconduct." *BMW v. Gore*, 1996 U.S. Lexis 3390 (S.Ct. May 20, 1996).

162 Chemical accident: *Wall Street Journal*, September 9, 1997.

163 Background of breast implants: "The Breast Implant Tragedy" (editorial), *Wall Street Journal*, May 19, 1995; *Daily Journal* (San Francisco), April 25, 1996.

163 "There has yet to be published": Joseph Nocera, "Fatal Litigation," *Fortune*, October 16, 1995, 62.

163 "Very weak risk factor": Marcia Angell, *Science on Trial: The Clash of Medical Evidence and the Law in the Breast Implant Case* (New York: W. W. Norton, 1996), 196–197.

164 *Journal of the American Medical Association* study: "The Risks and Awards of Implants" (editorial), *Wall Street Journal*, March 28, 1996.

164 Houston doctor: *New York Times*, September 18, 1995.

164 UCLA pathologist: Gary Taubes, "Silicone: Has the Truth Been Served?" *Discover*, December 1995.

164 Frye rule: *Frye v. U.S.*, 293 F. 1013 (D.C. Cir.1923).

165 "Gatekeepers": *Daubert v. Merrell Dow*, 113 S.Ct. 2786 (1993).

165 Judge Steinheimer: "Junk Science and Judges" (editorial), *Wall Street Journal*, November 8, 1995.

165 Judge Magess: *Los Angeles Times*, August 19, 1997.

165 Judge Schneider: *Los Angeles Times*, March 29, 1995.

165 Judge Jones: "A Sleazy Attack" (editorial), *Wall Street Journal*, February 18, 1997.

166 Agent Orange: *In Re "Agent Orange" Product Liability Litigation*, 818 F.2d 145 (2d Cir. 1987).

166 Richmond toxic cloud: Susan Hansen, "Money for Nothing?" *American Lawyer* (January/February 1996), 61.

166 "Pleural plaques": See Lester Brickman, "The Asbestos Litigation Crisis: Is There a Need for an Administrative Alternative?" *Cardozo Law Review* 13 (1992), 1853.

167 Asbestos: Max Boot, "Rule of Law: The Toxic Tort That Won't Die," *Wall Street Journal*, July 10, 1996.

168 "Good guy–bad guy": John P. Frank, "Thirty Years of Class Actions in Historical Perspective," paper submitted to the Judicial Conference's Advisory Committee on Civil Rules, April 28, 1994.

169 "While in theory": Statement of Senator William Cohen, 141 Congressional Record 207, December 22, 1996, S19250.

170 Texas insurance class action: Max Boot, "Rule of Law: A Texas-Sized Class Action Fraud," *Wall Street Journal*, May 22, 1996; "Taken for a Ride" (editorial), *Wall Street Journal*, October 23, 1996.

170 86 cents: The suit pertained to the escrow practices of M&T Mortgage Corp. in Buffalo, New York. The settlement was approved in 1996 by Federal Judge James B. Zagel.

171 "Glorified promotional fare offer": Quote from Cornish Hitchcock of Public Citizen, in *Washington Post*, December 23, 1994. See also *Washington Post*, March 20, 1995, Associated Press, November 3, 1996.

171 Cereal suit: *Star Tribune* (Minneapolis-St. Paul), May 23, 1995; *Los Angeles Times*, May 2, 1995.

171 Bank of Boston case: *Chicago Tribune*, March 21, 1996; *New York Times*, November 21, 1995;

171 Judge Posner: *In re Rhone-Poulenc Rorer Inc.*, 51 F.3d 1293 (7th Cir.), *cert. denied*, 116 S.Ct. 184 (1995).

172 *Castano* class action: *Castano v. American Tobacco Co.*, 84 F.3d (5th Cir. 1996).

172 Heart valve: *Washington Post*, March 8, 1996.

172 GM pickup trucks: *In Re General Motors Corp. Pick-Up Truck Fuel Tank Products Liability Litigation*, 55 F.3d 768 (3d Cir. 1995), *cert. denied*, 116 S.Ct. 88 (1995).

172 Ford Bronco II: Associated Press, February 28, 1997.

172 "I do not believe": *Arizona Business Gazette*, May 2, 1996.

174 Mosk opinion: Max Boot, "Rule of Law: The Mass Tort That Wasn't," *Wall Street Journal*, November 6, 1996.

Chapter 7: Justice for Rent

177 "Scintilla of evidence": *Mitchell Energy Corp. v. Bartlett*, 1997 Tex. App. Lexis 5900 (Tex.App.Ct. [2d Dist.], November 13, 1997).

179 Smelly-water case: "Smelly Verdict" (editorial), *Wall Street Journal*; "Smelly Verdict II" (editorial), *Wall Street Journal*; *Ft. Worth Star-Telegram*, June 1 and May 21, 1996; *Houston Chronicle*, July 26, 1996; *Texas Lawyer*, July 1, 1996; author's interview with Judge Fostel, February 23, 1998.

179 Defendant's request: *Mitchell Energy Corp. v. Ashworth*, 943 S.W.2d 436 (Tex. 1997).

180 Second smelly-water trial: *Houston Chronicle*, May 29, 1997; *Ft. Worth Star-Telegram*, July 16, 1997.

181 Ohio and Texas spending: *Wall Street Journal*, May 27, 1997.

183 Judge Starcher: "Injudicious Politics" (editorial), *Wall Street Journal*, July 8, 1996.

183 "Many people think": *Wall Street Journal*, May 27, 1997.

184 Harris County court clerk: *Houston Chronicle*, February 6, 1997.

187 Mary Klager: Max Boot, "A Tale of Silicone City," *Wall Street Journal*, November 29, 1995; "Victory for Plaintiffs" (editorial), *Wall Street Journal*, September 23, 1996; *Klager v. Worthing*, No. 04–95–00134-CV, 1996 Tex. App. LEXIS 3521 (Tex.App.Ct. [4th Dist.] Aug. 7, 1996).

188 "These days": *Houston Chronicle*, April 9, 1995.

188 $150 million: George L. Priest, "The Punitive Damages Phenomenon in Alabama: A Preliminary Report," October 24, 1996. Study in author's possession.

188 Robertson told me: Author's interview with William Robertson, November 4, 1997.

189 "Any jury anywhere": Author's interview with Robertson.

189 Judge Robertson's retirement: *Birmingham News*, October 4, 1996; *Ledger Enquirer*, October 20, 1996; *Montgomery Advertiser*, October 19, 1996; *Efaula Tribune*, October 23, 1996;

190 Class actions: Max Boot, "In the Land of Litigation," *Wall Street Journal*, October 30, 1996.

191 Alabama Supreme Court: Roger Parloff, "Is This Any Way to Run a Court?" *American Lawyer* (May 1997).

192 "I think we put an end": *Los Angeles Times*, October 19, 1996. For the rest of the San Diego scandal, see Walter Olson, "Will Trial-Lawyer Cash Corrupt Our Courts?" *Investor's Business Daily*, November 14, 1996; *San Diego Union Tribune*, April 14, 1996; *Los Angeles Times*, April 14, 1996; *United States v. Patrick R. Frega, G. Dennis Adams, James A. Malkus*, No. 96–698, Grand Jury Indictment (November 1994).

193 Judges' sentences: *San Diego Union Tribune*, August 20, 1997.

193 Judge Maloney: *Chicago Tribune*, June 3, 1994; *New York Times*, April 15, 1997. For Operation Graylord generally, see *Washington Post*, August 25, 1989. The Supreme Court allowed the defendant who didn't bribe Judge Maloney to proceed with his case challenging his murder conviction. *Bracy v. Gramley*, 117 S. Ct. 1793 (1997).

193 Operation Court Broom: *St. Petersburg Times*, August 11, 1991.

193 Nashville judge: *Tennessean*, October 8, 1995.

194 Judge Collins: *Dallas Morning News*, August 7, 1993; *New Orleans Times-Picayune*, August 7, 1993; *Baton Rouge Advocate*, June 12, 1993; Associated Press, June 29, 1991.

194 Judge Aguilar: *San Francisco Chronicle*, June 25, 1996; Associated Press, November 1, 1990; *Orange County Register*, August 23, 1990; *San Francisco Chronicle*, March 20, 1990.

194 Judge Hastings: *Seattle Times*, September 20, 1986; *Washington Post*, January 10, 1993; *Orlando Sentinel*, September 18, 1992; *San Diego Union Tribune*, October 21, 1989.

195 Judge Nixon: Associated Press, November 4 and 3, 1989.

195 Judge Claiborne: UPI, July 12, 1986.

Chapter 8: Dethroning the Juristocracy

200 "The lawyers' ideal": John O. McGinnis, "Legal Monopoly," *National Review* (September 1996).

202 "The impeachment clause": *National Law Journal*, June 30, 1997.

202 Bork's solutions: Robert H. Bork, "The Conservative Case for Amending the Constitution," *Weekly Standard*, March 3, 1997.

203 "Very plausible schemes": Edmund Burke, *Reflections on the Revolution in France*, ed. J.G.A. Pocock (Indianapolis: Hackett Publishing Co., 1987), 53–54.

203 Canada: *Weekly Standard*, March 17, 1997.

205 Upheld enforcement authority: *Ex Parte Young*, 209 U.S. 123 (1908).

206 Three-judge requirement: House of Representatives, *Report No. 179*, 104th Cong., 1st Sess. 1995, 1995 WL 427617 (Leg. Hist.)

206 Stenberg plan: Don Stenberg and Kimberli D. Bindewald, "A Vote of One Judge Undermining the Will of the People: A Call to Congress to Enact Legislation to Limit the Authority of the Federal Courts to Declare Laws Unconstitutional," comment submitted to *Harvard Journal on Law and Public Policy* (in author's possession).

209 Judge Ronald George: *Washington Post*, August 6, 1997; *National Law Journal*, June 2, 1997; Mark S. Pulliam, "Snatching Defeat from the Jaws of Victory," *California Political Review* (July/August 1996); Mark S. Pulliam, "George Watch," *California Political Review* (March/April 1997).

211 Clinton judges confirmed: Dan Carney, "Battle Looms Between Clinton, GOP over Court Nominees," *Congressional Quarterly*, February 8, 1997; Matthew Reese, "Judging the Judges," *Weekly Standard*, March 3, 1997.

211 James Ware: Associated Press, November 9, 1997; *Los Angeles Times*, November 7, 1997.

212 Activist judges: "Clinton judges generally are more likely to favor defendants in criminal cases and plaintiffs in civil rights and civil liability cases, and to view the power of the federal courts more expansively than judges appointed by Ronald Reagan or George Bush." Clint Bolick, "Clinton's Judges: An Analysis," April 2, 1996 (unpublished study in author's possession).

212 Judge Barkett: Thomas L. Jipping, "The Lessons of Rosemary Barkett," *Washington Times*, April 20, 1994; *Orlando Sentinel*, May 5, 1996; John Leo, "In Many Cases Judges Have Taken Leave of Their Senses," *Richmond Times-Dispatch*, March 24, 1996.

212 Cippolone case: *Haines v. Liggett Group*, 975 F.2d81 (3ʳᵈ Cir., 1992).

212 Judge Sarokin: *Star Ledger* (Newark), April 24, 1996; statement of Orrin Hatch before the U.S. Senate, October 4, 1994.

213 Changing Senate rules: *New York Times*, April 30, 1997.

213 *New York Judge Reviews*: *New York Times*, July 2, 1997.

214 Demoting judges: Author's interview with Judge Lipmann, October 28, 1997; *New York Daily News*, May 1997.

214 "Judges perform a constitutional": *State Government News*, August 1992.

215 Studies on TV: "Our review . . . did not find that the presence of cameras in New York interferes with the fair administration of justice." New York State Committee to Review Audio-Visual Coverage of Court Proceedings, *An Open Courtroom: Cameras in New York Courts* (New York: Fordham University Press, 1997), xv.

215 "Invisible to most Americans": John Leo, *First Things* (January 1997).

215 Only two of thirteen circuits: *New York Times*, June 7, 1997.

217 "Great disservice": *New York Times*, March 29, 1996; *Washington Post*, April 14, 1996.

217 "Un-American": *Washington Post*, August 6, 1997.

218 Burger's comments: Remarks to Ohio Judicial Conference, September 4, 1968.

218 "My own favorite object of mirth": H. L. Mencken, *A Second Mencken Chrestomathy*, ed. Terry Teachout (New York: Alfred A. Knopf, 1995), 90.

Acknowledgments

I SHOULD start by thanking my employer, *The Wall Street Journal*, for giving me the chance to write some of the stories that resulted in this book. I'm grateful to Dan Henninger, Melanie Kirkpatrick, and all of my colleagues at the editorial page, who have created the most congenial work environment imaginable. Above all, there is Robert L. Bartley. He has made the editorial page what it is today, and in some important sense has made me the newspaperman that I am today. I will always be grateful to Bob for giving me one of the best jobs in journalism.

This book would not exist were it not for one extraordinary man: Edward Hayes. I would dedicate this book to him were it not that Tom Wolfe has already paid him far greater homage with a dedication in *Bonfire of the Vanities*. Counselor Hayes is my agent, but much more than that: He is a force of nature who moves heaven and earth to accomplish his goals, and it was my great good fortune that publishing this book became one of Eddie's goals.

This book was made possible in part by a generous grant from the Lynde and Harry Bradley Foundation; I'm grateful to Michael Joyce and Dusty Rhodes at the foundation for their support. The Manhattan Institute has also backed this work; I thank Larry Mone, its president, for all his help. Elizabeth Dee was an industrious research assistant. David Conti was a great editor; he was so dedicated to this book that he stayed with it even after Basic Books switched corporate owners. At Basic, Marian Brown, Brian Desmond, and many others have done a tremendous job. Jack McKeown and John Donatich, president of Perseus and editorial director of Basic, respectively, have been wise guiding forces behind the whole project.

In researching this book, I had useful conversations with people too numerous to mention; indeed, some of them, especially the practicing attorneys, wouldn't want to be mentioned, for fear of getting on the wrong side of some judge. A number of people gave generously of their time in reading drafts of my manuscript or portions of it: Janet Hiller-Bailey and Ed Bailey, Lester Brickman, Erich Eichman, John O. McGinnis, Trevor Nelson, Walter Olson. Their comments improved the final product immeasurably. Robert H. Bork was kind enough to take time from his busy schedule to pen a wonderful foreword.

Finally, I owe thanks to the women in my life. My mother, Olga Kagan, raised me so that I would be capable of pursuing a life of words. My mother-in-law, Kathleen McCarty, has helped nurture me in recent years. My wife and consigeliere, Jeannette K. Boot, read all of my drafts, no matter how daft, and kept me going on the right track. She even had the good grace to tolerate my obsession with birthing this book, while she was in the process of birthing something far more important: a bouncing baby Boot. Perhaps someday Victoria E. Boot will become a judge. The good kind, I hope.

Index